THE SUICIDE SYNDROME

THE SUICIDE SYNDROME

EDITED BY RICHARD FARMER AND STEVEN HIRSCH

CROOM HELM   LONDON

© 1980 R.D.T. Farmer and S.R. Hirsch © 1979 Cambridge University Press Ch 3
Croom Helm Ltd, 2-10 St John's Road, London SW11

British Library Cataloguing in Publication Data

The suicide syndrome.
  1. Suicide — Congresses
  I. Farmer, R D T
  II. Hirsch, Steven Richard
  364.1'522   HV6545

ISBN 0-85664-868-X

Reproduced from copy supplied
printed and bound in Great Britain
by Billing and Sons Limited
Guildford, London, Oxford, Worcester

CONTENTS

ACKNOWLEDGEMENTS

We wish to record our sincere thanks to Mrs J. Rohde, Research Assistant for the Department of Community Medicine, Westminster Medical School, for her patient and considerable help in the preparation of this manuscript.

This book is a collection of papers that were presented at a conference that was held at Charing Cross Hospital Medical School in October 1978. We are grateful to Bencard for sponsoring the conference and for their help in its organisation.

R.D.T. Farmer
S.R. Hirsch

INTRODUCTION

Suicide and attempted suicide have been the subject of study and speculation for many years. In particular attemped suicide, or parasuicide, has attracted great attention during the past 25 years as its incidence is increasing throughout the western world. Paradoxically in England and Wales recorded suicide mortality has fallen and this phenomenon has generated considerable interest. This book brings together a wide range of carefully conducted investigations from England, and other European countries. The contributors include psychiatrists, epidemiologists, sociologists and social workers, resulting in a fresh approach to a complex series of problems. The authors challenge previous diagnostic concepts and the basis for recognising groups most at risk. They offer a variety of new approaches for assessing and managing patients who have been admitted to hospital following an overdose.

The first section of the book comprises a number of epidemiological studies. The relationship between suicide and attempted suicide is re-examined by Farmer. His tentative conclusion that the two are quite intimately connected, differs from the view widely held in Britain and in much of America. However, it is similar to a view that is held in continental Europe. Sainsbury *et al.* start with the assumption that suicide is a different syndrome from attempted suicide. Their important investigation seeks to explain the observation that suicide mortality in England and Wales has fallen, whereas in most other countries it has not. They examine the relationship between changes in mortality and a number of social and demographic variables. Their conclusions are a vindication of Durkheim's hypothesis. Kreitman and Schreiber's analysis of trends in morbidity from parasuicide amongst young women in Edinburgh shows that there has been an increase in both the numbers of persons attempting suicide and in the repeat rate. From these data it is hard to escape the conclusion that both primary and secondary preventive measures have been unsuccessful. Morgan's work is of particular interest since it adopts a demographic approach to the investigation of attempted suicide in a small geographical area. He is able to identify zones with particularly high morbidity and draws important conclusions regarding social factors which tend to increase the rates.

These initial papers set the scene for the detailed investigations of groups of individuals. Part Two comprises studies of the role of life events, and in Part Three the various authors present the results of their studies of the symptoms and other characteristics of parasuicide patients which predict the likelihood of a repeated episode and of associated clinical or social morbidity. Newson-Smith and Hirsch look at assessments at the symptom level; Paykel, Katschnig *et al.* and Turner identify groups with high and low risks of relapse according to other characteristics. Katschnig *et al.* and Paykel have each used very similar approaches to identify subgroups of patients by cluster analysis, a statistical technique for identifying groups of patients with similar symptom patterns. Katschnig *et al.* have gone further and reported a five-year follow-up of these different groups, and have shown that their model can separate parasuicide patients with no increased risk of killing themselves from other groups of patients with a very high risk of subsequent death by suicide. Their results are not inconsistent with those of Ettlinger who reports her 15-year follow-up of a very high risk group who were semi-comatose when admitted, a group that is somewhat different to most used in the UK studies. Jennings' review of the evidence of the effect of the Samaritans (a self-help phone-in-service) on the suicide rate in the UK is the only evaluation in this book of a service intended to prevent first occurrences as opposed to dealing with individuals who have already identified themselves by a previous parasuicide.

Traditional practice in Britain over the past 15 years, codified in guidelines set out by the Department of Health, Ministry of Health (1968) holds that every patient presenting to hospital following parasuicide should be assessed by a psychiatrist prior to discharge. The majority are admitted for this purpose and for medical observation. Parts Four and Five of this volume describe some recent departures from this practice and evaluate their success by carefully controlled investigations which compare the new approach to the traditional one. These studies represent important contributions because, in practice, psychiatrists are not always readily available for consultation and the consequent waiting period can delay discharge and waste scarce hospital resources. Personnel specially trained to assess or manage the parasuicide patient may not only be more skilled but also better motivated to deal with a problem which is unwelcomed by most physicians and many psychiatrists. The quality of care received by parasuicides is not always of the highest standard because it is often difficult to establish patients in treatment and maintain follow-up. If it can be demonstrated that a variety of approaches do not differ in their effectiveness, then local services can adopt the one most appropriate for themselves.

The authors in Part Four describe different services which rely for first-line assessment on nurses, social workers and junior non-psychiatric physicians respectively and use psychiatrists as back-up for consultation and, if necessary, treatment. In Part Five, the authors describe innovative services for treating patients using a task-orientated brief social work approach, a domiciliary service and a specialised in-patient self-poisoning unit which, although well established in Edinburgh, is still an exception of its kind.

In addition to describing novel approaches to assessment and management, each report of self-poisoning patients in Parts Four and Five includes a systematic evaluation of the new statistics. When drawing conclusions from the research the reader should be aware that different authors have adopted different criteria for both the selection of subjects, the length of follow-up and the criteria of outcome. The most indisputable criterion is the eventual suicide rate, but studies which employed this measure have used different time periods for follow-up. It is obvious that longer follow-up will be associated with a higher eventual mortality. For example, Ettlinger's study which both extends over 15 years and was limited to a group with a grave prognosis should not be directly compared with the others. Ultimate survival is not a sensitive measure of outcome unless the numbers of patients studied are large, as in the study by Katschnig *et al.*, and the follow-up period runs over several years.

Subsequent parasuicides would appear to be a more relevant test, but none of the treatment studies reported in Part Five shows an effect on this measure. The most powerful prediction of a repeated parasuicide is a history of previous parasuicides. If Farmer's theory that suicide and parasuicide are largely impulsive acts, the main determinant of death being the availability and lethality of method, is correct, then it would not be surprising that treatments which are aimed at the elimination of symptoms and the improvement of social functioning fail to alter the likelihood of a repetition. Newson-Smith and Hirsch show that while some groups had a considerable reduction in symptoms this was not related to a lower frequency of repeated parasuicide and Gibbons reports improved social functioning without an effect on the repetition rate.

Measurement of symptom levels are included in the evaluations of Hawton, Catalan and Gibbons, but not by Gardner, who compares the assessment of junior hospital physicians to that of psychiatrists. In addition to the level of symptoms and frequency of further parasuicide, Gibbons looks at the success of social workers in eliminating 'target' problems. Hawton looks at patient acceptance in terms of reliability in attending for treatment and whether patients thought it was helpful or were helped to resolve interpersonal and social difficulties. These indicators provide a more comprehensive and sensitive measure of change and are more likely to reveal differences between the effects of different treatments when they exist. It must be remembered that when differences in symptoms or social functioning are found they may not be due to the treatment, but to other differences between the groups such as their previous suicide history or the initial criteria by which they were selected.

The studies reported here provide a firm basis for concluding that there is much more scope for experimentation and innovation by a wide range of caring professions – nurses, doctors, social workers, psychiatrists and perhaps others – in providing the principal agent who will deal with the parasuicide patient. These chapters point the way to the means of assessment which will enable clinicians and counsellors to detect those who require one sort of help or another. We hope that these papers demonstrate the need for and value of research in this area. A really powerful therapeutic approach has yet to be developed. Greater understanding of the suicide syndrome and new techniques for helping patients should have their impact in the not too distant future.

PART ONE

Suicidal Behaviour in Different Groups

1 THE RELATIONSHIP BETWEEN SUICIDE AND PARASUICIDE

R.D.T. Farmer

Introduction

In successive years since the mid-1950s the annual numbers of suicide deaths recorded in England and Wales have fallen. Concurrently there has been a sustained and substantial rise in the numbers of hospital admissions for episodes of self-poisoning (Adelstein and Mardon, 1975; Alderson, 1974). Death by suicide is more common amongst males than it is amongst females. The converse is true of self-poisoning, the most common method of attempted suicide, which has a declining incidence after the age of 30 and occurs more frequently in females than males (Hospital In-patient Enquiry). At first sight these paradoxical secular trends and contrasting demographic characteristics cannot be assimilated into a single syndrome hypothesis. Thus the current view is that two more or less sharply delineated groups exist, a model initially proposed by Stengel *et al.* (1958) and quickly endorsed by leading psychiatrists. Later Kreitman *et al.* (1969) suggested that the 'term "attempted suicide" is highly unsatisfactory for the excellent reason that the great majority of patients so designated are not in fact attempting suicide'. They proposed the adoption of the word 'parasuicide', and this has now gained wide acceptance.

Though the dichotomous model has proved to be of some value in research and in clinical management, there is evidence to suggest that it does not describe the situation accurately. Within the broad area of self-harm there are undoubtedly many subcategories, but a primary division on the criterion of fatality may not be the most appropriate. An alternative primary division is between the impulsive and the planned suicide, a distinction first proposed by Morselli (1857). The outcome of self-destructive behaviour of either type may be death. It is suggested that the probability of survival will be greater in the case of an impulsive suicide since the preparation is less likely to be adequate. The evidence supporting the hypothesis is drawn principally from epidemiological data although the findings of many clinical investigations and post-mortem enquiries are not inconsistent with the proposition.

Sources and Quality of Data

The data that are available to examine the epidemiology of suicide and parasuicide are death records and hospital records. Each can be supplemented by special enquiries and neither are complete.

Death records have some important shortcomings. Whereas no difficulty arises in recording the fact of death, there are problems related to the assignation of cause. In the case of suicide the assignation of cause is more complicated than in other situations. The death must first be recognised as having been caused unnaturally before any further investigations can be initiated. When death from natural causes is expected and death occurs then it is readily assumed that it was the result of natural causes. Patel (1973) examined the findings from 15,000 medico-legal autopsies amongst which he detected 764 probable suicides. He reflected that

> The use of drugs requires no witnesses, they do not leave behind visible marks and present a picture similar to that of a natural death. The body being found anywhere in the house. . .Therefore, general practitioners when requested to call to attend dying or dead patients, have nothing to suspect and. . .issue certificates without hesitation.

Thus the variables that are likely to affect the recognition of a death as unnatural are the age and state of health of the deceased and the method chosen to procure death. The most difficult to detect would be poisoning in an elderly and sick person. The most likely to be recognised as unnatural is any death in a fit young person.

After the death has been recognised as being due to outside intervention, the cause has to be assigned by a coroner. In England and Wales the coroner is a member of the judiciary and as such is bound by rules that are quite different from those that govern a doctor's clinical practice. The most important rule governing the coroner in possible cases of suicide is that

> suicide must never be presumed. If a person dies a violent death, the possibility of suicide may be there for all to see, but it must not be presumed merely because it seems, on the face of it, to be the most likely explanation. Suicide must be proved by evidence, and if it is not proved by evidence, it is the duty of the Coroner not to find suicide but to find an open verdict (Widgery, 1975).

New hal

The effect of constraints such as these are inevitable underrecording.

By contrast, 'parasuicide' is a clinical diagnosis, a label applied to a patient following interview, and yet the ascertainment of parasuicide is also far from adequate. The coding of causes of death takes account of the nature of injury and the external cause of that injury. Thus a suicidal hanging will be coded as suicide (hanging) and as asphyxiation. Hospital morbidity records show only the nature of injury; in the case of parasuicides it is necessary to use the category 'poisoning by medicinal agents' as a proxy. Obviously, poisonings are not exclusively parasuicides nor do all parasuicides involve poison. Furthermore, not all episodes of parasuicide result in hospital admission, indeed some may not even come to medical attention.

One other difficulty arises in the study of morbidity and mortality from self-harm. It is not possible to use exactly the same criteria in investigations of fatal and non-fatal events. Clearly the dead cannot be interviewed. The living cannot be investigated as if dead as this would be likely to cause unnecessary distress to relatives, friends and to the victim himself. Many discussions of taxonomy have neglected these fundamental observations and have been built upon the assumption that both types of observation represent the truth, albeit gathered in different ways. It cannot be said that either or neither are the truth, for each is a different type of truth. This must be taken into account when using data to generate explanatory hypotheses.

Mortality

During the past 100 years there have been substantial variations in the annual numbers of recorded suicide deaths (Figure 1.1). There were falls during both wars, a rise in the early 1930s and a fall since the early 1960s. The variation in female suicide deaths was less marked than that for males except for the post-1960 fall.

The interpretation of suicide statistics for periods of war is difficult for many reasons. There were substantial and sudden changes in the size of the civilian population and this compounded the existing difficulties in estimating the size and age structure of the population. Military suicides were recorded separately from civilian suicides and it is possible that the military suicides were incompletely recorded. In a war with its disruption of the civilian population, there is an increased possibility of a suicide death not being ascertained — for example, in the case of a person who kills himself in a house that is bombed before the death is noticed. There may have been real decreases in mortality from suicide during both wars but the data are insufficient to be totally

Figure 1.1: Total Suicides, 1876-1975

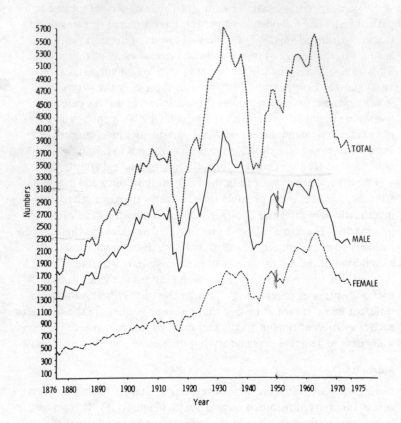

convincing (Farmer and Rohde, 1980).

Several methods of suicide can be followed independently over the hundred year period. The methods may be divided into two groups according to whether there has been any change in the availability of the instrument used to cause death.

Throughout the period there has been no change in the availability of instruments to cause a suicide by hanging (Figure 1.2). Hanging has always been much less common in women than in men. During both wars there was a fall in the numbers of suicidal hanging. There was no obvious rise in the 1930s. There was a modest fall in the 1950s followed by a rise that has been maintained for about ten years. The trends in suicide mortality by drowning (Figure 1.3) is quite different.

Figure 1.2: Suicide by Hanging

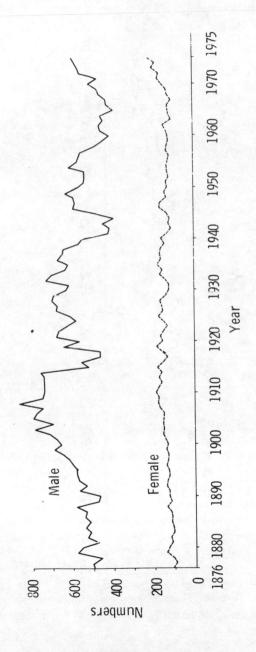

Figure 1.3: Suicide by Drowning

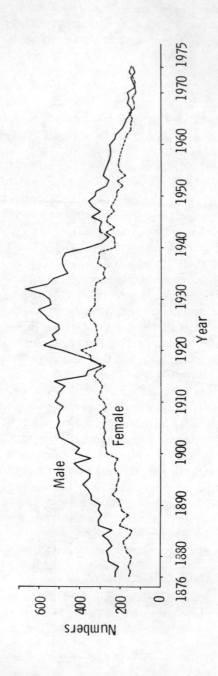

The male:female ratio is closer than for hanging. There was a marked fall in the number of recorded deaths during the First World War but a decline began in the early 1930s and continues to the present day. Because of this there is no obvious discontinuity during the Second World War. By the 1970s the male:female ratio is about one to one. The average age at death of modern suicidal drownings is about 10 years greater than that in the inter-war years. There has been little change in the annual numbers of suicidal jumpings. Suicides by cutting and piercing instruments (Figure 1.4) give a picture not dissimilar to that for drowning except that there is no major fall during the First World War.

The availability of instruments of death in three important methods of suicide has changed over the years. A possible causal association between the supply of toxic domestic gas and suicide mortality in post Second World War England and Wales has been suggested by Kreitman (1976) and by Hassall and Trethowan (1972). Figure 1.5 shows the annual numbers of deaths from suicide by coal gas during the 100 years beginning 1876. Although gas was manufactured from coal in England and Wales since the mid-nineteenth century it was used almost exclusively for public lighting. It was not until the early twentieth century that it was introduced to the domestic environment, first for lighting and subsequently for heating and cooking. This last change meant that it could be used in suicide. There was a sharp rise in suicidal gassings up until the early 1930s, and then this was followed by a relatively constant number of deaths each year for about 10 years. There was a fall during the Second World War which was more marked in men than in women. In the early 1960s a decline in suicidal gassings began, coincident with the introduction of some non-toxic oil-based gas. Thereafter manufactured gas was replaced by natural gas which, because of its low carbon monoxide content, is non toxic. Throughout the period the male:female ratio is closer than for most other methods.

Between 1876 and the early 1950s the annual number of suicide deaths by poisoning by solid or liquid substances (Figure 1.6) varied little, except for the periods of war. The male:female ratio was about 1:0.8.. In the early 1950s there was a sharp rise that continued until the early 1960s and thereafter remained static. After the Second World War the sex ratio reversed. The post-war increase was substantially caused by the increase in numbers of poisonings by medicines rather than domestic or household poisons. Suicides by firearms (Figure 1.7) are relatively uncommon and increased only during the wars and then only in members of the armed forces (dashed line in Figure 1.7).

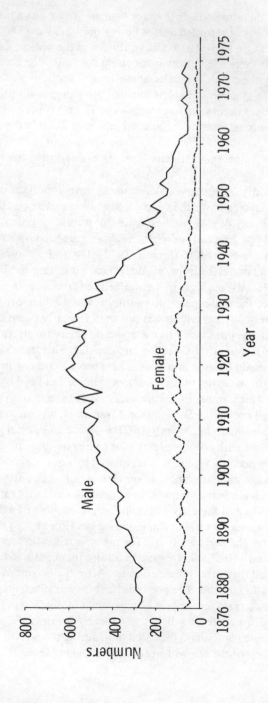

Figure 1.4: Suicide by Cutting and Piercing

Figure 1.5: Suicide by Coal Gas Poisoning

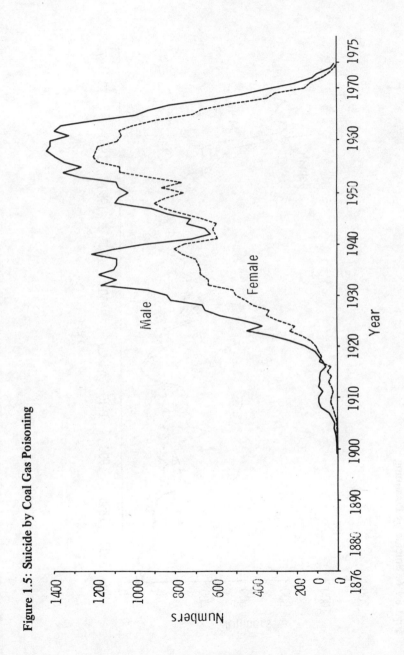

Figure 1.6: Suicide by Poisoning

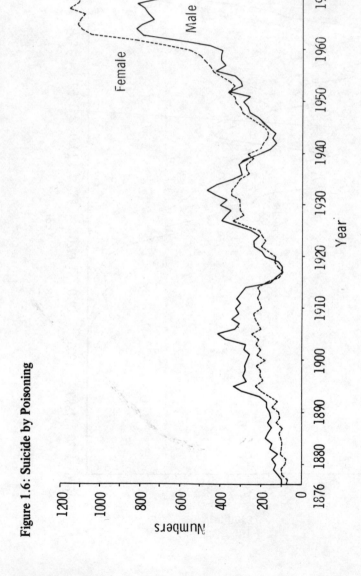

Figure 1.7: Suicide by Firearms

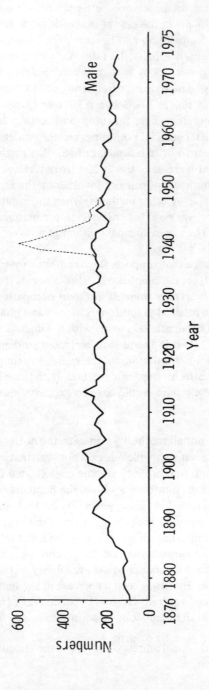

There is an obvious association between suicide mortality and the supply of instruments in the case of domestic gas poisoning, poisoning by solid or liquid substances and firearms. The principal question that arises from this observation is, does the availability of a method affect the proportion of suicides by particular methods rather than the total suicide mortality? The five most frequently used methods of suicide are shown together in Figure 1.8. Between 1876 and the early 1950s suicidal poisonings, hangings, drownings and cuttings tended to vary together. Thereafter suicidal poisonings changed independently. Coal gas suicides appear to be independent of all other methods throughout. During their great increase in the 1920s, there was not a significant decrease in the numbers of suicides by other methods, that is there is no hint of its replacing other methods. When the numbers of coal gas suicides fell there was no substantial rise in the numbers of suicides by other methods. The rise in suicidal poisonings was out of phase with the fall in suicidal gassing.

Further evidence that supports the hypothesis that the availability of substances affects the numbers of suicides comes from the investigation of mortality amongst different occupational groups. Medical workers, medical practitioners, nurses and pharmacists are amongst the ten occupational groups with the highest suicide mortality (OPC & S, 1978). This is due to their increased tendency to self-killing by medicinal agents. If variations in the availability simply determined the proportion of deaths by a specific method, then there is no reason to suppose that these groups would have an excessive mortality.

Morbidity

In part, because not all morbidity comes to the notice of doctors, and in part, because even that which does is not systematically recorded, the study of trends in morbidity is more complicated than the study of mortality. In the country as a whole, the numbers of episodes of poisoning has increased in recent years (Figure 1.9), and the increase has been greater amongst the younger than in the older age groups. The three most important drugs used in episodes of self-poisoning are the salycilates, the barbiturates and the psychotropic drugs. In recent years there has been no change in the availability of the principal salycilate, aspirin. There has been a decrease in the number of prescriptions issued for barbiturates (Department of Health, 1967-75) and an increase in the number of prescriptions issued for psychotropic drugs.

The estimated annual admission rates for the treatment of poisoning

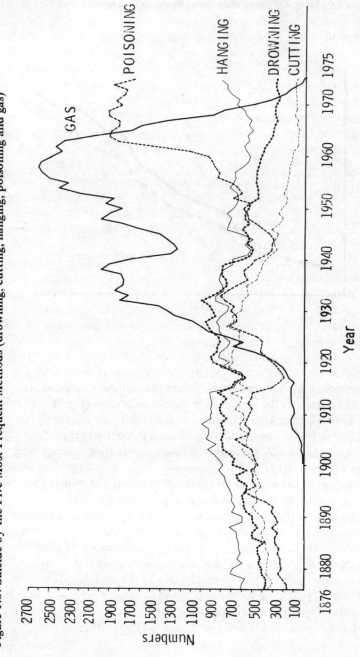

Figure 1.8: Suicide by the Five Most Frequent Methods (drowning, cutting, hanging, poisoning and gas)

Figure 1.9: Hospital Morbidity from Poisoning (England and Wales)

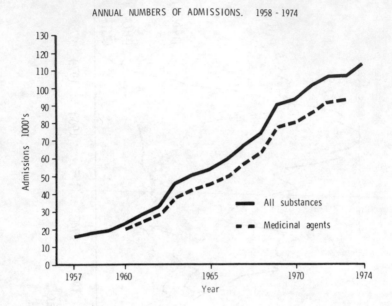

ANNUAL NUMBERS OF ADMISSIONS.   1958 - 1974

by various agents is shown in the figures that follow. Compared with the other methods the variations in aspirin poisonings (Figure 1.10) have been modest. After an initial rise the barbiturate poisoning rate fell (Figure 1.11) whereas there has been a steep rise in the rate of poisoning episodes by psychotropic drugs, especially amongst young women (Figure 1.12).

Once again, the question of substitution arises. The evidence seems to suggest that the rise in psychotropic poisoning episodes was independent of the fall in episodes of barbiturate poisoning. The ratio of poisoning episodes to deaths, the case fatality rate, has remained constant within age and sex groups for each substance over many years. The case fatality rate for barbiturates is considerably higher than that for the other substances. The explanation of the unchanged numbers of deaths from poisoning for the past ten years may lie here. Although the numbers of episodes of self-poisoning are rising the lethality of the substances being used is now less than it has been hitherto.

Figure 1.10: Admission Rates for Poisoning by Analgesics and Antipyretics, 1968-73

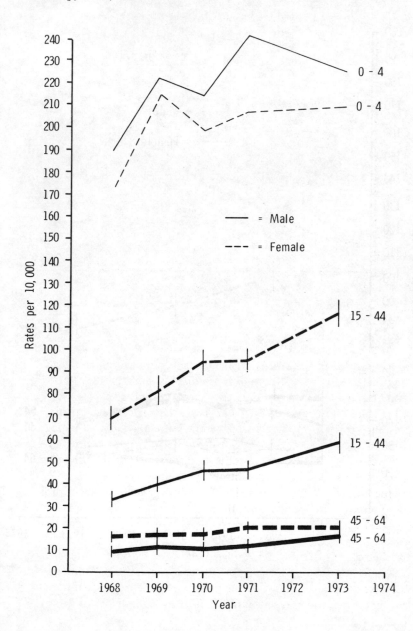

Figure 1.11: Admission Rate for Poisoning by Barbiturates and Other Hypnotics, 1968-73

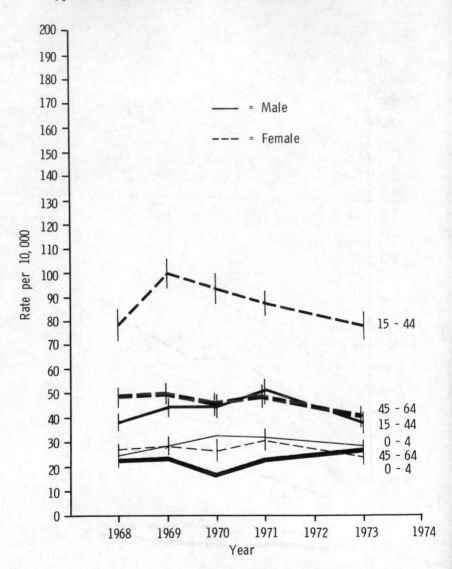

Figure 1.12: Admission Rate for Poisoning by Psychotropic Drugs, 1968-73

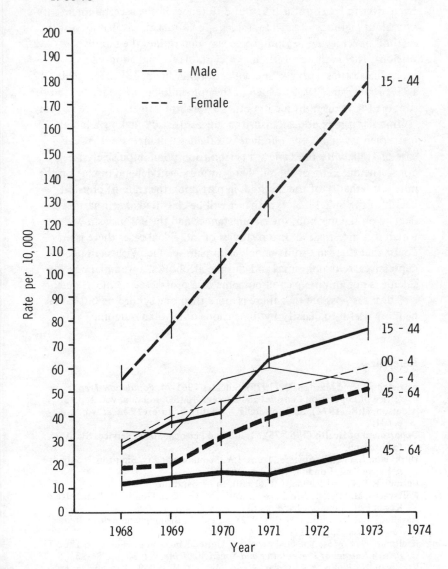

Discussion

Even after full account is taken of differences in the ascertainment rate of various methods of suicide it does appear that the availability of the method of achieving death in some way determines the numbers of suicides. The methods of suicides acceptable to, and adopted by, individuals varies with age and with sex (Durkheim, 1897; Morselli, 1857; Halbwachs, 1930). Much of the epidemiological evidence used to support the two-syndrome hypothesis does not withstand close scrutiny.

Initially it may appear absurd to suggest that by making a lethal instrument available the numbers of suicides will increase. However, ease of availability does allow a person to respond impulsively to a crisis. The outcome of the self-harm impulse will depend in part on the inherent lethality of the method, in part upon the state of physical health of the individual. Whether it will be classified as self-harm will depend on the method, the circumstances and the enthusiasm with which it is investigated. From studies of individual cases there is no doubt that there are some people who plan suicide. With such people, depressives, schizophrenics and chronic alcoholics, a well-planned suicide is not an unexpected outcome of a protracted mental illness.

Thus it is possible that there is more than one syndrome but it may be more useful to classify by dimensions other than outcome.

References

Adelstein, A. and Mardon, C. (1975). Suicides 1961-74. *Population Trends*, Office of Population Censuses and Surveys. HMSO, London, vol. 2, p.13.
Alderson, M.R. (1974). Self-poisoning – what is the future? *Lancet*, vol. i, p.1040.
Department of Health (1967-75). Health and Personal Social Services Statistics for England.
Durkheim, E. (1897). *Suicide*. Trans. J.A. Spaulding and G. Simpson. Routledge & Kegan Paul, London, 1957.
Farmer, R.D.T. and Rohde, J.R. (1980). In preparation.
Halbwachs, M. (1930). *The Causes of Suicide*. Trans. H. Goldblatt. Routledge & Kegan Paul, London, 1978.
Hasall, C. and Trethowan, W.H. (1972). Suicide in Birmingham. *British Medical Journal*, vol. 1, pp. 717-18.
Kreitman, N. (1976). The coal gas story: United Kingdom suicide rates, 1960-71. *British Journal of Preventative and Social Medicine*, vol. 30, pp. 86-93.
Kreitman, N., Philip, A.E., Greer, S. and Bagley, C.R. (1969). Parasuicide. Letter to *British Journal of Psychiatry*, vol. 115, pp.746-7.
Morselli, H. (1857). *Suicide*. 2nd edn., Kegan Paul, Trench & Co., 1883.
Office of Population Censuses and Surveys (1978). Occupational Mortality, 1970-72. HMSO, London.

Patel, N.S. (1973). Pathology of suicide. *Medicine Science Law*, vol. 13, p.2.
Stengel, E., Cook, N.G. and Kreeger, I.S. (1958). *Attempted Suicide, its Social Significance and Effects.* Maudsley Monograph, Oxford University Press, London.
Widgery (1975). From official report made of the judgement of the Lord Chief Justice of England, Lord Widgery, Mr Justice Milmo and Mr Justice Wien on 1 July 1975, Queen's Bench Division on the case The Queen v. HM Coroner for the City of London. *Exparte* Doris Barber.

2 THE SOCIAL CORRELATES OF SUICIDE IN EUROPE

P. Sainsbury, J. Jenkins and A. Levey

This chapter reports an investigation of an association between changes in the suicide rates of countries of Europe and changes in certain of their social characteristics. The study was carried out as part of a larger project commissioned by the World Health Organisation and undertaken in collaboration with Dr Baert (Sainsbury *et al.*, 1979). The aims were to describe suicide trends in Europe and against this background to test various hypotheses which we had put forward to account for the remarkable decline in the suicide rate in England and Wales between 1963 and 1974. In this way it was hoped clues to prevention could be obtained.

We began by comparing the mean suicide rates of 18 European countries for the two periods 1961-63 and 1972-74. The first three-year period was chosen because it immediately preceded the decline in suicide in England and Wales, while the second period was simply the last three years for which a complete set of data could be obtained. Using three-year means diminished the effect of minor year-to-year fluctuations in the rates.

The investigation was restricted to those European countries which report their suicide rate to WHO and which have populations which are

Table 2.1: Change in Suicide Rate for Overall Population, 1961-63 to 1972-74

Group 1 (decrease or low increase)		Group 2 (high increase)	
Rank	%	Rank	%
1. England and Wales[a]	− 33.9	10. Czechoslovakia	12.6
2. Greece[a]	− 21.1	11. Finland	13.4
3. Scotland[a]	− 2.8	12. Sweden	13.4
4. France	1.6	13. Norway	24.5
5. Italy	3.7	14. Poland	32.1
6. Austria	5.3	15. Netherlands	33.9
7. Switzerland	8.6	16. Denmark	34.2
8. Germany	9.1	17. Ireland	37.9
9. Belgium	9.2	18. Hungary	48.5

a. The group of countries whose suicide rates declined.

large enough to provide reliable age and sex specific rates.
Consequently, 18 European countries were examined. In 15 of these
the over-all suicide rate had increased, the three exceptions being
Scotland where the rate fell by 4 per cent, Greece by 21 per cent and
England and Wales where the fall was 34 per cent. In some of the other
countries the increase in the rate was of the same order as, or even
greater than, the decline in England — Denmark, Hungary, Ireland, the
Netherlands and Poland all had rises of more than 30 per cent.

In every country where the male rate increased so did the female
rate. But in two countries, France and Scotland, the male rate fell,
while the female rate rose. The increase in female rates continues a
trend which has been apparent in a large number of countries since the
beginning of the century, while over the same time changes in male
suicide rates show a less consistent trend.

The recent decline in the English rate was found in each age and sex
group with the single exception of females aged 15 to 24, and the sizes
of the fall were greater in the old age groups. In England the over-all
trend for male suicide since 1900 has been downwards, but in women
it has been increasing so the present decline represents an unexpected
reversal of this trend in women. In the other countries the greatest
percentage increases during 1961-63 to 1972-74 occurred in the young
of both sexes — notably in Finland, Ireland, Netherlands and Norway
(in Scotland the young male rate rose appreciably, but not that of
young women).

In women, in general, more countries showed increases than
decreases in every age group, although the sizes of the increases became
progressively less with age in most of them. In men this age effect was
greater, so that nearly as many countries showed decreases in the rates
of older men as showed increases.

The massive recent increases in the young in so many countries and
the almost universal increases in women's rates in contrast to those of
men since 1900, notably in the older age groups, all suggest that
trends in suicide are being determined by factors whose effects are age
and sex specific. That these effects may well be social and economic
influences becomes apparent when the trends in national suicide rates
are related to major economic and political events in Europe during the
first part of this century.

In both world wars the rates of nearly all European countries fell
sharply. Thus the 15 countries that published rates for 1938 and 1944
all show a decrease in their male rates of suicide and most of them a fall
in their female ones. Similarly, the rates of both sexes increased in more

Figure 2.1: Suicide Rates in England and Wales, 1900-74 by Age and Sex

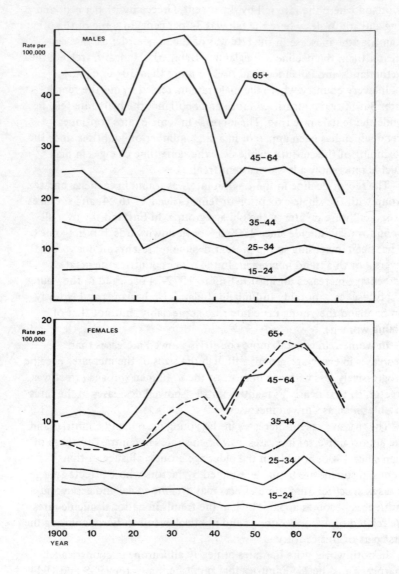

Table 2.2: **Effect of War on Suicide Rates by Sex in Selected Belligerent and Neutral Countries (suicides per 100,000 population aged 15 and over)**

Country	Male 1938	Male 1944	Male Percentage difference	Female 1938	Female 1944	Female Percentage difference
Belligerent Countries						
Union of South Africa	15.5	10.7	−31	5.0	3.4	−32
Canada	13.1	8.9	−32	3.7	3.2	−14
United States	23.5	14.9	−37	6.9	5.4	−22
Ceylon	10.1	8.2	−19	3.9	4.1	+ 5
Austria[a]	60.7	28.1	−54	28.6	13.8	−52
France	31.0	18.2	−41	8.9	6.1	−31
Italy	11.0	6.0	−45	3.6	2.0	−44
England and Wales	18.0	13.5	−25	8.2	5.8	−29
Scotland	12.3	9.1	−26	6.3	4.5	−29
Northern Ireland	6.9	5.6	−19	6.9	5.6	−18
Australia	16.4	9.9	−40	5.0	4.9	− 2
New Zealand	19.5	14.6	−25	5.1	5.7	+ 12
Belgium	27.6	18.1	−34	8.6	6.5	−24
Denmark	28.9	24.0	−17	12.9	20.5	+ 59
Finland	32.8	27.7	−16	7.3	5.3	−27
Norway	10.7	8.2	−23	5.3	9.8	+ 85
Netherlands	11.6	7.4	−36	5.4	5.6	+ 4
Japan[bc]	21.0	18.7	−11	12.9	12.9	0
Neutral Countries						
Chile	6.8	6.5	− 4	2.5	2.3	− 8
Ireland	4.7	4.6	− 2	1.8	0.6	−67
Portugal	16.6	13.9	−16	5.0	4.8	− 4
Sweden	25.0	20.6	−18	6.8	5.7	−16
Switzerland	38.4	37.2	− 3	11.6	14.7	+ 27
Spain[d]	6.9	8.8	+ 28	2.3	2.6	+ 13

Source: World Health Organization, 1956.

a. Nearest figures available for Austria were for 1946.
b. Nearest figures available for Japan were for 1947.
c. Japan was also at war in 1938.
d. Civil war in Spain in 1938.

countries than chance can account for during the economic depression in the early 1930s. Further, in England significant rises were apparent in all age groups, except for young women; and relevant to our present theme are that the contrary impacts of war and depression were most evident in the late middle-life, while the extent of the effects were comparable to the 35 per cent decline we are presently observing in England.

On the strength of these observations one of the hypotheses we

Table 2.3: Changes in the Incidence of Suicide by Sex and Age in
Selected Countries Between 1921-22 and 1931-32 (Economic
Depression) (percentage change − mortality around 1920-21 = 100)

Country	Males			Females		
	20-39	40-49	60+	20-39	40-49	60+
South Africa	+ 10	− 4	+17	+ 63	+104	+35
Canada	+ 29	+ 48	+33	+ 32	+ 15	+23
Chile	+ 96	+150	+41	+ 90	+200	N.K.
United States	+ 6	+ 28	+36	+ 19	+ 21	+20
Germany	− 3	+ 17	+ 1	+ 13	+ 28	+15
Belgium	+ 29	+ 19	+19	− 6	+ 18	+ 2
Denmark	+ 13	+ 22	− 9	+ 88	+ 6	+ 5
Spain	− 5	+ 36	+23	+ 14	+ 26	+33
Finland	+108	+ 58	+68	+ 39	+ 42	+13
France	+ 8	+ 3	0	− 5	+ 5	− 5
Italy	+ 5	+ 76	+55	− 4	+ 47	+52
Norway	+ 22	+ 35	+49	+ 63	+ 18	−24
Netherlands	− 14	+ 11	− 1	+ 15	+ 54	+38
Portugal	+ 14	+ 61	+54	− 10	+ 5	+46
England and Wales	+ 41	+ 20	+16	+ 42	+ 32	+45
Scotland	+ 56	+ 77	+76	+128	+ 91	+68
Sweden	− 9	+ 8	− 2	+ 3	− 2	−15
Switzerland	+ 13	+ 5	+ 5	− 4	+ 13	− 9
Australia	+ 25	+ 10	0	0	+ 17	− 7
New Zealand	− 10	+ 26	+19	− 5	+ 28	+47
Number which increased	15	19	15	13	19	14
Number which decreased	5	1	3	6	1	5
No change or number not known	0	0	2	1	0	1
Sign test two tailed p	.042	<.001	.008	.168	<.001	.064
Number of times age group had:						
Greatest increase	6	11	3	5	10	5
Greatest decrease	5	1	1	4	0	4

Source: World Health Organization, 1956.

proposed to explain the recent fall in the English suicide rate and its
increase nearly everywhere else was that it could be attributed to
socioeconomic changes during 1961-74. But besides examining the part
social factors might have played we also looked at three other possible
explanations. We will briefly refer to each of them in order to put the
socioeconomic one in perspective.

Firstly, we were able to dismiss decline in England as merely being
a statistical artefact due to changes in the procedures for ascertaining
and reporting suicide. Similarly our data also showed that national

differences cannot be ascribed to the countries' differing methods of ascertainment and registration of deaths.

Secondly, we investigated the hypothesis that changes in the availability of methods of committing suicide can affect changes in a suicide rate: for example, the popular view that the elimination of carbon monoxide from the domestic gas supply between 1961 and 1974 was found to have affected neither the decline of the rate in England nor the increase in Holland. In the latter instance, for example, the suicide rate increased as much in the Dutch Provinces where conversion to natural gas had been completed as those where this had not yet been achieved. It would appear that the availability of the means of suicide, whether it be carbon monoxide or medicinal drugs, appears only to determine the *extent* to which it is used rather than affecting the *incidence* of suicide in a population.

Thirdly, we considered the beneficial effect of improvements in psychiatric services in England, particularly in primary care and in the greater skill of the GP both in recognising the patients most at risk for suicide as well as in treating those conditions which so commonly accompany a serious intention to commit suicide. We found some evidence in support of this explanation which makes it one worth pursuing further.

On the other hand, when Barraclough and Jennings undertook a carefully controlled evaluation of an important lay organisation that befriends those in distress (The Samaritans), they concluded that the weight of the evidence was that the national decline in suicide could not be accounted for by the valuable services they provide (Barraclough *et al.*, 1977; Jennings *et al.*, 1978).

This brings us back to our fourth hypothesis, namely that the decrease in suicide in England and Wales and its increase in most other countries can be ascribed to changes in the social environment. More specifically we asked whether a set of social variables and the changes in them can predict the size and direction of change of the suicide rates of the 18 European countries for which we had the appropriate data.

Since Durkheim (1897) successfully tested his notions: (1) that those aspects of social life which increase the individual's integration with his family, neighbourhood and religious group protect against suicide, and (2) that suicide increases when society's control of its members is diminished ('anomie'), many researchers have confirmed and extended these associations. Sainsbury in his ecological study of suicide in the London Boroughs found operational measures of social disorganisation and isolation, such as divorce rates, immigration rates and the percentage of the population living alone, correlated highly with suicide, and then, for example, that suicides themselves were more often living alone and not London born than were the population at risk (Sainsbury, 1955). More recently, Ashford and Lawrence (1976) related the male and female suicide rates of 170 county boroughs in England and Wales to 88 social and demographic variables at two points of time. Using a step-wise regression analysis they found that the single variable, one person households, accounted for as much as 71 per cent of the variance of the male suicide rates between 1961 and 1967 and 48 per cent in the period 1968 and 1971. It was less prominent in females, but was still the major social variable.

Elsewhere in Europe similar results have been obtained. In Helsinki, Lönnqvist (1977) has shown that the incidence of suicide increases with social disorganisation; moreover, he found that in those areas of the city where his measures of integration had increased between 1961 and 1972, the suicide rate had decreased. Overall some 50 per cent of the variance of the changes in this time were accounted for by a combination of the social variables. This finding is of particular importance and may well be of relevance to England and Wales where a decline in suicides occurred during a similar period.

When it comes to seeing whether changes in social cohesion, in anomie or in economic well-being have been affecting national suicide rates, those concepts have to be restated in operational terms. We, therefore, needed first to select social variables that described these processes which are held to predispose to suicide, and secondly to find relevant statistics which are available for as many countries as possible.

Eventually, we obtained data on 15 suitable variables. These are listed in Table 2.4; some were selected as over-all indicators of anomie, some of the socioeconomic status of a country, while others refer to social changes affecting particularly vulnerable demographic categories whose suicide rates had altered most. You will gather from what we have already mentioned about age and sex trends in suicide that the ones that we were concerned with were: first, women and their changing status and role; secondly, the social predicament of young people who can be considered to have been especially exposed to the effects of changes in family structure and cohesion of an increasingly urbanised and affluent society; and thirdly, the elderly, whose occupational and domestic commitments have been greatly reduced.

There were some variables which we would have liked to have included, but they were either only available for a few countries or they were not consistently defined by the countries. Notably missing

Table 2.4: Social Variables

Social Variable	Social Indicators of:				
	anomie	family cohesion	status of women	alienation of aged	social economic status
1. Population < 15 years	*	*	*	*	
2. Population 65 years +		*		*	
3. Marriage	*	*	*		
4. Divorce		*	*		
5. Illegitimacy	*	*	*		
6. % births to women < 20 yrs	*	*	*		
7. % births to women >|30 yrs			*		
8. Women in tertiary education			*		
9. Female employment			*		
10. TV Sets/100,000 Population					*
11. Room occupancy					*
12. Unemployment	*				*
13. Deaths from cirrhosis of liver	*				
14. Homicide rate	*				
15. Road accident deaths	*				

Table 2.5: Pearson Product – Moment Correlations Between Social Variables and Suicide Rates in 18 European Countries, 1961-63

Social Variable	Over-all	Male	Female
1. Population < 15 years	−.4057**	−.3296*	−.5426***
2. Population 65 years +	+.1453	+.0848	+.2720
3. Marriage	+.2610	+.1891	+.4261**
4. Divorce	+.8492****	+.8198****	+.8061****
5. Illegitimacy	+.5790***	+.5581***	+.5810***
6. % births to women < 20 years	+.6849****	+.6544***	+.6866****
7. % births to women > 30 years	−.7211****	−.6797****	−.7453****
8. Women in tertiary education	+.2364	+.2916	+.0771
9. Female employment	+.4763**	+.4904**	+.4120*
10. TV sets/100,000 population	+.0638	+.0327	+.2476
11. Room occupancy	−.3170	−.2790	−.3670
12. Unemployment	−.3463	−.3813*	−.2201
13. Deaths from cirrhosis of the liver	+.2135	+.2184	+.2071
14. Homicide rate	+.4245**	+.4878**	+.2592
15. Road accident deaths	+.3486*	+.3310*	+.3707*

p = .10*   p = .05**   p = .01***   p = .0001****

are measures of living alone, migration and indicators of the social integration of old people.

Correlations between each social variable and suicide for the first period of time, that is 1961-63 (Table 2.5), were calculated and were much as predicted. Thus, suicide correlated inversely with two measures of family size, namely the proportion of the population aged less than 15 and the proportion of births to women over 30. And it related powerfully to such indicators of 'anomie' as rates of divorce and illegitimacy, though less strongly to homicide and road accident death rates. Of the indices of the female's role in society, the rate of women in employment and births to women below 20, were associated with suicide. These coefficients were remarkably similar for both sexes. Further, the base rates for suicide varied inversely with two of the socioeconomic measures: to a modest extent affluence begets suicide. In general, these findings accord with those of other ecological studies; though measures of female status do not appear to have previously been taken into account.

We next correlated the initial or basal values of the variables with changes in the suicide rates between the first and second periods to see whether they predicted the way national suicide rates would move in the ensuing 10 years (see Table 2.6). We found that two indicators of family cohesion were powerful predictors of an increase in suicide. They were: the proportion of children in the population and the divorce rate. On the other hand some of the measures of socioeconomic status, which indicated relatively low living standards in 1961, also foretold an increase in suicide in the latter period. In each instance these associations were stronger in men than in women.

Lastly, we correlated changes in the social variables with changes in national rates of suicide, since we had postulated that rapid social and economic developments in Europe would affect mortality rates (Table 2.7). We had, for example, designated a decrease in the proportion of young people as a measure of decreasing social cohesion and, in fact, found that national trends in suicide varied inversely with this measure. Also, as had been expected, three of the indicators of anomie increased concurrently with suicide. They were rates for illegitimacy, for road accident deaths, and for cirrhosis. The most striking finding with respect to indices of the changing role of women was that suicide in both sexes increased with the number of women in employment. The higher proportion of women in tertiary education, on the other hand, had no impact on suicide. One other measure of the altering role of women predicted change in their suicide rates: an increasing proportion

Table 2.6: Pearson Product — Moment Correlations Between Social Variables Base Rates (1961-63) and Change in Suicide Rates Between 1961-63 and 1972-74

Social Variable	Over-all	Male	Female
1. Population < 15 years	+.4141**	+.4408**	+.3503*
2. Population > 65 years	−.2290	−.3415*	−.0010
3. Marriage	−.3812	−.1457	−.3812*
4. Divorce	+.5510**	+.5996***	+.4108*
5. Illegitimacy	−.0739	−.0946	−.0489
6. % births to women < 20 yrs	+.2280	+.2937	+.0570
7. % births to women > 30 yrs	+.0330	−.0465	+.2347
8. Women in tertiary education	+.1665	+.2288	+.0928
9. Female employment	−.1057	+.0348	−.3595*
10. TV sets/100,000 population	−.5588**	−.5955***	−.4551**
11. Room occupancy	−.2859	−.1260	−.5298**
12. Unemployment	−.4034*	−.4153*	−.3362
13. Deaths from cirrhosis of the liver	−.2816	−.2878	−.2634
14. Homicide rate	−.0968	+.0311	−.2739
15. Road accident deaths	−.1962	−.2556	−.0822

$p = <.10*$ $p = <.05**$ $p = <.01***$

Table 2.7: Pearson Product — Moment Correlations Between Changes in Social Variables and Changes in Suicide Rates, 1961-63 to 1972-74

Social Variable	Over-all	Male	Female
1. Population < 15 years	−.4572**	−.5728***	−.2107
2. Population > 65 years	−.0323	−.1027	−.2949
3. Marriage	+.1385	+.1763	+.1203
4. Divorce	−.3786*	−.4225*	−.2924
5. Illegitimacy	+.1762	+.1057	+.3549*
6. % births to women < 20 yrs	−.3911*	−.3810*	−.3564*
7. % births to women > 30 yrs	−.1702	−.1549	−.2339
8. Women in tertiary education	−.0597	−.0621	−.0745
9. Female employment	+.4780**	+.4147*	+.5382**
10. TV sets/100,000 population	+.5573**	+.6155***	+.4239**
11. Room occupancy	+.2862	+.1834	+.3838*
12. Unemployment	+.3779*	+.3584	+.3349
13. Deaths from cirrhosis of the liver	+.3801*	+.4530**	+.1953
14. Homicide rate	+.1796	+.0983	+.3135
15. Road accident deaths	+.3715*	+.4306**	+.2480

$p = .10*$ $p = .05**$ $p = .01***$

of births to women under 20.

As regards economic change, increasing affluence as depicted by national rates of television ownership was also accompanied by an increase in suicide.

These results were sufficiently encouraging to lead us to examine further the combined effect of the variables by carrying out a discriminant analysis (Nie *et al.*, 1975). The purpose of discriminant analysis is to assess the relative contribution of the set of variables in allocating cases to some previously determined classification. In this instance, the cases were the suicide rates of the 18 individual countries and the variables the 15 social indicators already described. The analysis constructs a composite of the separate variables, each of which is also weighted for its contribution to the classification of interest.

If the 18 countries are listed in order of the change of their suicide rates starting with the largest decrease and progressing to the largest increase and then split at the median, two groups of countries are obtained; one in which suicide has decreased or has increased only moderately, and the other in which suicide has increased considerably (see Table 2.1).

As well as allocating each country to one group or the other, the analysis also predicts the relative size of increase or decrease in a country's rate, and this predicted order can then be compared with the original or observed rank order. Furthermore, the analysis classifies each of the social variables according to its discriminatory power or, in other words, its relative contribution to the composite of variables which prove most successful in discriminating between the groups. It is very important to note that the original discriminatory power of a measure may be greatly diminished or enhanced when it forms part of the composite variable derived from all 15 measures. Thus, the measures which separate the groups on their own before the discriminant analysis are not necessarily the best predictors in the discriminant function. This is because the composite reflects the joint effect of the variables and their tendency to reinforce each other; this is likely to differ from the isolated effect of any individual variable. Incidentally, any variable which fails to contribute to the classification is dropped from the analysis.

Results

In the first analysis we wanted to see to what extent the base values of the social measures in 1961-63 correctly predicted the changes in a country's suicide rate. Table 2.8 describes the extent to which the

The Social Correlates of Suicide in Europe

49

Table 2.8: Discriminant Function Analysis : Number One
Part A: Change in over-all suicide rate by base rates of the social
variables in 1961-63: continuous model.

Countries	Rank order of their suicide rates		Discriminant function score
	predicted	observed	
Group 1 (low)			
Germany[b]	1	8	6.04
France	2	4	6.03
Greece	3	2	5.73
Scotland	4	3	5.65
Italy	5	5	5.34
England and Wales[a]	6	1	5.24
Switzerland	7	7	5.11
Austria	8	6	4.36
Belgium	9	9	3.26
Group 2 (high)			
Denmark[b]	10	15	3.28
Norway	11	13	3.75
Ireland[b]	12	17	4.84
Finland	13	11.5	4.90
Czechoslovakia[a]	14	10	5.46
Poland	15	14	5.99
Sweden[a]	16	11.5	6.00
Netherlands	17	16	6.26
Hungary	18	18	6.27

a. Actual rank much lower.
b. Actual rank much higher.
Canonical correlation = 0.98 (correlation between suicide and composite variable).

countries are allocated to Group 1 (low increases or decreases in suicide)
or to Group 2 (high increases in suicide) by the base rates of the social
variables — that is their value in 1961-3. In other words, it describes
how efficiently the composite of the social base rates predicts a rise or
a fall in the suicide rate in the 18 countries in the following ten years.

All countries are correctly classified by the analysis. The observed
changes in the countries' suicide rates (whether they will increase
considerably or increase only a little or decrease) are therefore correctly
predicted by our social measures. Table 2.9 shows the DF coefficients
which measure the contribution each variable as part of the composite
makes to the discrimination. This part of the analysis shows that the
percentage of births to women below 20 and the related variable births
to women over 30, both measures of family integration, makes the
most poiwerful contributions to the combination of indicators which

Table 2.9: Discriminant Function Analysis: Number One
Part B: Order of magnitude of discriminatory power of base rates of
social variables (the standardised coefficients).

Social variable		Standarised coefficient
D6B	Births to women < 20	7.90
D7B	Births to women 30+	7.03
D10B	TV sets per 100,000 population	5.44
D12B	Unemployment	4.95
D1B	% population aged < 15	2.57
D11B	Room occupancy	2.13
D5B	Illegitimacy	1.39
D14B	Homicide	1.38
D3B	Marriage rate	1.08
D8B	Female education	1.03
D9B	Female employment	0.69)
D4B	Divorce rate	0.68) a
D2B	% population aged 65+	0.42)
D13B	Cirrhosis deaths	0.36)

a. Highly significant statistically but negligible quantitatively.

Variables on which Groups 1 and 2 differed significantly before DF analysis:
  D1B Population < 15 $p < .05$
  D13B Cirrhosis deaths $p < .01$
  D15B Vehicle deaths $p < .05$.

Variables excluded by the analysis (non-contributory):
  D15B Vehicle deaths (good single discriminator but differs from variable
       defined by DF analysis).

predict the size of a future rise of suicide. The socioeconomic
circumstances of a country are also seen to contribute substantially.
Thus, a high rate of room occupancy in 1961-63 predicts a large
increase in suicide, whereas a high wave of unemployment predicts a
decrease or a low increase.

The second analysis again involves all the social measures; but now
the changes in their values between the earlier and later periods are
applied to the changes in the country's suicide rates again split at the
median. This analysis also correctly classified each country according
to whether the increase in the suicide was low — below the median, or
high — above the median. But within the high and low groups, as can
be seen from the DF scores in Table 2.10, Germany was ranked too
low within Group 1 and Ireland too low within Group 2. Whereas
England and Wales were ranked too high in Group 1 and Finland too
high in Group 2.

The DF coefficients tell us that changes in the three principal
indicators of the changing status of women, the marriage rate, female

Table 2.10: Discriminant Function Analysis: Number Two
Part A: Change in over-all suicide rates by changes in social variables:
  continuous model.

Countries	Rank order		Discriminant function score
	predicted	observed	
Group 1 (low)			
Germany[b]	1	8	5.25
Scotland	2	3	5.13
Greece	3	2	4.48
Switzerland	4	7	4.16
France	5	4	4.04
Italy	6	5	2.96
England and Wales[a]	7	1	2.74
Austria	8	6	2.61
Belgium	9	9	2.10
Group 2 (high)			
Ireland[b]	10	17	2.41
Sweden	11	11.5	2.90
Czechoslovakia	12	10	3.02
Norway	13	13	3.45
Netherlands	14	16	3.85
Poland	15	14	4.13
Hungary	16	18	4.42
Finland[a]	17	11.5	4.50
Denmark	18	15	4.79

a. Actual rank much lower.
b. Actual rank much higher.
Canonical correlation = 0.96 (correlation of composite with criterion).

education, and females in employment contributed most to the
discrimination. In each case an increase determined an increase in
suicide. The other variable whose increase appears to determine the
extent to which a country's suicide rate will increase is unemployment.
It is of interest that before the analysis the two groups already differed
on four separate variables which we had selected as indicators of
anomie, namely changes in mortality from cirrhosis of the liver, road
accidents, homicide and the proportion of the population aged less
than 15 years; but in the discriminant function they are outweighed by
the other variables.

　　In conclusion, since the discriminant analysis enabled the countries
to be correctly assigned to the appropriate group, that is to say, the
group that they are observed to belong to, we have established the
pertinence of the social variables which were hypothesised as important
in affecting changes in national suicide rates. The social variables which

Table 2.11: Discriminant Function Analysis: Number Two
Part B: Order of magnitude of the discriminatory power of the
measures of social change (the standardised coefficients).

Social Variable		Standardised coefficient	
D3C	Marriage rates	4.39	
D12C	Unemployment	3.24	
D8C	Female education	2.99	
D9C	Female employment	2.08	Set I
D13C	Cirrhosis	1.75	
D15C	Illegitimacy	1.60	
D14C	Homicide	0.88	
D4C	Divorce rate	0.76	
D2C	Population 65+	0.60	
D1C	Population < 15	0.59	Set II
D11C	Room occupancy	0.50	
D6C	Births to women < 20	0.47	
D7C	Births to women 30+	0.21	

a. All 13 variables are highly significant statistically, but some are negligible
   quantitatively (Set II).

Variables on which the groups differed significantly before DF analysis:
   D1C   change in population < 15 $p < .01$
   D14C change in homicide rate $p < .05$.

Variables excluded by the analysis (non-contributory):
   D10C change in TV sets/100,000 population
   D15C change in vehicle deaths.

appeared to be having most effect in determining changes in the
incidence of suicide in the period we are considering are first, those
relating to the changing status of women, next those indicative of
increasing anomie and third, socioeconomic change.

References

Ashford, J.R. and Lawrence, P.A. (1976). Aspects of the epidemiology of suicide
   in England and Wales. *International Journal of Epidemiology*, vol. 5, p. 133.
Barraclough, B.M., Jennings, C. and Moss, J.R. (1977). Suicide prevention by the
   Samaritans: a controlled study of effectiveness. *Lancet*, vol. ii, p. 237.
Durkheim, E. (1897). *Le Suicide*. Paris. Nouv. ed. Alcan, 1930.
Jennings, C., Barraclough, B.M. and Moss, J.R. (1978). Have the Samaritans
   lowered the suicide rate? A controlled study. *Psychological Medicine*, vol. 8,
   p.413.
Lönnqvist, J. (1977). Suicide in Helsinki. Supplement to *Acta Psychiatrica
   Scandinavica*.
Nie, N.H., Mull, C.H., Jenkins, J.G., Steinbrenner, K. and Bent, D.H. Eds. (1975).
   Statistical Package for the Social Sciences. McGraw Hill, New York.

Sainsbury, P. (1955). *Suicide in London.* Maudsley Monograph No. 1, Chapman and Hall, London.
Sainsbury, P., Baert, A. and Jenkins, J. (1979). Suicide trends in Europe: a study of the decline in suicide in England and Wales and the increases elsewhere. WHO. In preparation.
World Health Organization (1956). *Epidemiological and Vital Statistics Report,* vol. 9, no. 4.

3 PARASUICIDE IN YOUNG EDINBURGH WOMEN: 1968-75*

N. Kreitman and M. Schreiber

Of the many purposes to which epidemiological monitoring may be put, two are of special relevance for parasuicide. The first and most obvious is that, since the rates are changing fairly rapidly, it is important constantly to update what has been established so that general conclusions from the over-all epidemiological pattern remain under scrutiny. The second is that monitoring serves to indicate which subgroups of the population are showing the most rapid change. The identification of such groups is important, since a dynamic situation should prove (in principle at least) more amenable to analysis than a static one as well as being more illuminating.

The problem of deciding which subgroup of the population is in fact showing most change is not trivial. Much depends on whether absolute or relative increases are being considered, and this in turn may depend on whether the chief interest is in service planning or in scientific enquiry. If *numbers* of cases are at issue, as is usual in service situations, then the absolute rather than the relative increases will be more important. If *rates* are being considered, the situation becomes more complex. A small increase, either absolute or relative, of the rate for some large population subgroup may lead to a psychiatric service being inundated but would suggest relatively little of scientific interest. On the other hand, a large increase in the rate of a rare disorder, or of one which occurs primarily in a small subgroup of the population may have little impact on service requirements but may point to important basic changes, for example, in the character of the disorder or an altered lifestyle of the section of the population manifesting the change. Even for scientific purposes, however, it remains to be decided, according to the question being posed, whether increase is more usefully defined in absolute or relative terms.

Scrutiny of the Edinburgh Regional Poisoning Treatment Centre records showed that between 1968 and 1975 the age-sex subgroup showing the greatest increase in numbers of parasuicides and in rates,

*First published in *Psychological Medicine*, November 1979 and reprinted by kind permission of Cambridge University Press.

each considered both absolutely and proportionally, was that of young
women. Most noticeable has been the age group 15-19, but those aged
20-24 have also shown a substantial growth. A review of the literature,
summarised in the discussion section, suggests that this is a general
finding and it is these two groups which will now be considered.
Attention will also be given to certain changes in patient characteristics
which cannot be expressed epidemiologically since general population
data are lacking.

Method

A parasuicide may be briefly defined as any individual who deliberately
initiates an act of non-fatal self-injury or who ingests a substance in
excess of any prescribed or generally recognised dose. This definition
does not involve ultimate intention, and therefore includes patients
suffering from acute effects associated with drug abuse or
experimentation; these patients are, however, considered separately
below.

The majority of parasuicides arising within the city of Edinburgh are
brought directly to the Regional Poisoning Treatment Centre (RPTC)
at the Royal Infirmary, Edinburgh, and it is official policy in the city
that all cases referred to any other hospital should be transferred there.
The RPTC operates a 100 per cent admission policy. A series of spot
checks over the years have confirmed that these principles have been
adhered to with a high degree of fidelity.

Information is routinely recorded on a pre-coded item sheet for all
cases with the exception of a few who discharge themselves prematurely.
Only those admitted between January 1968 and December 1975 and
whose addresses were within the boundaries of the city are considered
here.

The size and structure of the population at risk has been estimated
using the 1966 and 1971 censuses: for 1968 to 1970 estimates were
derived by linear interpolation between the census years and by
extrapolation for 1972 to 1975. This procedure has been reasonably
satisfactory, though certain difficulties were encountered which are
discussed below.

The definition of parasuicide and details of the Edinburgh system
have been presented at length elsewhere (Kreitman, 1977), while an
earlier report described the trends in parasuicide rates for the
population as a whole (Holding *et al.*, 1977). As in that study care has
been taken to distinguish admission rates (which refer to events), and
'first-ever' rates (referring only to those episodes which were the

individual's first parasuicide whether hospital treated or not).

Results

The trends in the rates for the two age groups of 15-19 and 20-24 are shown in Figure 3.1. The rates for the younger group climbed steeply between 1969 and 1973 with comparatively minor fluctuations subsequently. For the 20-24 group, the curves are less regular, but a steeper increase early in the study period can again be discerned. At the beginning of the period the rates for the two groups were not very different, but by the end the younger women were markedly ahead.

Table 3.1 gives comparative data on the number of cases as well as rates, presented as annual averages for the first two and the last two years of the period. Both age groups show a similar increase (of 88 and 83) in the number of admissions per annum. When expressed as rates, however, the picture is very different; the younger group shows an absolute increase of 631 per 100,000 of the population at risk as compared to a corresponding gain of only 270 in the older women, and this 'difference between differences' is highly significant statistically

Table 3.1: Admissions, Patients and 'First-evers' (numbers and rates per 100,000 by age group)

		Annual average 1968-69 (a)	Annual average 1974-75 (b)	Absolute difference — (b-a)	Proportional change — (b/a)
Younger Group — 15-19					
Admissions:	no.	77	165	88	2.14
	rate	421	1,052	631	2.50
Patients:	no.	71	144	73	2.03
	rate	385	918	533	2.38
First-ever:	no.	57	95	38	1.67
	rate	311	608	297	1.96
Older Group — 20-24					
Admissions:	no.	77	160	83	2.08
	rate	418	688	270	1.64
Patients:	no.	69	133	64	1.93
	rate	376	572	196	1.52
First-ever:	no.	48	75	27	1.56
	rate	262	321	59	1.22

The numbers of 15-19-year-old women in Edinburgh fell slightly between 1968-69 and 1974-75, while the numbers of 20-24-year-olds increased.

Figure 3.1: Female Parasuicide Rates per 100,000, 1968-75

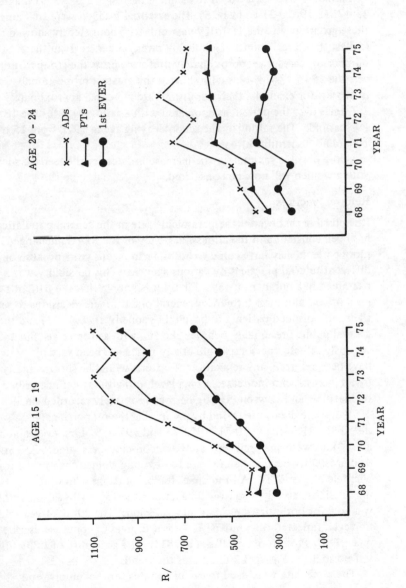

(p < .005). The patient and 'first-ever' data reflect a similar pattern, again with statistically significant greater increases in the younger group (p < .005 and < .02 respectively).

Similar analyses were used to examine narrower age bands (at ages 15-17, 18-19, 20-21 and 21-25). The essential findings were that among these groups it was the 18 to 19-year-olds who consistently showed the highest 'first-ever' and total admission rates. The increase in the numbers of cases was approximately uniform across the groups, but it was the 15 to 17-year-olds who showed the greatest proportional increases: for example, their admission rate increased approximately 2.7 times over the period, as compared with a ratio of 1.8 for the 18 to 19-year-olds. The raising of the school-leaving age in 1972 from 15 to 16 had no discernible effect.

Some possible reasons for the increase in rates for the teenagers and young women will now be considered.

Referral Practices

It is possible that even if the parasuicide rate in the general population has been constant and the admission policy of the RPTC unchanged, more patients may have come to hospitals in recent years because of different referral practices by various agencies. This possibility was examined in a number of ways. Firstly it is known that the patient's level of consciousness influences general practitioners' decisions to send their self-poisoned patients to hospital (Kennedy *et al.*, 1973) and the general public presumably behaves likewise with self-referrals. Since seriously affected persons would at any time have been very likely to have been referred, any relaxation of criteria would be shown chiefly by an increase in minor cases. Coma level, using the system described by Matthew and Lawson (1966), has been routinely recorded since 1970 and the data were tested by comparing the proportional distributions during 1970-71, 1972-73 and 1974-75. 'First-ever' and all admissions were analysed separately. Unconsciousness (grades 2, 3 and 4) consistently occurs less commonly in young women than in the total clientele of the RPTC. All the same, the proportions who were unconscious actually rose over time among the 15 to 19-year-olds: this was true for both 'first-ever' and all admissions. The 20 to 24-year-olds, however, reflected the tendency to lesser degrees of coma as described recently by Proudfoot and Park (1978) for the generality of Edinburgh self-poisonings. Figure 3.2 illustrates the trends.

The same data were used to calculate rates for the 'mildly' and

Figure 3.2: Proportion of all Poisonings Who Were Unconscious: 1970-71, 1972-73 and 1974-75

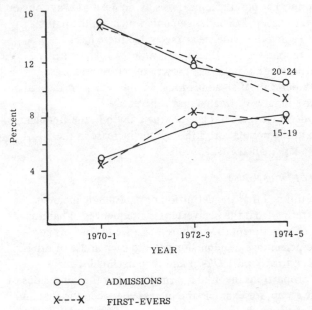

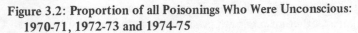

'severely' poisoned for the admissions and 'first-ever' in both age groups. Among the younger group both types of poisoning increased, the severely poisoned more steeply than the mildly poisoned. For the 20 to 24-year-olds, the mildly poisoned rate increased while the severely poisoned rate fell. Overall, then, firstly, there was no evidence of changing referral criteria having influenced the trend in total admission or 'first-ever' rates among the teenagers: for the older group, however, a change in practice might account for much of the trend in total rates.

Secondly, it is conceivable, though improbable, that agencies in some particular section of the city might have disproportionately increased their referrals in the more recent period. The geographical distribution of rates within the city was found, however, to have been highly stable over the study period.

Thirdly, a diffusion of awareness that the RPTC was concerned with all forms of parasuicide and not solely those due to poisoning might have led to more self-injury referrals in recent years. On comparing the first and second halves of the study period no evidence of any change was found, self-injuries consistently representing about 5 per cent of all admissions.

Lastly, the recorded source of referral, for example general practitioners, other hospitals etc., was also examined, but the data were found to be somewhat unsatisfactory; it is by no means always obvious after a crisis who initiated the arrangements which led the patient to the hospital.[1] Taking the evidence at face value there has been a disproportionate increase in self-referrals, which was statistically significant for both age groups. The growth of self-referrals, from about 25 to 45 per cent of all admissions, would explain at most about half the increase in rates of treated morbidity.

It is concluded that there has been a true growth in the frequency of parasuicide in the population, although the increase in the 20-24 group might be less than at first appears.

Acute Effects of Drug Abuse

It has been mentioned that the definition of parasuicide includes individuals suffering from the inadvertent consequences of habitual drug abuse or of experimentation. There was a trend towards an increase in the percentage of admissions due to such abuse of drugs, which continued to around 1972-73 and then declined slightly. However, the proportions involved are small; among the admissions of the 20-24-year group, for example the increase between the first and second halves of the study period was from 4 to 7 per cent.[2] Thus, although changes in drug misuse are of intrinsic interest, it is clear that they contribute little to the trends among young female parasuicides.

Marital Status

Age and civil status are so intimately linked that detailed standardisation procedures should ideally be used before any conclusions are drawn concerning the separate effects of either variable. The limitations of the census data precluded this. A simple stratification of the data by age and civil state is shown in Table 3.2, using only those cases clearly identified as single or married, and again combining the years into a first and second half of the study period (to accumulate sufficient cases of married women). From the upper part of the table, which refers to the younger group, it can be seen for both periods that most cases are of single girls as might be expected; however, the young married women have strikingly higher *rates* than the single, both for 'first-ever' and all admissions. Similarly the greatest contribution to the increased number of cases, however defined, is from the single girls, but the greatest absolute increase in rates is shown by the married. In terms of relative growth of rates there is not a great deal of difference,

Table 3.2: Numbers and Rates per 1,000 (1971 Census) for Admissions and 'First-evers' by Age Group and Marital Status, 1968-71 and 1972-75

		Annual average 1968-71 (a)	Annual average 1972-75 (b)	Absolute difference – (b-a)	Proportional change – (b/a)
Younger Group – 15-19					
Admissions:					
single	no.	83.8	138.5	54.7	1.65
	rate	5.2	8.5	3.3	
married	no.	12.8	23.0	10.2	1.80
	rate	11.3	20.6	9.3	
First-ever					
single	no.	55.5	80.8	25.3	1.46
	rate	3.4	5.0	1.6	
married	no.	9.5	13.0	3.5	1.37
	rate	8.2	11.5	3.3	
Older Group – 20-24					
Admissions:					
single	no.	50.0	75.0	25.0	1.51
	rate	4.6	6.9	2.3	
married	no.	40.5	68.3	27.8	1.69
	rate	4.4	7.3	2.9	
First-ever:					
single	no.	22.0	30.5	8.5	1.39
	rate	2.0	2.8	0.8	
married	no.	32.3	39.5	7.2	1.22
	rate	3.5	4.3	0.8	

although the proportional increase for all admissions is rather higher in the married population (80 per cent).[3]

The lower section of Table 3.2 concerning the 20 to 24-year-olds indicates that marital status in this group is of minor importance. The increased numbers of cases are drawn about equally from single and married alike, the rates do not differ strikingly between these groups and the pattern of increase in rates is more or less uniform.

Thus the younger married women appear to be showing particularly marked changes, which were investigated further using two different methods. The first extended the issue of civil status in general, and determined the number of women in what might be called a 'marginal' status, i.e. those who were divorced, living apart from, or cohabiting with someone other than their spouse. There are, of course, no population data for such a group, but the results are of descriptive interest. In 1968-71, 1.2 per cent of all 'first-ever' admissions in the younger age group were in this marginal category, while for 1972-75 the percentage was 6.7 per cent. It could, of course, be that young women have simply become more ready to admit to marginal status in recent years, but this is unlikely to be the whole story since the increase in those recorded as cohabiting, which is presumably the most sensitive category, was much the same as for those who declared that they were separated from their spouses, a designation carrying less social stigma. (Among older women the relative changes over time were less dramatic though all the percentages were higher. For example, over one in five of all admissions between 1972 and 1975 in this age group were in a 'marginal' category.)

The second approach focused on married women only, among whom the proportion was determined of ever-married women who at the time of admission were living apart from their husbands or were divorced. Between the two halves of the study period teenagers showed a ten-fold increase for 'first-evers' from 2.6 per cent to 20.4 per cent and for admissions from 2.0 per cent to 29.0 per cent. The older age group (aged 20-24) were similarly analysed, but although the proportions affected were generally higher, there was no consistent pattern over time. Less extreme indicators of marital stress and the conclusions that can be drawn, will be considered later.

Familial Aspects

Two family features were examined, namely permanent separation from mother and/or father before the age of 15, and the frequency of parasuicide in a close family member. Neither showed any trend.

Psychiatric Features

Few of the 'first-ever' cases in either age group had received previous psychiatric in-patient or out-patient treatment, and neither they nor the 'all admissions' showed any increase over time in the proportion which received such care.

Clinical diagnosis was considered under the separate headings of illness and personality disorder. Uniformity of diagnosis is not easily maintained with changing junior staff, especially in an emergency setting, but as noted elsewhere (Holding *et al.*, 1977) there has been a reasonably high consistency over the years in RPTC diagnoses. For present purposes diagnosis was considered under three broad headings. 'None' refers to an absence of recognisable illness but includes acute situational reactions; 'depressive illness' refers to both reactive depression and, much less commonly, to endogenous depression; 'other' comprises all remaining diagnoses. Table 3.3 shows that the pattern has changed over time though not uniformly for all groups. As proportions, the 'none' and 'depressive illness' categories have in general remained static or have increased while the 'other diagnoses' have consistently fallen. In so far as these changes can be interpreted they suggest an increase in minor pathology rather than in major illness.

Personality disorders, of various kinds but categorised for current purposes simply as present or absent, were also examined. The 15-19-year group showed a small *decrease* in the proportion recorded as abnormal personalities, from 36 to 27 per cent for 'first-evers' ($p < .02$) and from 51 to 43 per cent for all admissions ($p < .02$). The older group showed no change.

Taken together these findings suggest there has been no increase in major illness among either group, and that especially among the

Table 3.3: Illness Diagnosis by Age Group for 'First-evers' and All Admissions, 1968-71 and 1972-75 (percentages)

	1968-72	1972-75	
Age 15-19			
First-evers:			
None	72	67	
Depressive illness	19	28	$\chi^2 = 7.42$
Other diagnoses	9	5	$p < .05$
(N)	(261)	(393)	
All admissions:			
None	65	65	$\chi^2 = 10.91$
Depressive illness	24	29	$p < .01$
Other diagnoses	11	6	
(N)	(391)	(684)	
Age 20-24			
First-evers:			
None	44	56	$\chi^2 = 2.89$
Depressive illness	35	42	p N.S.
Other diagnoses	21	2	
(N)	(218)	(306)	
All admissions:			
None	48	54	$\chi^2 = 14.74$
Depressive illness	37	38	$p < .001$
Other diagnoses	15	8	
(N)	(401)	(633)	

younger patients situational disturbances and minor depressive
reactions in normal personalities have been noted more frequently in
later years.

The Role of Alcohol

Alcohol may be implicated in parasuicide either as acute intoxication
or by 'alcoholism', here taken to include habitual excessive drinking as
well as withdrawal states and physical damage from alcohol.

The consumption of alcohol within four hours of the parasuicidal
act was found to have become more common in both age groups, and
among both 'first-evers' and admissions. When individual years were
studied the build-up was found to be smoothly progressive. Summary
data for the first and second halves of the study period are compared in
Table 3.4, which shows that for the 15 to 19-year-olds seen between
1972 and 1975 nearly one-third had been drinking, with a higher
proportion among the 20-24-year group. The absolute and relative
increases in the proportions who had been drinking were similar for the
two age groups. Chronic alcohol abuse was, of course, less common but
also showed some increase in frequency.

**Table 3.4: Alcohol Before Act and Chronic Alcohol Abuse, 1968-71
and 1972-75 (percentages)**

Age		Alcohol before act			Chronic alcohol abuse	
		Years			Years	
		1968-71	1972-75		1968-71	1972-75
15-19	First-ever	17.2	28.7	***	2.3	3.3
	Admissions	18.9	30.0	***	5.1	8.6*
20-24	First-ever	21.6	36.3	**	4.6	5.3
	Admissions	23.2	37.3	***	10.5	13.0

Significance of difference from earlier period by CR.
* = p $<$.05   ** = p $<$.01   *** = p $<$.001

Selected Social Problems

Information was available for the whole study period concerning
certain social difficulties including (i) whether the patient was in arrears
of rent or had other serious financial problems irrespective of actual
legal actions pending against her, (ii) whether the patient had been the
recipient of physical violence, sufficient to cause damage, from their
spouse or other relatives over the preceding five years and (iii)

overcrowding, defined as a living density of 1.5 persons per room or greater; patients living in hostels or admitted from a psychiatric hospital were excluded from the calculation. Current trouble with the police, and having a criminal record were also examined but too few instances were found among young women to be of much help for present purposes.

In view of what has already been noted concerning the increasing rates of parasuicide among married teenagers, it seemed of interest to see how any changes in the proportions scoring positively with respect to the items just listed were distributed by civil status. Figure 3.3 illustrates the findings for 'all admissions' of 15-19-years of age; drinking alcohol before the act has also been included in this diagram. It can be seen that among the married being in debt has always been a notable feature, and has increased markedly in comparison with a very modest increase for the non-married. Being the victim of recent violence was in the earlier period about equally common in both groups, but has since increased substantially among the married, as compared to a small increase among the others. Alcohol ingestion before the act has always been a feature principally of the non-married, and has remained so, with similar increases in both categories.

Thus the patterns of social problems show a difference, and have changed differently, according to marital status. It will be recalled that teenage married girls have shown a much faster rise in the parasuicide rate than the non-married. It now emerges that debt and being a victim of violence have both increased markedly as a feature of the former group; alcohol abuse, on the other hand, has increased in both categories. The data on 'first-ever' admissions show a similar picture.

In contrast, the increase in rates among the 20 to 24-year-olds was shown (Table 3.3) to have been much the same among married and non-married women. Findings on social difficulties and alcohol are given in Figure 3.4. Debt, once again, is a consistent feature of the married and so too is violence in this age band. Drinking before the parasuicide has in both periods tended to characterise the non-married. But the point of chief interest is the absence of any conspicuous change in these features between the two halves of the study period and the only variable to show a significant increase, namely alcohol ingestion, has increased about equally (roughly doubled) in both subgroups. There is therefore no evidence of *differential* change according to marital status in this age group. The 'first-ever' data support this view.

The findings for overcrowding have not been illustrated because they present some peculiar difficulties (see below); in essence the

Figure 3.3: Selected Social Problems Among Admissions, 15-19 by Civil Status, 1968-71, 1972-75

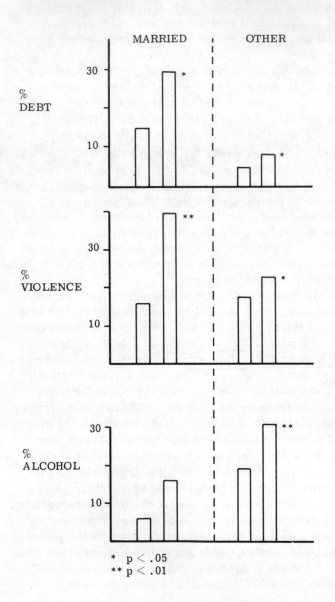

* p < .05
** p < .01

**Figure 3.4: Selected Social Problems Among Admissions, 20-24 by
Civil Status, 1968-71 and 1972-75**

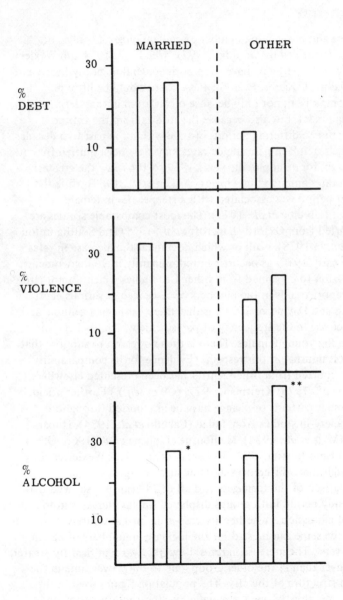

proportions classified as overcrowded have shown a decline in both the married and other categories for both age groups.

Discussion

Of the large and burgeoning number of epidemiological studies of parasuicide (reviewed by Goulding, 1971, Weissman, 1974 and Wexler *et al.*, 1978) relatively few have been both epidemiologically-based and longitudinal in character. Even for these there would be little point in detailed comparison, not only because of variation in case definition and ascertainment, but also because the studies from the United Kingdom refer to differing periods of time within the past two decades, during which trends in parasuicide rates may have been quite different. In Edinburgh, for example, the years 1962 to 1967 saw the greatest increase in rates among young males (Aitken *et al.*, 1969) while the subsequent period was associated with a steeper rise in female parasuicides (Holding *et al.*, 1977). The most comparable studies are those reported from Oxford (Bancroft *et al.*, 1975) and Southampton (Gibbons *et al.*, 1978), both of which document the increase in rates during the early 1970s as occurring predominantly in young women. The impression to be gained from other UK studies which do not cite rates but report trends in the numbers of cases seen at various centres (e.g., Smith and Davidson, 1971), is that there has been a genuine and marked increase in the frequency of parasuicide which has been most evident among young females. There is thus no reason to suppose that Edinburgh is unusual in this respect. (Evidence for its comparability with rates reported from other centres has been presented elsewhere (Bancroft *et al.*, 1975; Kreitman, 1977, p. 9 *et seq.*).) Further afield, broadly similar patterns of change have been reported throughout Western society in studies from Milan (Cazullo *et al.*, 1974), Hobart, Tasmania (Mills *et al.*, 1974), Melbourne (Linnane *et al.*, 1966, Oliver *et al.*, 1971) and Boston, USA (Weissman *et al.*, 1973; Wexler *et al.*, 1978) though some differences in detail also emerge.

A comparison of the teenagers and 20 to 24-year-olds showed that over the study period both groups displayed similar increases in the *numbers* of admissions, whether increase is defined absolutely or relatively; the same can be said for the increase in numbers of patients and 'first-evers'. The increase in *rates*, however, was significantly greater in the younger than in the older group, due to shifts over time in the population structure of the city. The population figures used in the calculation of Table 3.1 were estimated by linear interpolation and extrapolation as explained. As a check the calculations were repeated using the Registrar General's annual estimates for Edinburgh which are principally derived from birth and death statistics subsequent to the latest census. These analyses yielded an essentially similar picture; the increase in rates among teenagers was still greater than the increase among 20 to 24-year-olds, albeit less dramatic. Thus the general conclusions hold, though uncertainties about the exact population size (however estimated) between census years, warrant caution concerning the precise accuracy of the rates quoted. The Registrar General does not supply estimates by civil state.

High rates for married teenage women have been noted by other workers. Evans (1967) and Bancroft *et al.* (1975) reported an annual person rate per 100,000 of 1,640 and 1,027 respectively; the Edinburgh values were 925 for 1968-71 and 1,233 for 1972-75. Table 3.2 confirms that married girls of this age have higher rates than the single and the figures are conservative since cases with uncertain marital status have been omitted rather than redistributed. For admissions of married 15 to 19-year-olds the absolute increase in rates for the two halves of the study period of 9.3, is significantly greater than the increase of 3.3 for the single. The data on marital breakdown suggest, though do not prove, why this differential increase has occurred. The increasing vulnerability to parasuicide of married teenagers together with the national trend towards earlier marriages, and hence larger numbers at risk, must be contributing to the rising rate of parasuicide in this age group: the magnitude of the 'marital factor' contribution to the general increase (i.e., the attributable risk) cannot yet be assessed precisely. Meanwhile a point made earlier may be reiterated: although the rates for married teenagers have apparently accelerated more rapidly than those for the non-married, it is single girls who have contributed most to the increase in numbers of cases now being seen. The findings on 'marginal civil status' are relevant here, indicating what everyday observation confirms — that for the single as well as the married social-sexual relationships are problematic for a growing proportion of girls.

For the 20 to 24-year-olds the picture is different. There is little difference in the rates considered by marital status, no evidence of differential increase and since marriage is much commoner in this age group, the growth in numbers for recent years is derived about equally for both the single and the married. In line with these findings the data on social-sexual roles show that changes over time have been much more limited than was found among the teenagers. The reasons for the increase in parasuicide rates in the 20-24 group are presumably to be found in other areas; the increasing frequency with which alcohol is taken before parasuicide may be a pointer.

The findings on the changing composition of the patient cohorts with respect to debt and the receipt of violence buttress the epidemiological results. Both debt and violence were reported more commonly latterly by the married but not by the non-married teenagers, while among the 20 to 24-year-group there has been little change and no pattern of differences to reflect marital status. Drinking alcohol before parasuicide has become commoner in both civil status groups to about an equal degree, and this is so for both age groups. Thus the increase in alcohol consumption, though of great importance, does not emerge as explaining the differential patterns noted.

Overcrowding has also been considered. A previous report (Holding *et al.*, 1977) indicated that there was a marked excess of parasuicide rates (for all ages combined) among the overcrowded in the late 1960s but by 1974 the difference had disappeared. Data for subsequent years have re-established the disparity; however, on a long perspective the gap is narrowing rapidly, not because the rate for the overcrowded has fallen but because that for the non-overcrowded has risen. Young women reflect these trends in that the proportions among successive cohorts who are overcrowded have fallen, and presumably factors unassociated with overcrowding have become more salient in recent years.

Details on social class have also been omitted from this report although they are clearly important. The problems here are not only the usual difficulties of the social class determination of women but also that abrupt changes in categorisation may occur on marriage which have little to do with the realities of lifestyle.

It remains to be underlined that the data presented in this study are essentially of two kinds. Some, such as those on age and marital status, can be reported as rates over time thereby allowing for changes in the population. Other variables however, such as debt, violence and alcohol consumption prior to parasuicide are descriptive of patient cohorts; it cannot be concluded that such factors are causal in the absence of either general population data or case controls neither of which are available. Thus however plausible the causal role of the second group of variables might be on clinical grounds, their significance must remain unproven at present. But whether causal or coincidental it does emerge that two age groups which are directly adjacent have manifested different and specific changes and only one change (increased alcohol consumption) which is similar in both. The analysis of parasuicide trends in other sections of the population may similarly require special rather than general factors to be taken into account.

Notes

1. In the early years, source of referral was scored 'not known' in nearly 20 per cent of admissions, but this fell to below 5 per cent for the later part of the study period. The results quoted refer to proportional distribution after discounting the 'not knowns'.
2. Details are available on request.
3. Formal testing for the significance of the difference in rates (each based on four years data) shows that for the 15-19-year group, the increase in the 'first-ever' rate for the single was $p < .0001$. For the married girls, the much larger increase fails to reach statistical significance presumably because the number of cases is small. For admissions, the increase for both the single and the married is significant at $p < .001$ or better, and the magnitude of the increase for the married married is significantly greater ($p < .05$) than the increase for the single.

References

Aitken, R.C.B., Buglass, D. and Kreitman, N. (1969). The changing pattern of attempted suicide in Edinburgh, 1962-67. *British Journal of Preventive and Social Medicine*, vol. 23, pp. 111-15.

Bancroft, J.H.J., Skirmshire, A.M., Reynolds, F., Simkin, S. and Smith, J. (1975). Self-poisoning and self-injury in the Oxford area: epidemiological aspects. *British Journal of Preventive and Social Medicine*, vol. 29, pp. 170-77.

Cazzulo, C.L., Invernizzi, G. and Vitali, A. (1974). Ricerche epidemiologiche ed ecologiche in tema de tenativo di suicidio in eta giovanile. *Minerva Psichiatrice e Psicological*, vol. 15, no. 3, pp. 113-20.

Evans, J.G. (1967). Deliberate self-poisoning in the Oxford area. *British Journal of Preventive and Social Medicine*, vol. 21, no. 3, pp. 97-107.

Gibbons, J., Elliot, J., Unwin, P. and Gibbons, J.L. (1978). The urban environment and deliberate self-poisoning: trends in Southampton, 1972-77. *Social Psychiatry*, vol. 13, pp. 159-66.

Goulding, R. (1971). Self-poisoning. *British Journal of Hospital Medicine*, vol. 5, pp. 249-60.

Holding, T., Buglass, D., Duffy, J. and Kreitman, N. (1977). Parasuicide in Edinburgh: a seven-year review 1968-74. *British Journal of Psychiatry*, vol. 130, pp. 534-43.

Kennedy, P. and Kreitman, N. (1973). An epidemiological study of parasuicide ('attempted suicide') in general practice. *British Journal of Psychiatry*, vol. 123, pp. 23-34.

Kreitman, N. (1977). *Parasuicide*. J. Wiley.

Linnane, J., Buckle, R.C. and McConaghy, N. (1966). A comparison of patients seen at the Alfred Hospital after suicidal attempts in 1959-60 and 1963-64. *Medical Journal of Australia*, vol. 1, pp. 665-9.

Matthew, H. and Lawson, A. (1966). Acute barbiturate poisoning: a review of two years' experience. *Quarterly Journal of Medicine*, vol. 35, pp. 539-52.

Mills, J., Williams, C., Sale, I., Perkin, G. and Henderson, S. (1974). The epidemiology of self-poisoning in Hobart, 1968-72. *Australian and New Zealand Journal of Psychiatry*, vol. 8, p. 167.

Oliver, R., Kaminski, Z., Tudor, K. and Hetzel (1971). The epidemiology of attempted suicide as seen in the Casualty Department, Alfred Hospital, Melbourne. *Medical Journal of Australia*, vol. 1, pp. 833-39.

Proudfoot, A. and Park, J. (1978). Changing pattern of drugs used for self-poisoning. *British Medical Journal*, vol. 1, pp. 90-93.

Smith, J.S. and Davidson, K. (1971). Changes in the pattern of admissions for attempted suicide in Newcastle upon Tyne during the 1960s. *British Medical Journal*, Hospital Topics, pp. 412-15.

Weissman, M. (1974). The epidemiology of suicide attempts. *Archives General Psychiatry*, vol. 30, pp. 737-46.

Weissman, M., Paykel, E., French, N., Mark, H., Fox, K. and Prusoff, B. (1973). Suicide attempts in an urban community, 1955-70. *Social Psychiatry*, vol. 8, pp. 82-91.

Wexler, L., Weissman, M.M. and Kasl, S.V. (1978). Suicide attempts, 1970-75: updating a United States study and comparisons with international trends. *British Journal of Psychiatry*, vol. 132, pp. 180-85.

4 SUICIDE AND ATTEMPTED SUICIDE AMONG ADOLESCENTS IN FRANCE

M. Choquet, F. Facy and F. Davidson

Since 1972 our research team has concentrated much of its effort on the epidemiological study of suicide among young people in France. The studies that have been carried out attempted to find out how widespread the phenomenon is, what causes it and what socio-demographic factors are associated with it. We have also tried to grasp its meaning in order to identify risk factors and thus to organise prevention more rationally.

This chapter summarises the progress made in our research. It falls into two parts: (i) a description of the secular trends of suicide and attempted suicide in young people and (ii) a more analytical part drawn from the results of several surveys carried out among teenagers.

Suicide Morbidity and Mortality in Young People

Mortality

The study of the death certificates completed by medical practitioners over a period of eight years (1968-76) shows that there has been little change in suicide rates in most age and sex groups (see Figure 4.1). However, there is a definite increase in the suicide rate for men aged 15-24; it has risen from 8.4 per 100,000 in 1968 to 13.3 per 100,000 in 1976 (i.e. a relative increase of 58 per cent). During the same period, there is very little variation in the rates for young women. Figure 4.2 shows the proportionate contribution of suicide to total mortality between 1968 and 1976.

For all age groups combined the proportion of deaths by suicide did not change between 1968 and 1976. Throughout the period it has contributed more to male than to female mortality. Among people aged 25-34, suicide is responsible for an even higher proportion of deaths (13 to 24 per cent) but its importance rapidly decreases with increasing age. The way young people commit suicide is different from the way in which people in all age groups do. The methods chosen have changed between 1968 and 1976 (see Figures 4.3 and 4.4).

Among women one out of three used drug overdose (one out of four if all the age groups are considered). There has been a decrease in the frequency of drowning since 1968. Hanging and drowning are not

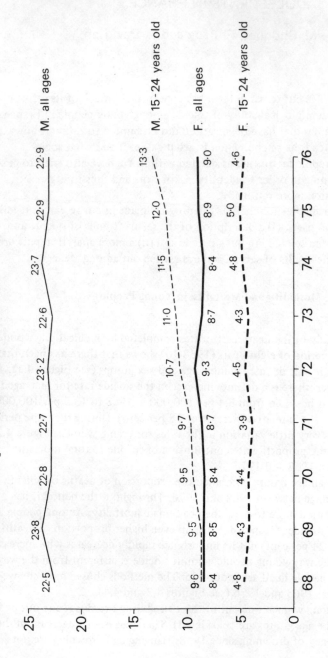

Figure 4.1: Suicide Death Rates per 100,000 from 1968 to 1976

Figure 4.2: Suicides per 1,000 Deaths

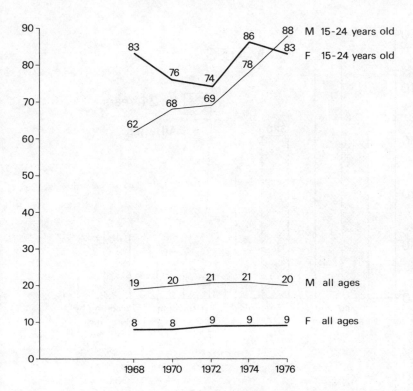

Figure 4.3: Method of Suicide (percentage of distribution of total suicides)

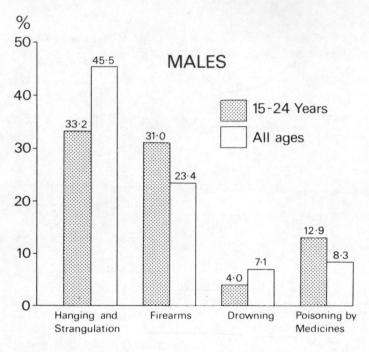

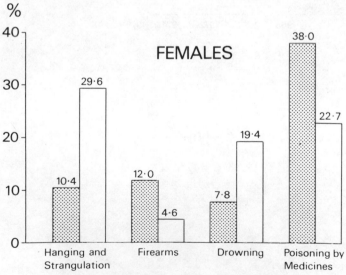

Figure 4.4: Method of Suicide in Young People, 15-24 Years Old
(percentage distribution of total suicides)

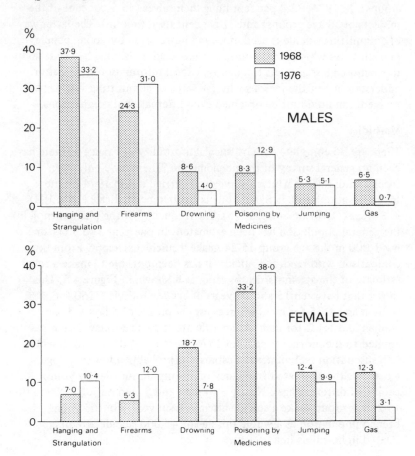

frequent among young women and young men more often resort to violent means (this trend has been noticed among men of all age groups). In 1976, 33.2 per cent hung themselves (45.5 per cent of the subjects of all age groups) and 31 per cent used firearms. The latter way of committing suicide is used more and more often by young people of both sexes whereas drowning, and above all, poisoning by gas seem to be chosen less and less frequently. Useful information for a better understanding of the reasons why the ways of committing suicide have evolved, can no doubt be obtained from international comparisons.

Morbidity

There are no complete data of suicidal morbidity in France as there has been no general survey of the phenomenon. There have only been special studies from which a survey was carried out in 1974 by the Institut Nationale de la Santé et de la Rechèrche Medicale (INSERM) in 3 areas (Davidson *et al.*, 1975). The frequency of the phenomenon in the general population has been estimated. In one year 3 to 5 persons per 1,000 in the age group 15-24, make a suicidal attempt. From the comparison with recorded suicides it has been possible to make a rough estimate of the attempts/deaths ratio, as is shown in Figure 4.5. This shows that between 15 and 24 years of age the ratio is 1:160 for women and 1:25 for men, whereas for people over 65 it is 1:3 for women and 1:1.2 for men. As an estimate these ratios have been applied to the mortality data for 1976. Because of the improvements in resuscitation techniques the estimate is probably a low one. Figure 4.6 shows the estimated frequency of attempted suicides by young people of different ages. Nearly 7 women and 3 men out of 1,000 in the 15-24 age group make a suicide attempt each year. For the young French population as a whole this means 45,000 suicide attempts treated in hospitals in a year.

An Analytical Study of Suicide among Adolescents

With such high figures for mortality and morbidity it seemed relevant to carry out epidemiological research taking into account the various social, cultural, demographic, psychiatric and psychological aspects of the suicidal act. It is indeed important to identify risk and predictive factors in order to foresee and prevent any attempted suicide. Such research has been carried out recently in other countries: Bagley and Greer (1971), Buglass and Horton (1974), Henderson *et al.* (1977), Kreitman (1976), Katschnig and Sint (1973), Paykel and Rassaby (1978).

Figure 4.5: Ratio Attempted Suicide/Suicide by Age and Sex

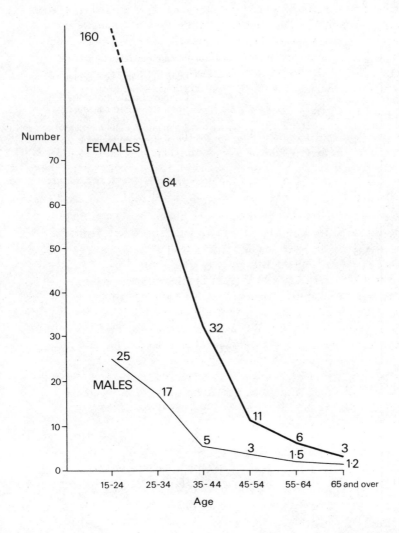

Figure 4.6: Suicide and Attempted Suicide (estimated) (Rate per 100,000, 1976)

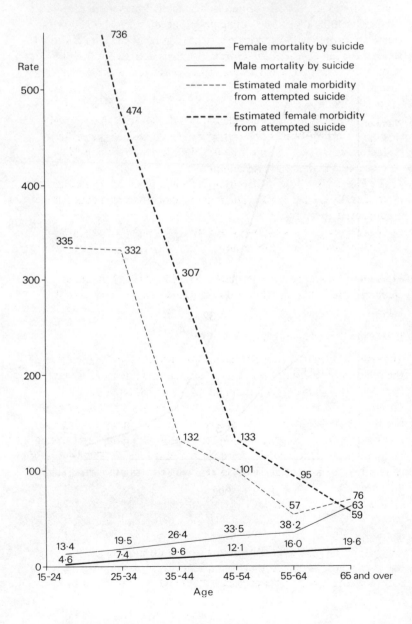

We carried out two surveys among young people. The first one, in 1971, was amongst teenagers: 2,339 secondary school pupils, a representative sample from three French regions, who answered questions about their consumption of psychotropic drugs and gave their opinions about these products. The second survey questioned a 'deviant' population of 535 young people aged 15-19 who had been treated in hospital after a suicide attempt. Some of the data collected were of the same nature; therefore a comparison between the two populations was possible. The analysis of these data was directed towards:

(1) The comparison of the suicidal population with the 'normal' population. From this risk factors can be derived. Some of these factors were also characteristic of other deviant behaviour, for example, drug taking and delinquency.
(2) The comparison of first attempters and repeaters in an attempt to identify a scale of risk. The reliability of this scale needed to be improved and validated.
(3) The search for a typology of suicide attempters, using a method of classification into four groups.

The method used has been developed by Diday (1971). Its main characteristic is that it makes it possible to determine very definite types.

Risk Factors in Attempted Suicide

The risk factors are first explained and then related to the family and the relationships within the family. Our team has published several papers on this subject (Davidson and Angel, 1978; Davidson and Choquet, 1976; and Davidson, Choquet and Facy, 1976). They bear out the results of other clinical epidemiological studies on suicide attempters which show that coming from a broken family and having unhappy parental relationships are outstanding factors. The importance of family size and family history is also worth mentioning (see Tables 4.1 and 4.2).

If we study the importance of various sociological factors that are pathogenic — for example, some difficulty in the matrimonial situation of the parents or in the family history, then we come to the following conclusion: 64 per cent of the young suicide attempters carry at least one pathogenic factor. Among them, 32 per cent carry only one pathological factor, 22 per cent carry two factors, 8 per cent three

Table 4.1: Size of the Families of Young Suicide Attempters

Size of families	Census data (15)	Suicide attempters
	%	%
Only child	18.0	10.6
2 or 3 children	50.0	39.8
More than 4 children	32.0	49.6

Table 4.2: Pathological Family History

Percentage with family history of:

	%
Suicide	10.3
Attempted suicide	25.8
Mental diseases	17.1
Alcoholism	31.9
Young people having at least one family member with one of the above characteristics	44.0

Table 4.3: State of Health

	Suicide attempters	Control population secondary school children
	%	%
Are in poor health	40	12
Have been seriously ill	29	15
Have been treated in hospital several times	36	15
Take sedative tablets	37	10
Take sleeping tablets	48	13

factors and 2 per cent four factors. This family pathology is therefore important and nearly one out of three young people carries several factors.

Among the risk factors that have been studied relating to this, the past medical history of the subject is of particular interest (Table 4.3): the young suicide attempters feel that their health is poor; they have been treated in hospital more often than others; they are more likely to have been seriously ill and have taken psychotropic substances. Eleven per cent of the suicide attempters had been treated in hospital during the six months preceding the last attempted suicide and among them, nearly one out of five was treated for mental disorders. It should be noted that 6 per cent of the suicidal teenagers had been treated in hospitals for psychiatric or nervous disorders (the figure is ten times lower in the reference population), 58 per cent had taken sleeping or sedative tablets and 9.3 per cent were under the follow-up care of a psychiatrist, psychologist or psychotherapist. Moreover, the analysis reveals that 46 per cent of the subjects had difficulties at school during their childhood or adolescence; 52 per cent had behaviour difficulties which had led them to see a specialist.

Studies on young drug addicts, delinquents or young people taking psychotropic substances have shown that these sociodemographic, psychological, medical or family variables are risk factors of deviant behaviour in general (Taleghani, 1979; and Choquet *et al*, 1977). Complementary studies on the different deviant groups should help analysis of the specific character of the suicidal act.

Scale of Risk of Repeated Attempted Suicide

The fact that repeated attempted suicide is very frequent amongst suicide attempters makes it necessary to build up a scale of risk to enable more appropriate care of primary suicide attempters to be provided. Among all the factors which have been studied, some are particularly meaningful for repeaters and clearly differentiate them from the first attempters (Davidson and Choquet, 1976). These factors are:

psychiatric diagnosis or pathological personality;
belonging to a family of four children or more;
alcoholism in the previous history of the family;
disturbed relationship with the family;
school and behaviour difficulties;
depressive tendencies.

The subjects who carry the first factor and who carry at least three of the other factors carry a high risk of becoming repeaters; 48 per cent of them have already attempted suicide.

Using a method of segmentation it has been noticed that the highest risk is to be found in the specific association of these factors (Davidson, Choquet and Facy, 1976). For example, among those who have had behaviour difficulties, a psychiatric diagnosis and who consider that their parents have too much or not enough authority, 62 per cent are repeaters. The accumulation of factors is important, but their specific association is an outstanding warning sign.

Typology of Suicide Attempters

Using cluster analysis the subjects are classified according to the
sociodemographic and family variables. The other variables, namely
the information provided by the medical practitioner (description of
the suicidal act) or by the subject himself (self-portrait or description
of his way of life) are then used to characterise the different groups
(Facy *et al.*, 1979). Four reasonably distinct groups of suicide
attempters have thus been identified (see Figures 4.7 to 4.10). Of the
four groups, Types I and II include the subjects who had made a
particularly serious attempt. They carry a high risk of repetition partly
because of adverse family and social factors and partly because of
difficulties in their personal situation and strong self-destructive
tendencies. Social integration has been poor, intellectual and
educational levels are low, poor health and mental disturbances are
common and the subject has often resorted to violent means or taken
several medicines in his or her suicide attempt. Those who belong to
Type II are younger and mainly characterised by the absence of one of
the parents and the presence of step-brothers and sisters and have only
made one attempt, but are otherwise similar to those in Type I. Types
III and IV carry a lower risk of repetition because they have more
integrated relationships and do not suffer from mental disorders. But
some subjects in Type IV carry the risk of repeating their 'appeal
suicide' because of the aggressiveness of the family though the suicidal
tendencies are not as serious as for the other types. Indeed, the subjects
in Type IV often make a suicidal attempt with only one medicine.

It is clear that males more often belong to Types I and II and
females to Type IV. This enables us to say that attempts by males,
even if they are less numerous than those made by females, are more
serious, which might explain why the mortality through suicide is
higher for males.

Conclusion

The main aim of all the studies, which have been briefly summed up in
this chapter, is to gain a better understanding of the factors predisposing
to suicide in order to propose preventive action and follow-up care in
this field. In view of these results it seems important to emphasise the
necessity of undertaking research on an international level to help
understand this alarming phenomenon more fully.

Figure 4.7: Suicide Attempters (Type I)

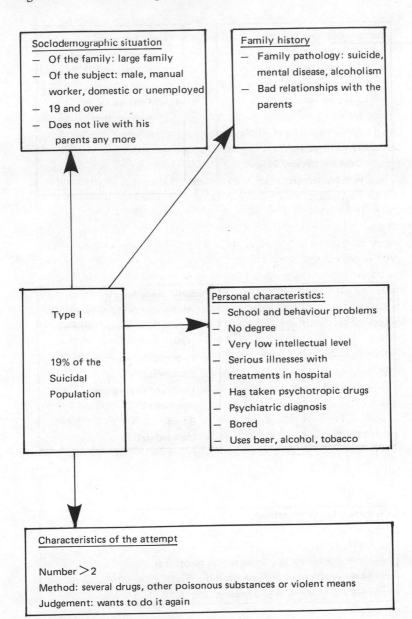

Sociodemographic situation
— Of the family: large family
— Of the subject: male, manual
  worker, domestic or unemployed
— 19 and over
— Does not live with his
  parents any more

Family history
— Family pathology: suicide,
  mental disease, alcoholism
— Bad relationships with the
  parents

Type I

19% of the
Suicidal
Population

Personal characteristics:
— School and behaviour problems
— No degree
— Very low intellectual level
— Serious illnesses with
  treatments in hospital
— Has taken psychotropic drugs
— Psychiatric diagnosis
— Bored
— Uses beer, alcohol, tobacco

Characteristics of the attempt

Number > 2
Method: several drugs, other poisonous substances or violent means
Judgement: wants to do it again

Figure 4.8: Suicide Attempters (Type II)

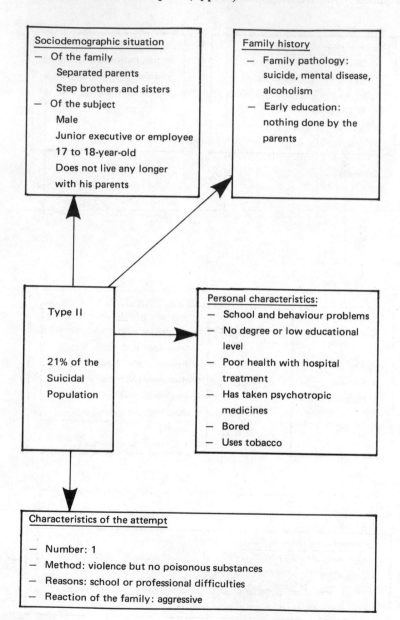

Sociodemographic situation
— Of the family
    Separated parents
    Step brothers and sisters
— Of the subject
    Male
    Junior executive or employee
    17 to 18-year-old
    Does not live any longer
    with his parents

Family history
— Family pathology:
    suicide, mental disease,
    alcoholism
— Early education:
    nothing done by the
    parents

Type II

21% of the Suicidal Population

Personal characteristics:
— School and behaviour problems
— No degree or low educational level
— Poor health with hospital treatment
— Has taken psychotropic medicines
— Bored
— Uses tobacco

Characteristics of the attempt

— Number: 1
— Method: violence but no poisonous substances
— Reasons: school or professional difficulties
— Reaction of the family: aggressive

Figure 4.9: Suicide Attempters (Type III)

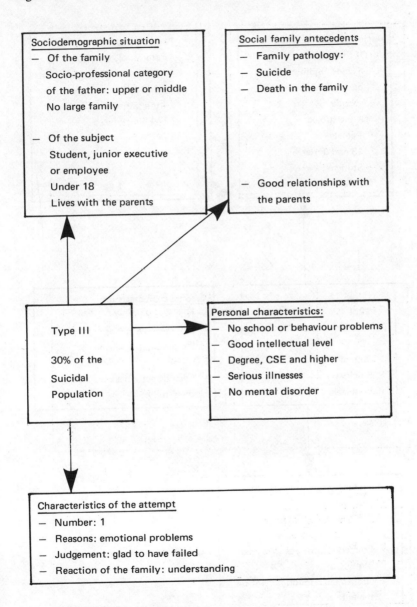

Sociodemographic situation
- Of the family
  Socio-professional category
  of the father: upper or middle
  No large family

- Of the subject
  Student, junior executive
  or employee
  Under 18
  Lives with the parents

Social family antecedents
- Family pathology:
- Suicide
- Death in the family

- Good relationships with
  the parents

Type III

30% of the
Suicidal
Population

Personal characteristics:
- No school or behaviour problems
- Good intellectual level
- Degree, CSE and higher
- Serious illnesses
- No mental disorder

Characteristics of the attempt
- Number: 1
- Reasons: emotional problems
- Judgement: glad to have failed
- Reaction of the family: understanding

Figure 4.10: Suicide Attempters (Type IV)

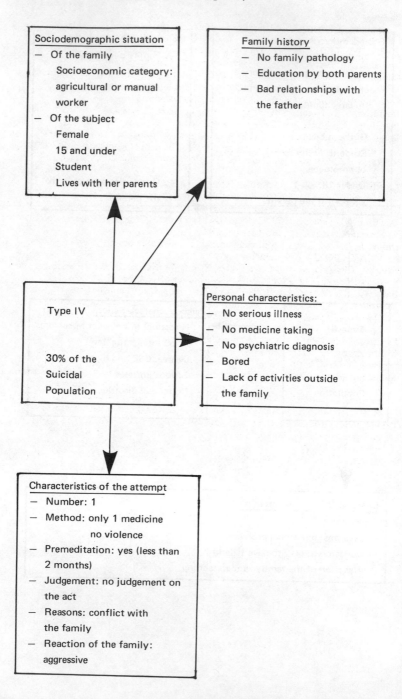

Sociodemographic situation
— Of the family
　Socioeconomic category:
　agricultural or manual
　worker
— Of the subject
　Female
　15 and under
　Student
　Lives with her parents

Family history
— No family pathology
— Education by both parents
— Bad relationships with
　the father

Type IV

30% of the
Suicidal
Population

Personal characteristics:
— No serious illness
— No medicine taking
— No psychiatric diagnosis
— Bored
— Lack of activities outside
　the family

Characteristics of the attempt
— Number: 1
— Method: only 1 medicine
　　　　 no violence
— Premeditation: yes (less than
　2 months)
— Judgement: no judgement on
　the act
— Reasons: conflict with
　the family
— Reaction of the family:
　aggressive

References

Bagley, C. and Greer, S. (1971). Clinical and social predictors of repeated attempted suicide: a multivariate analysis. *British Journal of Psychiatry*, vol. 119, pp. 515-21.

Buglass, D. and Horton, J. (1974). A scale for predicting subsequent suicidal behaviour. *British Journal of Psychiatry*, vol. 124, pp. 573-8.

Choquet, M., Facy, F. and Davidson, F. (1977). Consommation de médicaments et risque de déviance chez les adolescents. *Bulletin de Médicine Légale, Urgence Médicale, Centre Anti-poisons*, vol. 20, pp. 374-89.

Davidson, F. and Angel, P. (1978). Prévoir et prévenir le suicide des adolescents. *Cahiers Médicaux*, vol. 38, pp. 2247-53.

Davidson, F. and Choquet, M. (1976). Etude épidémiologique du suicide de l'adolescent: comparaison entre suicidants primaires et suicidants récidivistes. *Revue d'Epidémiologie, Médecine Sociale et Santé Publique*, vol. 24. pp. 11-26.

Davidson, F., Choquet, M. and Facy, F. (1976). La notion de risque dans le domaine du suicide de l'adolescent. *Revue d'Epidémiologie, Médecine Sociale et Santé Publique*, vol. 24, pp. 283-300.

Davidson, F., Taleghani, M., Courtecuisse, N. *et al.* (1975). *Morbidité et mortalité par suicide*, Editions INSERM, Paris.

Diday, E. (1971). Classification automatique – méthode des nuées dynamiques. IRIA/LABORIA Rocquencourt.

Facy, F., Choquet, M. and Lechevallicr, Y. (1979). Recherche d'une typologie des adolescents suicidants. *Social Psychiatry*, vol. 14, pp.75-84.

Henderson, A.S., Hartigan, J., Davidson, F., Lance, G.N., Duncan-Jones, P., Koller, K.M., Ritchie, K., McAuley, H., Williams, C.L. and Slaughuis, W. (1977). A typology of parasuicide. *British Journal of Psychiatry*, vol. 131, pp. 631-41.

INSEE (1968). General Census of Population, Households, Families.

Kreitman, N. (1976). Age and parasuicide (attempted suicide). *Psychological Medicine*, vol. 6, pp.113-21.

Katschnig, H. and Sint, P. (1973). Are there different types of attempted suicide? A cluster analytic approach. In *Proceedings of the Seventh International Conference for Suicide Prevention.* Amsterdam, 1973. Eds. N. Speyer, R. Diekstra and K. Van der Loo. Swets and Zeitlinger BV. Amsterdam.

Paykel, E.S. and Rassaby, E. (1978). Classification of suicide attempters by cluster analysis. *British Journal of Psychiatry*, vol. 133, pp.45-52.

Taleghani, M. (1979). Passe médical des toxicomanes et modalites de prise en charge des troubles de la santé. Personal communication.

5 SOCIAL CORRELATES OF NON-FATAL DELIBERATE SELF-HARM

H. Gethin Morgan

Previous studies in Bristol, England, have examined the social correlates of deliberate self-poisoning and self-injury in two ways. In the first, the ecological approach was used to establish the distribution of the problems throughout the urban area. The second study involved direct interviews with patients soon after their admission to hospital following an episode of deliberate self-harm. The aim of the study described here is to examine critically some of the problems which were encountered in applying these two approaches and to outline those lines of investigation which appear to be worth exploring further. Throughout this chapter non-fatal deliberate self-poisoning and self-injury will be referred to collectively as deliberate self-harm or *DSH*.

Determining Social Correlates

The Ecological Approach

Bristol forms a discrete urban area with a population of just over half a million, surrounded by relatively sparsely populated rural areas and bordering on the Bristol Channel (Figure 5.1). The city shows marked social zoning. The poorest and most overcrowded residential part is found centrally in the St Paul's and City Road areas. The best quality residential area is mainly on the north-west side of Clifton; the artisan residential area is to the east and south; private and council house estates are found in newer residential areas especially in the outer northern and southern suburbs.

During 1972 and 1973 the DSH problem in the whole of the Bristol area was evaluated by means of our case register which was designed to detect all DSH patients who attended hospital accident and emergency departments and/or were actually admitted to one of the three general hospitals in the area. DSH inception rates were calculated using data from the 1971 National Census for the various electoral wards; a very marked centripetal distribution was found for both 1972 and 1973, and later by a similar survey in 1975 (Figures 5.2 and 5.3).

Taking the age-specific rates for the 15-39 age groups, in which the peak incidence of DSH occurs, it was shown that the rates for persons living centrally were between 1.2 and 2.8 times greater than the city average. In the St Paul's area (ward 20) 1.6 per cent of females in this age group showed some form of DSH each year. The centripetal pattern was highly significant statistically and there seemed no reason to believe that it reflected a differential availability of hospital services throughout the city. It was not possible to be certain, however, of the extent to which it might be explicable in terms of a greater population mobility which seemed likely in the central areas. This would of course increase the population at risk and render ward population estimates, based on a single census count, too low thereby leading to artificially inflated DSH rates.

Using social data derived from the national census it was found that the high rate inner-city area was divided into two zones. That around St Paul's was characterised by substandard housing, overcrowding and poor amenities, containing one third of all Bristol's New Commonwealth immigrants and a high proportion of unskilled manual labourers. In contrast the western part of the high rate central area contained a large number of students, young professionals and a high proportion of rented accommodation. It may be noted in passing that these central city areas correspond closely to those in which Hare found a high incidence of schizophrenia twenty years before (Hare, 1956). We have also found that alcoholism, drug addiction and actual suicide are all found there more often than in other parts of the city. The city planning department has long regarded the city centre to be one of high living stress where social problems abound and where crime against persons is most common. The contrast of more peripheral areas of low DSH inception rates (wards 5 and 27) is striking: these have a high proportion of owner-occupied households with many more professionals, employers, managers and manual workers. The age-specific rates in the high and low rate wards differed by up to a factor of eight for females and six for males.

The DSH distribution was correlated with various social indices available through the national census (Table 5.1). The findings suggested that overcrowding, lack of domestic amenities and the proportion of immigrants were important concomitant factors. Such an approach is of course grossly limited by the fact that only a few crude social indices are available through the national census. We were also particularly disappointed to find that the census appeared to be least reliable in the central areas of the city where DSH was most common: in St Paul's as many as 21.8 per cent of residents could not be allocated to a socioeconomic group, compared with the city average

Figure 5.1: Bristol Residential Areas

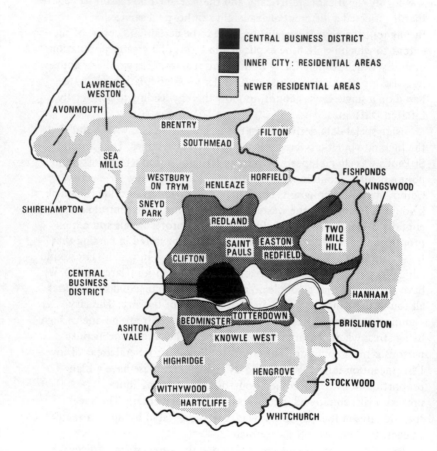

**Figure 5.2: Self-poisoning and Self-injury Inception Rates, Bristol
County Borough, 1972 and 1973**

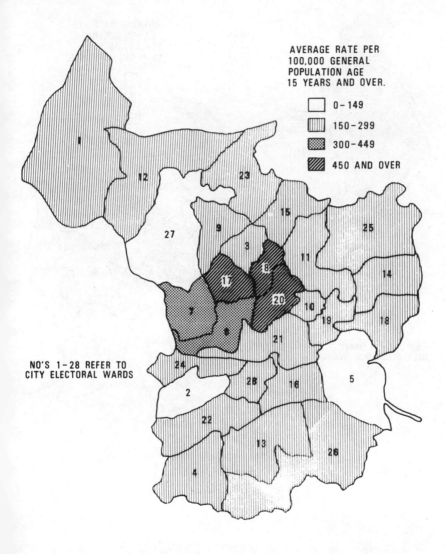

Figure 5.3: Self-poisoning and Self-injury Inception Rates, Bristol County Borough, 1975

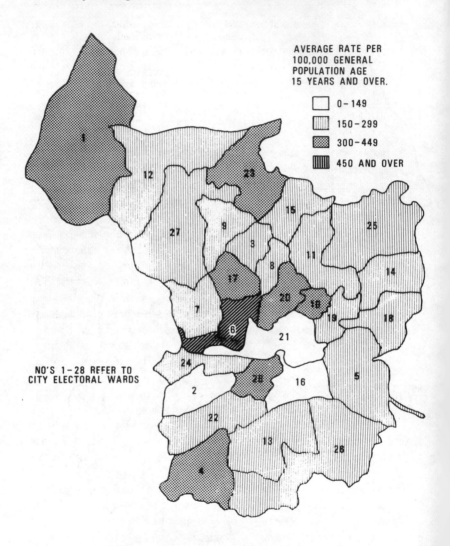

Table 5.1: Socioeconomic Correlates of Deliberate Self-harm
(Spearman rank correlation coefficient)

Year	Overcrowding	Lack of amenities	Proportion of immigrants	Lack of car
1972/73	0.76 (p < 0.01)	0.45 (p < 0.01)	0.60 (p < 0.01)	0.49 (p < 0.01)
1975	0.69 (p < 0.01)	0.41 (p < 0.05)	0.69 (p < 0.01)	0.37 (p < 0.05)

of 12.4 per cent.

Direct Interview Data

In parallel with the area survey, a series of 368 patients admitted to one of the Bristol general hospitals following DSH in 1972 was interviewed in detail. The relevant socioeconomic findings are shown in Table 5.2. It was found that although overcrowding is certainly more common in DSH patients than would have been expected (6.8 per cent compared with the city average of 1.3 per cent) the vast majority do not live in overcrowded conditions and less than 2 per cent believed that accommodation difficulties were a significant upset leading to DHS. The relationship between immigrant status and DSH which the ecological study suggested also appeared insignificant in this second approach; it was found that immigrants were not represented amongst DSH patients any more often than would have been expected from their proportion of the city population as a whole. This must mean that the positive correlation between the proportion of immigrants in a ward population and its incidence of DSH must indicate only an indirect relationship between the two. These two examples serve to illustrate how ecological studies, useful as they are in delineating areas of greatest service need, can lead to misleading conclusions regarding the individuals at risk unless their findings are interpreted in the light of information obtained directly from a representative sample of the patients themselves.

The recent upsetting events mentioned by DSH patients during direct interview soon after the event are summarised in Table 5.3 which illustrates that although 20 per cent do not recollect any upset, 64 per cent describe recent upsets, the most common of which is disharmony with key others and with relatives. A sense of personal isolation, which can of course be experienced whatever the living density, was very common. Forty-five per cent regarded themselves as not having a close friend and 35 per cent felt a sense of personal loneliness at all times. Perhaps the most important 'at risk' social factor consisted of visiting a

Table 5.2: Direct Interview Data: 368 Patients

		Patients	City average (census data)
Ethnic Group	Caucasian	97.8	97.0
	Indo-Pakistani	0.8	0.6
	West Indian	1.4	1.0
Overcrowded		6.8	1.3
Living alone		10.1	8.4

Table 5.3: Recent Upsetting Events in Non-Fatal Deliberate Self-harm (n = 368)

	%
No recent upset	20
Disharmony: key other person	40
relative	10
Depression	9
Work and employment problems	5
Financial problems	5
Social isolation	5
Physical illness, pain	4
Miscellaneous	2
Total	100

medical practitioner in order to obtain some form of psychotropic drug; 67 per cent of our series used such drug prescription for the self in order to take a deliberate drug overdosage. The precise significance of a so-called 'upsetting event' is of course often only understandable to the individual concerned. To an outsider it may in some cases have the superficial appearance of being trivial.

Causal Significance of Social Correlates

Before it can be concluded that the statistical association between a social event and DSH has causal significance it is necessary to apply very stringent criteria. One approach concerns the principle of concomitant variation (i.e., the changing incidence of one is shown to vary directly over a period of time with the strength of the other (Susser, 1973)). To illustrate an application of this, the particular problem of DSH in young males in Bristol can be considered.

In the three years covered by the ecological studies males aged 20-25 years showed a progressive and statistically significant increase in DSH incidence (Figure 5.4). The way in which young males differed

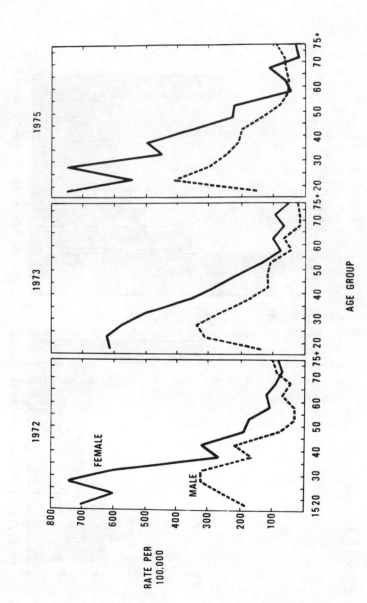

Figure 5.4: Deliberate Self-harm Rates: Bristol County Borough (persons referred to hospital casualty)

Figure 5.5: Unemployment by Age

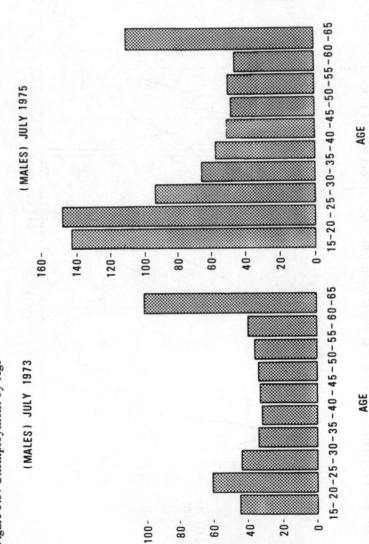

Table 5.4: Unemployment and Job Satisfaction

		Whole series n = 368	Males 15-25 years n = 36	Remainder of series n = 332	Significance level between groups (χ^2)
a	Employees	258	28	230	
	Unemployed at any time in past year	110	19	91	$\chi^2 = 13.50$ P $<$ 0.001
	Percentage unemployed	43%	68%	40%	
b	Worked at some time in past year	258	34	224	
	Dissatisfied with job in past year	86	19	67	$\chi^2 = 7.38$ P $>$ 0.01
	Of those who worked % dissatisfied	33%	56%	30%	
	Difficulties as a result of unemployment in the family	136 (37%)	19 (53%)	117 (35%)	$\chi^2 = 46.62$ P $<$ 0.001

a. At work or registered unemployed. b. Includes students and schoolchildren.

Table 5.5: Direct Interview Data: Age-specific Characteristics for Males 15-25 Years, Problems with Alcohol and the Law

	Whole series n = 368	Male 25 years+ n = 85	Male 15-25 years n = 36	Females 15 years+ n = 247	Significance level between groups (χ^2)
Alcohol intake increased in last 3 months	83 (23%)	37 (44%)	12 (33%)	34 (14%)	$\chi^2 = 6.45$ P $<$ 0.05
Alcohol taken less than 6 hrs before DSH	128 (35%)	47 (55%)	19 (53%)	62 (25%)	$\chi^2 = 7.35$ p $<$ 0.01
Court proceedings at any time	114 (31%)	76 (89%)	15 (42%)	23 (9%)	$\chi^2 = 21.41$ P $<$ 0.001

from the remainder of the series in terms of socioeconomic and life situation problems was therefore examined. It was found that they had experienced significantly more unemployment and job dissatisfaction as well as had family problems resulting from unemployment (Table 5.4). Their use and abuse of alcohol greatly exceeded that in female patients and approached a degree found in older male DSH patients who are well recognised as having a high incidence of alcohol related difficulties. The alcohol abuse in young males included problem drinking (22 per cent) besides its frequent use less than six hours before episodes of DSH (53 per cent) and an increased intake during the last three months (33 per cent) (Table 5.5).

The significance of these findings in young males who resort to DSH is of course uncertain; they may be fortuitous and even if there is a causal relationship this could be indirect rather than immediate. The case for a causal relationship between employment difficulties and DSH is strengthened by the fact that these increased at the same time as did the incidence of DSH in young males (Figure 5.5).

If this situation continues then it might be predicted that the incidence of DSH in the young male will continue to rise progressively as one index that he is a major casualty in our current economic recession. The relation between alcohol abuse in young males and DSH is much more a matter of conjecture. It is again tempting to suggest a causal association, though here we are dependent on less direct evidence of parallel changes in the two factors over a period of time. An increase in alcohol related problems in young males during the period of our study is suggested however, by the finding that the proportion of deaths (predominantly male) in drivers in the 20-40 age group killed in road accidents and found to have had an excess of blood alcohol rose from 20 per cent in 1968 to 50 per cent in 1974 in the United Kingdom (Transport and Road Research Laboratory 1977).

Conclusions

1. Patient recall is of course a crude method of studying social correlates and causes. There is a great deal to be done both in the categorisation of social factors (for example, along the lines of life event studies) and in determining their causal significance.

2. We need to be particularly rigorous in the interpretation of statistical associations between the incidence of DSH and its circumstances before concluding that they may be causally related.

3. There is clearly no single stereotype of the setting in which DSH may occur and the factors which may precipitate it. No part of an urban area is likely to be free from it, even though it seems to be concentrated in certain zones such as city centres and local authority housing estates. In fact we should beware of forming general conclusions based on small unrepresentative patient samples. The studies reported here have emphasised the high DSH morbidity rates in

Table 5.6: Characteristics of Patients from Central 'High Rate' Area Compared with Those from Remainder of City

	Patients from central area (n = 67)	Patients from rest of city (n = 301)	Significance of difference
Below 35 years of age	55 (82%)	188 (62%)	<0.01
In bedsitters	14 (21%)	12 (4%)	<0.001
At present address less than six months	32 (48%)	64 (21%)	<0.001
Living away from relatives	32 (48%)	81 (27%)	<0.01
Overcrowded conditions	9 (13%)	16 (5%)	<0.05

Bristol city centre though the number of DSH cases found there accounts for only a fifth of all those in the entire city.

A study of the way in which social correlates vary throughout different parts of the city might be useful in providing guides to its management and prevention in a way similar to work carried out in Edinburgh where it has been shown that social correlates of DSH vary markedly with age and sex (Kreitman, 1977). The findings from Bristol suggest that in socioeconomic terms marked differences in DSH do exist throughout various parts of an urban area. Table 5.6 shows for example, that the central city DSH patients when compared with those living elsewhere in a city area are likely to be younger, living in bedsitters, more socially mobile, living away from relatives and in overcrowded conditions. Alcohol related problems were particularly common in female DSH patients living in the city centre (28 per cent compared with 10 per cent elsewhere) but not in males though here the numbers were far fewer.

4. Each urban area probably needs to evaluate its own distinctive pattern of DSH distribution. We have focused our attention on Bristol city centre in an attempt to clarify the causal factors peculiar to it. Certain themes have emerged. Although morbidity rates are high there is a low rate of referral from the central area to psychiatric clinics and a high default rate amongst persons so referred. There are several questions to which we would very much like answers, perhaps the most pressing of which is the rate of psychotropic drug prescription throughout various parts of the city. It is time that the rate at which DSH complicates prescription of a psychotropic drug, especially the way it varies with social conditions, should be included as part of the data sheet for each preparation. It is indeed remarkable that such

information does not appear to be available, nor is it easy to obtain the relevant basic data.

These examples illustrate how the study of social correlates may generate a variety of hypotheses regarding the causes of DSH. In my view such an approach is also likely to be fruitful in determining its most effective treatment and prevention.

References

Hare, E.H. (1956). Mental illness and social conditions in Bristol. *Journal of Mental Science*, vol. 102, p.349.

Kreitman, N. (1977). *Parasuicide.* John Wiley, London.

Susser, M. (1973). *Causal Thinking in the Health Sciences.* Oxford University Press, London.

Transport and Road Research Laboratory (1977). Alcohol and Road Accidents: Blood Alcohol Level in Fatalities. Leaflet LF634. Crowthorne, Berkshire.

PART TWO

The Role of Events in Suicidal Behaviour

6 RECENT LIFE EVENTS AND ATTEMPTED SUICIDE

E.S. Paykel

Many people who have studied or treated suicide attempters have remarked that the attempt is frequently a response to a situational crisis. Although descriptive studies have sometimes listed the apparent precipitating factors, surprisingly few studies have made comparisons with control groups. A few studies have concerned specific types of events. Birtchnell (1970) found that suicide attempters had more commonly experienced the recent death of a parent than had other psychiatric patients. Levi et al. (1966) obtained similar findings for a variety of recent separations.

However, at the time my colleagues and I in New Haven, Connecticut, were carrying out a series of studies of life events in psychiatric patients and general population controls, we could find no published studies which had compared occurrence of a spectrum of recent life events in suicide attempters with any control groups, much less the general population. Our original published comparison used both the general population and mixed depressives as controls (Paykel et al., 1975). Subsequent data have enabled schizophrenics to be incorporated to set the findings in a wider context.

Subjects

The suicide attempters were 53 patients aged 18-65 admitted following unsuccessful suicide attempts to a general hospital emergency room providing the main crisis resource in New Haven (Paykel et al., 1974). They were an approximately 1:4 sample of all suicide attempters admitted to this facility over a six-month period. They spanned a spectrum of severity, including relatively mild suicidal gestures, but these had to involve some kind of act, rather than merely a threat. Like most such samples they were predominantly female and young.

The depressive controls were obtained from a study we had carried out earlier which incorporated 185 heterogeneous depressed patients. Only 18 per cent of these patients had made a suicide attempt in the recent illness. From these depressives, 53 were selected, each matched with a suicide attempter on age, sex, marital status, social class and race. The general population controls were part of a large epidemiological community survey carried out in New Haven. Fifty-three subjects were matched on the same variables. The schizophrenics were 50 patients admitted to hospital with a first illness satisfying research criteria for schizophrenia (Jacobs *et al.*, 1974). The schizophrenics were not matched on demographic variables with the suicide attempters, but they were approximately comparable.

Life Events Recorded

We recognised the familiar pitfalls of obtaining reliable information regarding life events (Paykel, 1974). The technique used in these studies involved a list of 61 events (condensed for analyses to 33) and each carefully defined. Information was obtained from the patient by a trained research assistant. The interview was semistructured; every event was enquired for, unless clearly inapplicable, by an initial question which was followed by further enquiry to establish full details. The interview was postponed until a week or more after initial presentation in the suicide attempt, and longer for other patient controls, to diminish reporting distortions due to psychiatric illness. The time period for which events were recorded was carefully limited to six months. For schizophrenics and depressives it was the six months prior to symptomatic onset; for suicide attempters six months prior to attempt; for the general population, six months immediately prior to intervie

Total Number of Events

The first comparison, which also set the general pattern of findings, involved mean frequencies of occurrence of all events in the six months. The greatest number of events, with a mean of 3.3 in six months, was reported by suicide attempters. Next in rank came depressives (2.1), and below that schizophrenics (1.5). All reported significantly more events than the general population mean of 0.8. This general pattern of ranking was to be found in most of the analyses. Events were experienced by suicide attempters at four times the rate in the comparable general population, a very impressive difference.

Individual Events

Frequencies of occurrence of individual events were next examined. These are shown for suicide attempters and controls in Table 6.1. Suicide attempters reported five events significantly more frequently than general population subjects: serious arguments with spouse; having a new person in the home; serious illness of family member; serious personal physical illness; and having to appear in court for an offence.

Table 6.1: Frequencies of Individual Events[a]

Event	Suicide attempters	General population	Significance[b]
Serious arguments with spouse	19	0	$<.001$
New person in home	11	0	$<.001$
Serious illness of close family member	17	4	$<.01$
Serious personal physical illness	15	1	$<.01$
Court appearance for offence	10	2	$<.05$
Lawsuit	7	1	NS
Move house	15	7	NS
Engagement	7	4	NS
Marital separation due to discord	6	2	NS
Start new type of work	5	1	NS
Pregnancy	4	1	NS
Unemployed for one month	5	3	NS
Divorce	3	0	NS
Major financial problems	3	1	NS
Death of close family member	2	0	NS
Family member leaves home	2	0	NS
Birth of child (for father)	2	0	NS
Stillbirth	2	1	NS
Birth of child (for mother)	2	1	NS
Son drafted into armed forces	1	0	NS
Marriage	1	1	NS
Child engaged	0	0	NS
Child married	0	0	NS
Change college or university	0	0	NS
Retirement	0	0	NS
Demotion	0	0	NS
Gaol sentence	0	0	NS
Business failure	0	0	NS
Fired	0	1	NS
Promotion	0	1	NS
Finish full time education	0	3	NS
Major change in work conditions	2	7	NS

a. Number of subjects reporting event at least once.
b. By Chi square, with Yates' correction.

Most other events were also reported more frequently by the attempters but at too low rates for differences to achieve statistical significance. Four events at the bottom of the list were reported more often by suicide attempters but here too differences were too low for significance. For the depressive controls and schizophrenics, findings have been omitted from the table for simplicity. They tended to follow the ranking seen previously.

Event Categories

The frequencies of most of the events were too low for useful analysis. In order to explore whether or not there were specific patterns for different types of events, events were grouped into categories in several alternative but partly overlapping ways. In each categorisation, two or more mutually exclusive categories were separated on the basis of event definition. Events that could not clearly be assigned to a category were omitted. For each category, numbers of individuals experiencing at least one event in that category were calculated.

Table 6.2 shows findings for three sets of categories used in several other studies. The first categorisation reflected an evaluative dimension. In terms of commonly shared values, one group of events was clearly undesirable — for instance, going to gaol, being demoted. A second and smaller group of events was socially desirable — for instance, promotion. All groups of patients reported undesirable events significantly more frequently than did the general population, the excess being most marked for suicide attempters. Neither suicide attempters nor any of the other patient groups reported significantly more desirable events than the general population. Only undesirable events preceded psychiatric disturbance, and that effect was more marked for suicide attempters than other patient groups.

A second and more specific categorisation referred to events involving changes in the immediate social field of the respondent. Two classes of events were defined. Entrances referred to those events involving introduction of a new person into the social field, such as birth of a child or new person in the home; exits involved departures, such as marital separation, death. Once again exits were reported significantly more frequently by all patient groups than by the general population. Here suicide attempters and depressives were closely similar; schizophrenics reported these events less frequently. For entrance events, there was a change of pattern; only suicide attempters experienced these events to an excessive degree. The entrance-exit dichotomy bears a somewhat specific relationship to the onset of depression: only exits preceded depression, and they preceded a quarter of onsets. For suicide attempts, both classes of events were involved. Exits of course correspond to the familiar concept of loss, and these findings suggest that loss bears a more specific relationship to depression than to suicide attempts or schizophrenia.

The third category was a single one. Several specific events referred to arguments and difficulties with various people in relationship to the

Table 6.2: Event Categories: Per Cent of Patient Group Reporting Events in Category at Least Once in Six Months

	Suicide attempters	Depressives	Schizophrenics	General population
Undesirable	60[a]	40[a]	42[a]	21
Desirable	15	4	8	11
Exits	21[a]	25[a]	14[a]	4
Entrances	34[a]	13	16	11
Interpersonal arguments (61 event list)	75[a]	62[a]	18[a]	3

a. Patient group reports event category significantly more frequently than general population

patient — spouse, relatives, friends and those at work. This kind of event is difficult to define precisely and to report accurately: it was particularly suspected that those who had experienced psychotherapy might report such events more readily than the general population. Except for the relatively clear-cut item of serious marital arguments, they were therefore omitted from the main analyses. However, on separate analysis, there were striking findings. All patient groups reported these events more frequently than the general population, but particularly depressives and, most strikingly, suicide attempters. Seventy-five per cent of attempts were preceded by an event from this class, a finding corresponding well to the clinical experience of a high incidence of difficulties and disruptions of interpersonal relations prior to the attempt.

Overall these findings suggested that suicide attempts were particularly highly related to the various classes of events which to a lesser degree also preceded the other psychiatric disorders with one exception: in changes in the social field, the relationship was not specific to losses.

Additional Categories

For suicide attempters, depressives and general population controls, but not schizophrenics, two additional categorisations were examined. These are shown in Table 6.3. One, based on over-all stress, was derived from another study in which subjects scaled the degree to which each of the events was regarded as upsetting (Paykel *et al.*, 1971). Events were divided by these scores into three groups: major, intermediate and minor. Depressives reported more events than the general population

Table 6.3: Additional Categories: Per Cent of Patient Groups Reporting Events in Category at Least Once in Six Months

	Suicide attempters	Depressives	General population controls
Major upset	68[ab]	45[a]	23
Intermediate upset	53[ab]	26[a]	4
Minor upset	49[a]	45[a]	25
Uncontrolled	66[ab]	40[a]	21
Controlled	34[a]	32[a]	17

a. Patient group reports event category significantly more frequently than general population.
b. Suicide attempter group reports event category significantly more frequently than depressives.

controls in all these groups. The expected excess in suicide attempters compared to depressives was found for major and intermediate events, but not minor events.

The second categorisation concerned the degree to which there was control or choice in the circumstances initiating the event. Some events — such as engagement, marriage, changing jobs and ceasing education — are likely to offer the respondent some control or choice. Others — such as being fired, serious personal physical illness and events occurring primarily to other people — do not. Controlled events showed a similar pattern to events of minor upset. Suicide attempters and depressives both tended to report more events than the general population, but were closely comparable. However, uncontrolled events were reported more by suicide attempters than depressives.

The general pattern here appeared to be that the suicide attempters experienced more events than depressives only in the more threatening categories — uncontrolled events, and events of major and intermediate rather than minor perceived stressfulness. Overall, suicide attempts emerge as responses to a wide variety of life events — all the classes examined except desirable events — but particularly those events with more threatening qualities.

Time Pattern

The findings so far concern events reported over the whole six-month period. The month of occurrence of the events within that period was also recorded for all groups except schizophrenics, and Figure 6.1

Figure 6.1: Mean Number of Attempts Reported Over Each One-Month Period

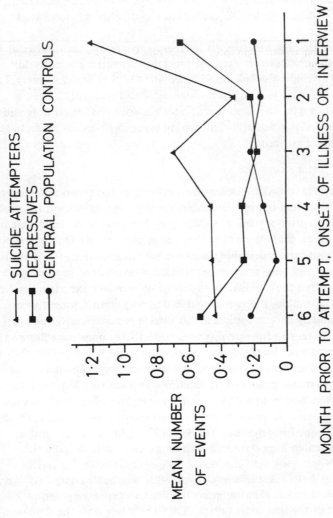

Source: Modified from Paykel *et al.*, 1975.

shows mean numbers of events reported month by month. For the general population the event rate was approximately constant over the six months. The depressives showed a moderate peak in the month before onset. For the two previous months the event rate was approximately that of the general population, but in the earlier months it was clearly elevated. For suicide attempters the striking feature was a very marked peak in the month prior to the attempt. Almost one-third of the events they reported occurred in that month. Quite a large proportion of these were in fact in the week before the attempt. For preceding months the rate tended to fall, although somewhat irregularly.

These findings indicate, via a retrospective frame, the manner in which the link between event and reaction operates. Evidently for suicide attempts the link is an immediate one. The attempt emerges as a rapid response to a highly threatening situational crisis. Mixed depression is much less so. Event rates for both conditions were still elevated six months earlier, suggesting that more persisting effects of stress also contribute.

Trigger or Causative Factors

One criticism often levelled against claims that life events are important causative factors in psychiatric disorder concerns the magnitude of the effect. It is often argued, particularly by the more biologically-oriented psychiatrists, that events are at best mere precipitants. One telling point in this argument is derived from the nature of the events reported. It has frequently been pointed out that close scrutiny of these events indicates that they are within the range of everyday experience rather than catastrophic. It seems probable that they must frequently be negotiated by other people without suicide supervening. Some other factors, in terms of personality and vulnerability must contribute to the development of the response.

This criticism has some force. It is easy to forget the importance of base rates in the general population. Where a disorder is uncommon, single events cannot be very plausible explanatory factors if they are common in the general population. A simple calculation, modelled on an earlier one for depression (Paykel, 1975), illustrates the problem. Exits appeared important in our findings: they were actually the category grouping with the highest frequency ratio in depressives to general population, excluding the possibly unreliable arguments. About 21 per cent of suicide attempters reported an exit as opposed to 3.8 per cent of the matched controls. Let us however refer the figures to the general population. The annual incidence of suicide attempts is about 200 per 100,000, giving 10 per 10,000 in the six months under consideration. Among 10,000 subjects in the general population, there will therefore be 9,990 who do not attempt (normals) and 10 who do attempt suicide. Among the former, approximately 4 per cent experience an exit, that is 400. Among the latter, 21 per cent do so, that is 2. A total of 402 (400 + 2) persons experience an exit, of which only 2 result in suicide attempts. Only 0.5 per cent of exits result in a suicide attempt; 99.5 per cent do not. Exits will not help much in predicting an attempt, a familiar problem in prediction.

This calculation does not, however, really mean the events are not important. Can we estimate in any way the magnitude of event effect in the causation of suicide? One useful index is an epidemiological concept of relative risk. It is the ratio of the disease rate in the population exposed to a causative factor to the rate in those not exposed, i.e., the degree to which the causative factor increases the risk of the morbid process developing. Strictly speaking, it requires an epidemiological study, but it can easily be calculated from data of the kind presented here, using an approximation (Paykel, 1978).

Table 6.4 shows the results of calculation in the six months after the occurrence of an exit event. The risk of a suicide attempt occurring is increased between six and seven times. The risk for depression is comparable; that for schizophrenia considerably lower. For any event in the list, the risk of a suicide attempt is increased about six times. The immediate peak of events in the month before the attempt, from the retrospective frame, indicates a large and rapid effect which then falls off, and in the month after the event the risk of an attempt is increased to ten times that of the general population. These findings indicate causative factors which, over the short term, make an

Table 6.4: Relative Risks

Exits in last six months	
Suicide attempts	6.7
Depression	6.5
Schizophrenia	3.9
All events in last six months	
Suicide attempts	6.3
Depression	5.4
Schizophrenia	3.0
All events in last month	
Suicide attempts	10.0

important contribution to the development of the attempt.

At the same time, the event must interact with a host of other factors, such as coping mechanisms, personality problems and even pre-existing psychiatric disturbance, so that it is a complex causative chain which determines whether the event is followed by a suicide attempt. We are really dealing with multifactorial aetiology, but the event is one important factor in producing the attempt and determining its timing.

It is not central to my main argument, but these data appear to have therapeutic implications. In recent years, provision of help to suicidal persons has increasingly become bound up with emergency availability and with techniques for crisis intervention. The evidence that suicide attempts are often immediate reactions to stressful personal and interpersonal crises would certainly suggest the value of rapid response to the distress, aimed at identification and control of the stressful circumstances, mobilisation of support from the family, and marshalling of personal resources for reintegration. Such an approach, seeking to modify the consequences of the events and to provide alternative modes of communication and help-seeking, may offer preventive possibilities for interrupting the suicidal crisis before it culminates in the attempt. This would most profitably be combined with identification of special high-risk groups of whom those who may have made a previous suicide attempt are clinically the most obvious. I would not yet abandon this approach, in spite of the negative findings of some therapeutic studies.

Conclusion

To summarise, the findings from this group of studies go some way to support clinical experience regarding the relationship of the suicide attempt to recent situational stress. Suicide attempters experience more life events before the attempt than any other patient group studied. The peaking of events in the month before the attempt indicates a particularly imminent relationship between events and reaction. The events are quite diverse, but it is particularly the more threatening classes — exits, undesirable events, events with higher rated stressfulness and events outside the patient's control — which distinguish suicide attempters from other patient groups. In keeping with an emphasis on marital difficulties in a number of descriptive studies, serious arguments with spouse comprised the single event reported most frequently by suicide attempters, and the group of interpersonal arguments in general were reported by a substantial majority of the attempters. Although, as common sense and ordinary life experience would confirm, only a very small proportion of exits are followed by a suicide attempt, the magnitude of the causative effect is sufficient to render it important and there may be therapeutic implications.

References

Birtchnell, J. (1970). The relationship between attempted suicide, depression, and parent death. *British Journal of Psychiatry*, vol. 116, pp. 307-13.

Jacobs, S.C., Prusoff, B.A. and Paykel, E.S. (1974). Recent life events in schizophrenia and depression. *Psychological Medicine*, vol. 4, pp. 444-53.

Levi, L.O., Fales, C.H., Stein, M. and Sharp, V.H. (1966). Separation and attempted suicide. *Archives of General Psychiatry*, vol. 15, pp. 158-65.

Paykel, E.S. (1974). Recent life events and clinical depression. In *Life Stress and Illness*, eds. E.K.E. Gunderson and R.H. Rahe. Charles C. Thomas, Springfield, Illinois.

Paykel, E.S. (1975). Environmental variables in the aetiology of depression. In *Nature and Treatment of Depression*, eds. F.F. Flach and S.C. Draghi. John Wiley, New York.

Paykel, E.S. (1978). Contribution of life events to causation of psychiatric illness. *Psychological Medicine*, vol. 8, pp. 245-53.

Paykel, E.S., Hallowell, C., Dressler, D.M., Shapiro, D.L. and Weissman, M.M. (1974). Treatment of suicide attempters: a descriptive study. *Archives of General Psychiatry*, vol. 31, pp. 487-91.

Paykel, E.S., Prusoff, B.A. and Myers, J.K. (1975). Suicide attempts and recent life events: a controlled comparison. *Archives of General Psychiatry*, vol. 32, pp. 327-33.

Paykel, E.S., Prusoff, B.A. and Uhlenhuth, E.S. (1971). Scaling of life events. *Archives of General Psychiatry*, vol. 25, pp. 340-47.

7 MEASURING LIFE STRESS: A COMPARISON OF TWO METHODS

H. Katschnig

Introduction

Reactivity as an aetiological psychiatric concept is as old as scientific psychiatry itself. Until recently, however, the evidence for its applicability to psychiatric disorders (mainly for depression), was not based on sound empirical research. Ten years ago the publication of standardised life change units (LCUs) for the items of the Schedule of Recent Experience (SRE) (Holmes and Rahe, 1967), signalled the advent of the numerical approach in life event research, and promised a change. Life event research, as understood by its advocates, should now confirm conjectures about the role of life events in the aetiology of somatic and psychiatric diseases, making an end to speculation about the significance of biographical events. The publication of life event papers using the SRE or its derivatives has in the meantime reached epidemic proportions. However, whether life event research has been successful in proving its hypotheses should remain a question of debate, as there are still methodological drawbacks in the instrument as used.

Among at least a dozen published or quoted methods for measuring life stress caused by life events, Holmes and Rahe's Schedule of Recent Experience (SRE) has remained by far the most widely employed. It is a *self-rating list* used to quantify life changes. It is widely published, easily applicable, by others as well as its authors, and economical both in terms of the amount of money and time needed to employ it — properties which clearly qualify it for the role of leader in the market of life event methods despite the fact that its use has been criticised for oversimplifying complex issues. Many of the other instruments used so far in life event research are complex, and it is cumbersome and time consuming to acquire the skills of applying them correctly. One of these is Brown's (1974) Life Event Schedule (LES), a lengthy interview with several hundred pages of rating instructions. Results obtained with such methods — while accounting for the complexities of human life — are not easily replicable, as few of us are in a position to acquire a thorough knowledge of these instruments.

Design of Study

The methodological study presented here is part of a more comprehensive research project on the classification of depressive disorders using the life event approach to clarify the notion of reactivity in the concept of depression, as opposed to the endogenous concept of depression.

In order to arrive at a rational basis for the decision as to which life event method to use, a comparative study of the Schedule of Recent Experience and Brown's Life Event Schedule was carried out. A population of attempted suicides was chosen in order to have a large number of life events to study. Among the 42 patients included in the study there were 410 life changes picked up by the SRE and 326 life events recorded by Brown's LES in the year preceding the attempted suicide.

The primary intention of this study was not to come to a conclusion about the aetiological significance of life events for attempted suicides. A matched control group, if not an epidemiological design, would have been necessary, and the question of the independence of the event of an ongoing pathology would have been crucial. Instead, not two populations, but two methods, were compared on the same population. This design yielded two measures for the life stress evoked by life events and experienced by this population in the 12 months preceding the attempted suicide. The study took place at the Regional Poisoning Treatment Centre of the Royal Infirmary in Edinburgh with 42 patients admitted consecutively with an attempted suicide ('parasuicides') who agreed to participate in the study and were able to fill out a self-rating questionnaire.

After the patients had been given notice of their imminent discharge (so that it could be assumed that they were not motivated to distort their reports in order to be discharged), they were approached by a registrar who secured their participation in this study and gave them the Recent Life Change Questionnaire (RLCQ) developed by Rahe (1974) out of the SRE (in fact it also covers all items of the SRE). After the patients had filled in the RLCQ, an interviewer of Brown's group who had participated in his major studies interviewed the patients and made the relevant ratings on the Life Event Schedule (LES). The average duration of these interviews was approximately one hour, depending on the number of life events and the difficulties encountered, whereas it took only a couple of minutes for the patient to fill in the RLCQ.

Results

In the framework of this presentation only a few points of this comparison can be mentioned. Other problems, such as the re-rating reliability, the statistical methods employed, the rating of independence for events, the dating of events and the quantification of the aetiological impact are omitted here for brevity.

Results of the Schedule of Recent Experience

Results of studies employing life change units (LCUs) are usually presented in the following way: a person's life experience, expressed in a series of single LCU scores for each life change over a period of several months, is collapsed into one parameter supposed to indicate the life stress evoked by the life changes experienced by that person in a given time period. These LCU totals for each individual in the group under study are then collapsed into one single mean score which indicates the life stress experience by the group as a whole. This LCU total mean is then calculated for different time periods before disease onset, usually for three or six months periods and the life stress experienced in these different time periods is then compared. The aim is to find a rise in the LCU total mean.

Using this procedure with our population of attempted suicides, the mean total life events was 106.8 at 0-6 months before the suicide attempt. There is a clear rise in the LCU total mean for the whole group of attempted suicides from the distant six-months period to the proximal six-months period, a result consistent with the basic hypothesis put forward by life event researchers. We found the same result by simply averaging the number of boxes ticked per patient. The average number of boxes ticked by patients in the 7-12 months before the attempted suicide was 3.5, and in the 0-6 months before the attempt was 6.2. The Spearman rank correlation between the number of boxes ticked and the LCU totals assigned to each individual is .96.

Results in the light of Brown's Life Event Schedule (LES)

The LES similarly presents its results in terms of an indicator representing the amount of life stress experienced by a whole group of persons. The statistic used is quite simple, consisting of the percentage of persons who have experienced at least one life event implying a certain degree of threat during a specified time period (how to arrive at a rating in an individual case is defined in detailed instructions of several hundred pages). The time grid used with Brown's LES is much

Figure 7.1: Percentage of Patients With at Least One Long-Term Threat on Brown's Life Event Schedule

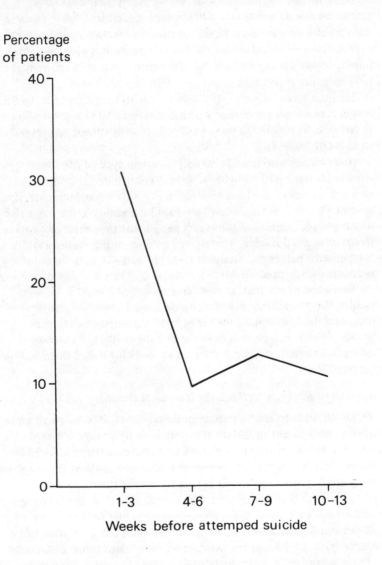

Percentage
of patients

Weeks before attemped suicide

narrower than that employed when the SRE is used, as it is easier in an interview to date life events exactly.

Using Brown's approach to measuring life stress the following picture emerged for our group of attempted suicides. There is a clear rise (toward the suicidal attempt) of the percentage of persons experiencing at least one severely threatening event (with long term implications). Taking six-month (rather than three-week) periods as the reference, the percentage of patients with one or more severely threatening event becomes strikingly similar to that found for the SRE, 30 per cent of the patients at 7-12 months rising to nearly 60 per cent at 0-6 months before the attempted suicide with at least one severely threatening life event.

However, we also found that only a certain type of life event, namely an event with 'long-term threat', contributed to this rise; 'short-term threat' events do not make any difference. Moreover, simply counting life events would have produced the same picture, i.e. a rise in the average number of life events per patient the nearer one comes to the attempted suicide. The average number of life events was 2.8 at 7-12 months before the attempted suicide, and 4.1 at 0-6 months before the attempted suicide.

We can conclude that, as they have produced basically the same results, the two methods could have been used interchangeably when analysing the contribution of life events for groups of attempted suicides. Further, we could have avoided the costly and cumbersome interview method of George Brown and could have used the much simpler SRE.

Agreement Between Methods for Individual Patients

Yet, if we want to clarify pathogenetic processes, it is no use to know the average amount of life stress experienced by groups, we need rather to know the amount of stress from life events experienced by individuals. A striking picture emerges when one looks at the life stress attributed by the respective methods to each of the 42 patients.

Looking only at the *proximal six-month* period, of the 20 patients with a total LCU score above the group mean of 182.8 only ten, i.e. 50 per cent, had a severe long-term threat event using Brown's LES. Similarly of the 23 persons with a severe long term threat event only 10, i.e. 43 per cent, had a Rahe's LCU score above the group mean. The high scores of the group are contributed by only a part of the group, a different part for the respective methods of measuring them, and the pooled result obtained in this way does not reflect the

Table 7.1: Life Events in Previous Six Months (comparison of Brown's LES and Holmes-Rahe LCU on individual patients, n = 42)

		Patients with severe long term threat (Brown)		
		Present	Absent	Total
Patients with life change units (Holmes-Rahe) above the mean of 183 LCUs	Present	10	10	20
	Absent	13	9	22
	Total	23	19	42

$$R_B = 0.11$$

Table 7.2: Relation of Life Event to Attempted Suicide with Different Schedules

		Brown's LES		
Occurrence of life event		12-7 months only	same[a]	0-6 months only
Holmes-Rahe Schedule of Recent Experience	higher 0-6 months	10	17	1
	same[a]	2	0	0
	lower 7-12 months	4	5	3
			Agreement 13/42 ns	

a. Same means equal frequency for each patient in 7-12 months and 0-6 months period.

importance of life events for a significant proportion of the members of the group. The biserial correlation coefficient between the two instruments is only 0.11.

If we look at the rise of life stress from the distant to the proximal six-month period (so neatly demonstrated by both methods for the whole group), an equally disappointing result emerges for the individual persons. Only 28 patients out of 42 had higher LCU scores in the proximal compared to the distant period, and only 16 patients out of 42 had a severe long-term threat event in the proximal period without having one in the distant period, i.e. showed a rise in the life stress measure. As far as agreement between the two methods is concerned, only ten patients showed the expected rise from the distant to the proximal six-month period congruently in both methods; thus, agreement was reached in less than 25 per cent of our population of parasuicides with regard to the basic hypothesis of life event research, implying a rise of life stress before the onset of a pathological phenomenon.

The conclusion can be drawn from this data, that whatever agreement may exist between results obtained by the SRE and Brown's LES respectively for *groups*, the discrepant results for *individuals* show that these methods measure *different phenomena.* This discrepancy is all the more astonishing since the design of the study— the two instruments were presented to the patients immediately one after the other — would have tended to create a bias in the sense of producing similar results.

The apparent agreement between the two methods when studying group phenomena and the implicit assumption of the validity of this agreement also for individuals, is a fallacy, which has long been recognised in another area, namely in epidemiology, where the extrapolation of correlations based on populations or geographical areas to implications for individuals has been called the 'ecological fallacy' (Robinson, 1950). Scheuch has generalised this problem calling it 'group fallacy'.

Conclusions

The following conclusions can be drawn from the above comparison. One must be more cautious in pooling the results of life event studies carried out with different methods. The reduction of a wide variety of phenomena into one single figure — a life change unit mean score or a simple percentage of persons experiencing at least one event — generates the problem of comparability: Is like really placed with like in different studies as far as the independent variable 'life event' is concerned? The problem psychiatrists are already aware of for diagnosis, i.e. for the dependent variable, applies also to alleged independent variables: in recent years we have become increasingly aware of the need for standardisation of diagnosis in psychiatry, and we must now be equally aware of the need for standardisation of the measurement of independent variables across different research groups. A uniform terminology would be the essential first step toward such a standardisation of measurement of life event.

One suggestion is to become more specific in life event research and to use global life event measures only in addition to more detailed information about individual events and their stressfulness, thus avoiding the problem that different global measures may possibly measure different phenomena. This should also help to create links between life event research and other research which can already rely on a body of sound empirically based hypotheses, such as behaviour theory. Finally, a more specific and individualised approach should make the life event approach more useful in clinical work as well.

References

Brown, G.W. (1974). Meaning, measurement and stress of life-events. *Stressful Life Events*, eds. B.S. Dohrenwend and B.P. Dohrenwend. John Wiley, New York, p.217.
Holmes, T.H. and Rahe, R.H. (1967). The social readjustment rating scale. *Journal of Psychosomatic Research*, vol. 11, p.213.
Rahe, R.H. (1975). Epidemiological studies of life change and illness. *International Journal of Psychiatry in Medicine*, vol. 6, pp. 133-46.
Robinson, W.S. (1950). Ecological correlations and behaviour of individuals. *American Sociological Review*, vol. 15, pp. 351-57.

8 THE ROLE OF LIFE EVENTS IN THE AETIOLOGY OF EPISODES OF SELF-POISONING

S.E.M. O'Brien and R.D.T. Farmer

Introduction

During the past twenty years there has been a considerable increase in the annual number of hospital admissions for self-poisoning. Now it is one of the most common reasons for a young adult being admitted to hospital. The trend is partly explained by an increase in the repeat rate (Alderson, 1974). In part because of the peculiarities of its population and in part for other reasons central London has a high incidence of both suicide (Farmer, Preston and O'Brien, 1974) and of attempted suicide. Any intervention strategy that could be introduced to reduce either morbidity or mortality would be of importance. This chapter reports some of the findings from a study of self-poisoning patients in central London. It is concerned with the evaluation of the possible role of life events in the aetiology of an episode.

Method

Over a six-month period, 195 consecutive patients aged between 15 and 30 years who were admitted to one of two hospitals in central London were interviewed within 24 hours of admission. The hospitals used for the study were St Stephens Hospital Chelsea, and Westminster Hospital. Together they provide the emergency services for the southern part of the borough of Kensington and Chelsea and the city of Westminster. In addition to asking a series of questions in a standard history questionnaire a life events schedule was administered. This schedule was adapted from Rahe (1975).

At attempt was made to re-interview the patients three months and one year after the index admission. Despite considerable effort only 57 per cent were traced and re-interviewed at three months and 59 per cent were traced and interviewed at one year. The principal reason for the apparently poor follow-up rate was the high mobility of the population investigated, 77 per cent having changed their address at least once by the time of the first follow-up interview.

Comparative data were obtained by interviewing young people attending general practitioners in the area for any reason other than self-poisoning. It was expected that they would have experienced a higher number of events than the general population, as some events would have preceded the need for consultation. Thus any differences between these people and the self-poisoning patients are of great significance.

Method of Analysis

The self-poisoning patients were divided into two groups. The index admission of patients in the EI group was their first ever episode of self-poisoning. Patients in the EN group had had at least one previous episode (N = *non*-first). There were two reasons for dividing the patients in this way. Firstly, the EI group comprises a sample of people who have episodes of self-poisoning as opposed to a sample of episodes of self-poisoning. Secondly, certain life events, for example, hospital admission, could be the direct result of a previous episode. The comparison group recruited from general practice were matched for age, sex, whether ever married and by father's social class, two to one to the EI group. They were called the general practice reference group (GPR). The sizes of the groups are given in Table 8.1.

Table 8.1: The Distribution of the EI, EN and GPR Groups by Sex

	GPR n = 152	EI n = 76	EN n = 117
Male	42	21	34
Female	110	55	83
Total	152	76	117

Results

The frequency with which individual events were reported in each group was compared by calculating the *prevalence ratio* of the reporting of events. The prevalence ratio is the ratio of the frequency of report in the study group to its frequency of report in the control group. In the case of comparisons between the two self-poisoning groups the prevalence ratio was calculated by dividing the frequency of report in the EN group with its frequency in the EI group. Table 8.2 shows a list of those events for which the prevalence ratio was significantly different from 1 by descending order of significance. There are few significant differences between the two self-poisoning groups. The average number of events experienced by members of each group in the six weeks preceding interview was calculated. The control subjects (the GPR group) reported an average of 1.60 events. The EI group gave an

Table 8.2: Prevalence Ratio of Life Events

$p < 0.001$	Prevalence ratio (of reporting EI/GPR)	Prevalence ratio EN/EI	Sig. level (only where $p < 0.1$)
Substantial change in sleeping habits (males)	16	1.0	
'Falling out' of a close relationship	13	0.8	
Change of usual level of physical activity (at work as well as during leisure time)	13	1.0	
Substantial change in eating habits	8.2	1.1	
Difficulties (other than sexual) with spouse (ever marrieds)	7.8	0.7	
Problems (other than sexual) with boy, or girlfriend	4.1	1.2	
Financial difficulties (females)	3.3	1.3	
Substantial change in sleeping habits (females)	3.0	1.3	$p < 0.05$
Concern over health or activities of a family member (major illness, accidents, drug addiction, disciplinary problems etc.)	1.7	1.1	
$p < 0.01$			
Difficulties (sexual) with spouse (ever marrieds)	13	0.7	
Marital separation (ever marrieds)	13	0.7	
Loss of a close friend by death	7.2	1.8	
Problems (sexual) with boy – or – girlfriend	6.2	1.5	
Move of home (males)	3.4	1.0	
Financial difficulties (males)	3.0	1.4	
$p < 0.025$			
Being sacked or laid off work (males)	1.6	1.6	
New close personal relationship	3.0	1.1	
Change to a new kind of work	2.0	1.1	
$0.05 < p < 0.1$			
Abortion (single females)	12	0.7	
Pregnancy (single females)	8.0	1.2	
Engagement to marry	3.0	0.6	
Illness (other than the index self-poisoning episode) involving bed rest for at least a week, or hospitalisation	1.8	2.0	$p < 0.001$

Table 8.2 *(contd.)*

>0.1	Prevalence ratio (of reporting EI/GPR)	Prevalence ratio EN/EI	Sig. level (only where p<0.1
Marital reconciliation (ever marrieds)	8.3	1.0	
Abortion (ever married females)	4.3	0.7	
Divorce (ever marrieds)	4.2	1.0	
Major success (including awards at work)	2.8	0.7	
Being sacked or laid off work (females)	2.1	6.0	0.05 < 0.1
Remarriage of mother or father	2.1	0.7	
Divorce of parents	2.1	0.0	
Change of social (group) relationships	1.9	1.9	0.05 < 0.1
Move of home (females)	1.7	1.3	
Pregnancy (ever married females)	1.3	0.7	
Miscarriage (ever married females)	0.0	1.4	
Loss of child by death (ever marrieds)	0.0	–	
Events not reported by either EI or GPR			
Death of father or mother	–	2.6	
Death of brother or sister	–	–	
Birth of a child (ever marrieds)	–	5.3	
Loss of spouse by death (ever married)	–	–	

average of 6·10 events compared with 7.04 from the EN group. The EI group differed significantly from the GPR group but EN and EI were not significantly different.

The life event data collected at the follow-up interviews were compared with those accumulated during the index interview. Because of the poor follow-up rate both self-poisoning groups were pooled. It was, however, feasible to separate those who had an episode of self-poisoning between the index and the follow-up interview. These were considered separately from those who did not. Patients were assigned to one of three categories according to whether the number of events they had experienced during the three months preceding interview had increased, remained the same or had decreased. The significance of any change in the numbers of events experienced was tested using Wilcoxon's matched-pairs signed-ranks test (Table 8.3).

At the three-month follow-up interview there were no significant changes in the numbers of events reported, irrespective of whether an interim episode of self-poisoning had occurred. One year after the index

Table 8.3: Change in Score Between Interviews

		Change in score				
		Increase	Decrease	No change		
Interview 1 v.						
3-month follow-up	n = 107	58	49	0	Z = − 0.78	N.S.
Interim overdose	n = 25	12	12	1		N.S.
No interim						
overdose	n = 84	46	37	1	Z = − 0.91	N.S.
Interview 1 v.						
one year follow-up	n = 113	36	75	2	Z = −4 .74	p < 0.001

episode there was a significant decrease in events experienced.

Twenty-three events studied here had been used by Rahe. He assigned a score to each event, based on the amount of adjustment necessitated by the event, irrespective of the desirability of the event. These scores were used to give some idea of the possible external weighting of the events at the index interview (Table 8.4). The EI group score was higher than the GPR group. The EN groups scores tend to be higher than EI scores and the distribution of scores from the two groups are significantly different $(\chi_4^2 = 10.11 : p < 0.05)$

Table 8.4: Distribution of Groups by Weighted (Severity) Score Categories (based upon Rahe's life event scores)

Score range		Control (GPR)	First episode group (EI)	Non-first episode group (EN)	Total
1st quartile	0- 29	75 (49%)	8 (11%)	4 (4%)	87 (26%)
2nd quartile	30- 79	52 (34%)	11 (15%)	16 (14%)	79 (23%)
3rd quartile	80-149	22 (14%)	31 (42%)	33 (29%)	86 (25%)
4th quartile	150-229	3 (2%)	19 (26%)	49 (43%)	71 (21%)
95th percentile	> 229	0 (0%)	5 (7%)	11 (10%)	16 (5%)
Not known		0	2	4	
Total		152	74	113	

Discussion

The 'control' group (GPR) used in this investigation cannot be said to be representative of the general population. People consult general practitioners for reasons that may themselves be related to life events. The differences between this group and the self-poisoning patients admitted with their first ever episode are remarkable.

The majority of the events in which there was a significant difference in report between the patients and the controls were 'soft events'. This term is used to describe those events that may be affected by the perception of the individual and which are often difficult to date precisely. For example, 'emotional difficulties with a boy friend or girl friend' is a much less precise event than is 'loss of a close personal friend by death'. There are two ways of interpreting this observation. All events could be regarded as being similar in nature. Alternatively the explanation of the observations regarding 'life events' could be that the expectations from life differed between groups. Thus the 'control' group would not perceive a particular event in the same way as the study group.

It was thought possible that the self-poisoning patients might offer more events at their first interview as a way of explaining their own episode. In fact there was remarkably little difference between the two self-poisoning groups. The continued high reporting rate of events at the three-month follow-up suggests that the episode itself is not necessarily precipitated by a particular event.

The findings are compatible with the hypothesis that both the events measured and the episode of self-poisoning had the same underlying cause, for example depression. Few events were reported significantly more frequently by the patients who were receiving treatment for a non-first episode (EN) than by those who were being treated for their first episode (EI). However, the EN group produced higher over-all scores than the EI group. There are several possible explanations for this. The differences may be entirely due to the small sample size, that is a larger sample may have shown more significant differences between the two groups when reporting individual events. It is possible that the EN group actually reported more high scoring events.

The follow-up data suggest that patients experience events after the episode that are similar in quantity and in quality to those experienced before the episode. This may indicate that the episode itself does not change the life situation. One year after the index episode there is a decrease in the numbers of events experienced.

Conclusions

Self-poisoning appears to be associated with increased experience of life events. The measures used here are brief descriptions of complex experiences and they do not take account of their intimate meaning for each individual. No conclusions as to cause may be drawn from these data. However, the data do suggest that the patients were undergoing a period of turmoil in their personal lives. It may be that the events measured were an expression of that turmoil rather than its cause. This could have important implications for management strategies particularly in relation to early intervention by general practitioners.

Acknowledgement

This research was funded by the Small Grants Committee of the DHSS, London.

References

Alderson, M.R. (1974). Self-poisoning – what is the future? *Lancet,* vol. i, p.1040.
Farmer, R.D.T., Preston, T.D. and O'Brien, S.E.M. (1977). Suicide mortality in Greater London: changes during the past 25 years. *British Journal of Preventive and Social Medicine*, vol. 31, no. 3, pp. 171-77.
Rahe, R.H. (1975). Epidemiological studies of life change and illness. *International Journal of Psychiatry in Medicine*, vol. 6, pp. 133-46.

PART THREE

Diagnosis and Prediction of Outcome

9 PSYCHIATRIC SYMPTOMS IN SELF-POISONING PATIENTS

J.G.B. Newson-Smith and S.R. Hirsch

There is long standing controversy whether the majority of parasuicide patients are mentally ill. Stanley (1969) reports that when the 1961 Suicide Act was debated at the Bill stage in Parliament, it was assumed that all persons attempting suicide were mentally ill. There is general agreement that depression is the most common diagnosis and that only a very small minority suffer from schizophrenia, organic mental states, etc. Weissman (1974) reports that different series give figures as varied as 39 to 70 per cent for those suffering from depression. A major problem is establishing at what level a person's reactive unhappiness reaches the level of mental illness. It must be assumed that this distinction is relevant in clinical practice. Situational crises, often in the setting of personality difficulties with poor coping mechanisms, are more likely to respond to counselling help (if help is needed outside the patient's primary family and social group, which may be instrumental not only in causing the parasuicide but also in resolving the crisis). Definite psychiatric illness may require treatment other than psychotherapy and social intervention.

The background to our work is that during the course of another study we noted the high level of psychiatric symptoms occurring over the four weeks before the overdose. This suggested that for some patients the overdose was the final event after a distressed interval of time. We also noted that one week later a considerable number of patients, as judged by improvement in their mental state, had actually benefitted from the event. This improvement is difficult to assess in normal clinical practice as clinic follow-up is often for more than one week after the event and there is universally a poor attendance rate (Goldney 1975).

We therefore set out to look at various issues: (1) The type and magnitude of psychiatric disorder in these patients together with its short term clinical course. (2) Which patients are deriving most benefit from the self-poisoning and attention received (without specific psychiatric help) and which patients are gaining little early relief from their mental distress. (3) Whether the patients as a group resemble any other type of psychiatric patients (again with reference to their symptomatology).

Method

The study was carried out at Charing Cross Hospital, London, on patients admitted to medical wards who had deliberately taken an excess of a substance thought to be harmful. The first three patients fit for assessment on any one day were studied. They were interviewed when fully recovered from the effects of self-poisoning. (The research interviews were additional to and independent of psychiatric assessment and management by the regular psychiatrist.) The first research interview covered the four weeks leading up to the self-poisoning. The mental state was examined with the full version of the ninth edition of the Present State Examination (PSE) (Wing, *et al.,* 1974) and the patient was asked to complete the 60-item version of the General Health Questionnaire (GHQ) (Goldberg, 1972).

The PSE was administered by the research psychiatrist. It is a semi-structured interview which has been extensively used in studies of acutely ill patients and in general population studies. The GHQ is self-administered and aims to provide information about the present mental state and has been found to discriminate effectively between psychiatric patients and normal controls. Goldberg advocates a cut-off score of 11, above which the patient is likely to be a psychiatric case. At first interview instruments covered the time-span of four weeks before the self-poisoning. The first interview was also aimed at establishing sufficient rapport between the patient and the research psychiatrist to make follow-up possible. The second interview, including a personal history, occurred one week later, usually at home or wherever else was convenient, e.g. other hospitals, public places, etc. The standardised mental state assessment was repeated for the intervening week. The patient was finally interviewed three months after the self-poisoning. Details were requested of professional help received and any repeat parasuicide acts. The standardised mental state assessment was repeated, which covered the four weeks preceding this three-month final interview.

Results

Seventy-nine patients were studied in order to obtain three interviews on 51 subjects. Differences in results to be reported between the 51 patients interviewed three times and those only interviewed once or twice are very small. Therefore it is unlikely that results are severely biased by the absence of drop-outs. Thirty-seven per cent of the 51 patients were male and 63 per cent female, and the mean age was 30 years. Complete sets of GHQ were obtained from 48 of the 51 patients.

Neurotic Scores

At first interview the mean GHQ score was 32 (approximately three times the cut-off score of 11), 18 at second interview (i.e. almost reduced by one half) and 12 at third interview (i.e. almost reduced to one third of its original value). The mean PSE neurotic scores (obtained from the sum of the two neurotic sub-scores) show a similar pattern of reduction with mean scores at 16, 9 and 5. These mean scores thus confirm that these patients generally do experience high levels of neurotic symptomatology prior to the self-poisoning well into the realms of psychiatric morbidity, and also the cathartic effect of the event is shown by subsequent reduction in levels. A control group of 78 hospital employees had mean GHQ scores of four on each of three occasions, covering the same time-span as the patient series.

A highly significant correlation of 0.8 (p < .0001) was obtained at all interviews between the patient's PSE neurotic scores and GHQ scores, so for this group the two scores appear to measure the same type of disorder since correlation between them is so high.

Index of Definition Levels

We used the index of definition level derived from symptoms rated at the PSE interview to determine whether the patient was a psychiatric case, i.e. could be classified to one of the conventional functional psychoses or neuroses. There are eight levels: levels 1-4 are below threshold and no diagnosis is obtained. Levels 5-8 are at threshold and above, the patient is a PSE case and a psychiatric diagnosis is obtained.

Sixty-one per cent of the series are identified as PSE cases at first interview, which means a diagnosis was obtained. This reverses at second interview, i.e. 61 per cent are not cases. Only 22 per cent are PSE cases at three months.

Clinical Course Based on Initial GHQ Score

The patients were placed into categories based on their initial GHQ scores, i.e. 0-20, 21-40 and 41-60. Mean GHQ scores were examined for each range. At second interview one week later the majority of patients in the middle and high ranges remain GHQ cases. Seventy-nine per cent of patients in the low range had reduced their GHQ score by 60 per cent or more at one week whereas only 38 and 33 per cent of

Table 9.1: Changes in Clinical Indices Over Time Related to Initial GHQ Scores (n = 48)

Initial GHQ scores	0-20	21-40	41-60
Interview I			
No. of patients	14	16	18
Mean GHQ			
Interview I	12	27	46
Interview II	3	20	28
Interview III	6	18	11
GHQ 'cases' − % with GHQ above 11			
Interview I	64	100	100
Interview II	7	63	72
Interview III	14	50	28
Repeat overdose by Interview III			
(3 months)	2 (14%)	4 (25%)	0 (0%)
Psychological help by Interview III			
(% treated by social workers or doctors)	14	69	73

patients, in middle and high score ranges respectively, had done so. More persons in the middle and high score ranges had taken previous overdoses. At three-month follow-up 14 per cent had repeated in the low range, 25 per cent in the middle range and none in the high range. Only 14 per cent of the low scorers had received any professional psychological help at three months, whereas 69 per cent and 73 per cent of patients in the middle and high score ranges had received help.

Diagnostic Results

As previously mentioned 61 per cent of the series, i.e. 31 patients, were PSE cases at the first interview. Depressive disorders were diagnosed for 30 patients and one patient was diagnosed as 'other effective psychosis'. Figure 9.1 shows the prevalence of the eleven most frequent individual PSE (neurotic) syndromes for this series at the first interview, which covered the four weeks before the self-poisoning. (A PSE syndrome uses the clinical concept of grouping symptoms of a similar kind, and the PSE criteria for establishing the presence of a syndrome are given in the PSE manual.) The syndrome 'worrying' has the highest prevalence in this series at 84 per cent (constituent symptoms are worrying, tiredness, nervous tension, neglect through brooding and delayed sleep). The next most frequent syndrome is simple depression which has a prevalence of 73 per cent. Other PSE depressive syndromes are somatic features of depression (59 per cent), special features of depression (29 per cent) and depressive delusions

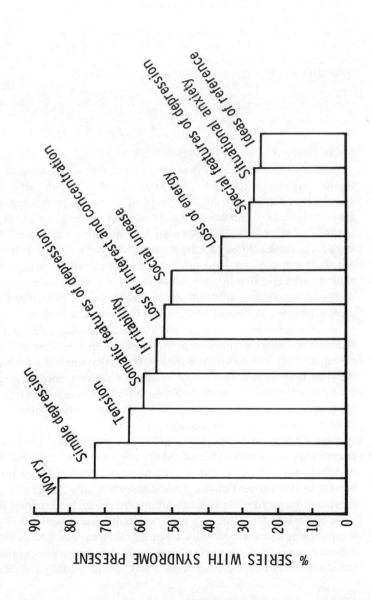

Figure 9.1: Rank Order Frequency of the Eleven Most Common PSE Syndromes in This Series (n = 51)

Table 9.2: PSE Depressive Syndromes at Interview I (n = 51)

Syndrome	Constituent symptoms	Prevalence
Simple depression	d mood, hopelessness, suicide plans or acts, d on examination, inefficient thinking.	73%
Somatic d.	morning d, loss of appetite, early waking, loss of libido, PMT.	59%
Special features of d.	Self depreciation, guilty ideas of reference, path. guilt, dulled perception, lost emotions.	29%
D delusions and hallucinations	d hallucinations, guilt delusions, hypochondriacal delusions, delusions of catastrophe.	0%

d = depression

and hallucinations (0 per cent) (see Table 9.2).

Other syndromes present in at least 50 per cent of the series are tension, irritability, loss of interest and concentration and social unease. Those present in 20 to 50 per cent are loss of energy, situational anxiety and ideas of reference. Syndromes present in less than 20 per cent of the series at first interview are depersonalisation, general anxiety, obsessional neurosis, hysteria and hypochondriasis. It is noteworthy that general anxiety (constituent symptoms are anxiety, panic attacks and anxiety on examination) is not a common syndrome.

Figure 9.2 shows graphically the syndrome profile at each of the three interviews. As would be expected from reductions in the neurotic scores over time, the per cent of the series experiencing individual syndromes reduces at subsequent interviews. Worrying is most prevalent at all interviews. A change after the first interview is that the syndrome somatic features of depression become more prevalent than the syndrome of simple depression. Tension remains a prominent syndrome (constituent symptoms for tension are tension pains, muscular tension and restlessness).

Figure 9.3 shows the profile of individual symptoms at the three interviews, i.e. the prevalence of the ten most common individual PSE symptoms for this series. The symptom suicidal plans or acts was rated present in 100 per cent of the series initially but only 22 per cent and 6 per cent respectively at subsequent interviews. It changes from first place by rank order initially to ninth and tenth places later. The symptoms of depressed mood and hopelessness, expected to be closely related to suicidal plans or ideas, rank in third and four places initially. Subjective feelings of nervous tension rank second initially and first

Figure 9.2: Syndrome Profiles of the Eleven Most Common PSE Syndromes for This Series at Each Interview

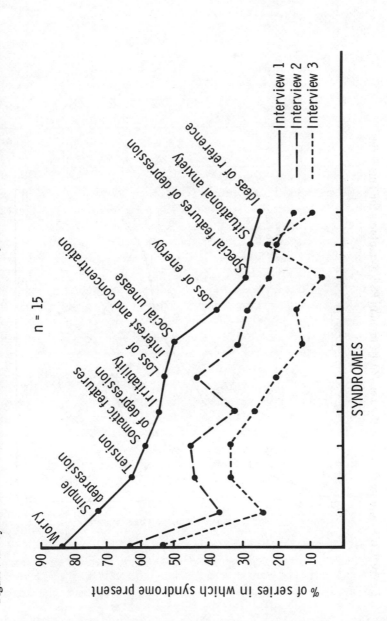

Figure 9.3: Symptom Profile of the Ten Most Common PSE Symptoms for This Series

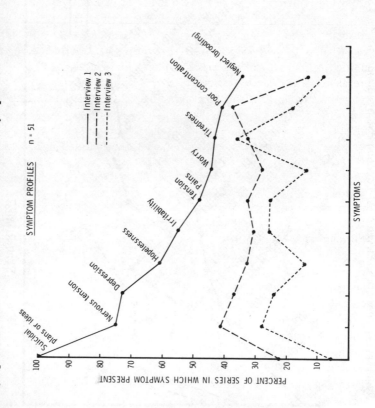

place subsequently. Generally symptoms represent minor neurotic disturbance with depressive features.

A major question we sought to answer was whether this group of self-poisoning patients resembles any other group of psychiatric patients. We were able to compare (by courtesy of Professor Wing) our PSE data with data on a series of in-patients and out-patients being treated for depression and a group of persons identified in a community study using the PSE as being depressive cases. The mean PSE scores for the self-poisoning series at 16 is very similar to that for the community cases at 15. In-patients and out-patients being treated for depression have higher scores at 26 and 24 respectively.

We then looked at selected symptoms (Table 9.3). Only 73 per cent of the self-poisoning series were rated as having depressed mood as opposed to 100 per cent by definition in the other series. The self-poisoning patients resemble the treatment patients for the symptom hopelessness. The proportion of self-poisoning patients affected by inefficient thinking and self-depreciation fell between the higher prevalence of patients in treatment and the lower prevalence of community cases. The remaining symptoms (pathological guilt, lack of energy, loss of weight, early waking and retardation) occurred relatively infrequently in self-poisoning patients and community cases as compared to the psychiatric patients having treatment for depression.

Table 9.3: Comparison of the Frequency of Selected PSE Symptoms in Other Series and Overdose Patients

PSE symptom	In-pts n = 55 (%)	Out-pts n = 14 (%)	Cases in the gen. population (%) n=19	Overdose pts n = 51 (%)
Depressed mood	100	100	100	73
Hopelessness	63	71	11	61
Inefficient thinking	46	43	22	31
Self-depreciation	38	36	22	28
Pathological guilt	21	21	6	2
Lack of energy	63	79	28	37
Loss of weight	46	71	11	26
Early waking	42	21	28	20
Retardation	21	7	0	0

Source: reproduced by courtesy of Professor J. Wing (Wing, 1976).

Discussion

This study has confirmed our initial impression that the vast majority of self-poisoning patients do experience a high level of depressive and neurotic symptoms before the self-poisoning act. Our technique was to interview patients as soon as possible after admission once they were mentally alert. This allowed little time for memory falsification. We have also shown that the act of self-poisoning can have a beneficial effect on psychiatric symptomatology, but this is much less likely in patients with high initial levels of symptoms. Apart from the direct and indirect gains accruing from the act, we must remember that spontaneous remission may also be an important factor.

Patients with initial low levels of disturbance (GHQ scores 0 to 20) do well. Few receive psychological help although repetition does occur. We would hope early screening would detect those patients most at risk of repetition so that the appropriate socially-orientated help could be made available. Patients with moderate and high levels of symptoms show a different pattern. Patients at the highest levels show much less resolution at one week. At three-month follow-up the majority of all these patients (initial GHQ scores 21 to 60) have received psychological help.

Our results suggest that earlier help than the standard clinic appointment a week or more hence is needed to deal with the continuing psychological distress. A further point spontaneously mentioned by many patients at one-week follow-up was that they saw little point in going to the clinic to see a different psychiatrist from the one they had met in the medical ward.

Study of diagnostic PSE results has yielded interesting results. The symptom profile has revealed that they more closely resemble depressive 'cases' discovered in the community than patients actually receiving treatment for depression. Interestingly neither the depressive 'cases' nor the self-poisoners at the time of self-poisoning are seeking help for psychological distress in a conventional way.

Certainly further research work is needed to evaluate the different types of early intervention after an act of self-poisoning. Our study has focused on psychiatric symptoms. The need for early follow-up has been shown by the continuing levels of psychiatric distress.

References

Goldberg, D. (1972). *The Detection of Psychiatric Illness by Questionnaire.* Oxford University Press, London.

Goldney, R.D. (1975). Out-patient follow-up of those who have attempted suicide: fact or fantasy. *Australian and New Zealand Journal of Psychiatry,* vol. 9, pp. 111-13.

Stanley, W.J. (1969). Attempted suicide and suicidal gestures. *British Journal of Preventive and Social Medicine,* vol. 23, pp. 190-95.

Weissman, M.M. (1974). The epidemiology of suicide attempts 1960-71. *Archives of General Psychiatry,* vol. 30, pp. 737-46.

Wing, J.K. (1976). A technique for studying psychiatric morbidity in in-patient and out-patient series and in general population samples. *Psychological Medicine,* vol. 6, pp. 665-71.

Wing, J.K., Cooper, J.E. and Sartorius, N. (1974). *The Measurement and Classification of Psychiatric Symptoms.* Cambridge University Press, Cambridge.

Wing, J.K., Mann, S.A., Leff, J.P. and Nixon, J.M. (1978). The concept of a case in psychiatric population samples. *Psychological Medicine,* vol. 8, pp. 203-17.

10 A CLASSIFICATION OF SUICIDE ATTEMPTERS BY CLUSTER ANALYSIS

E.S. Paykel

It is evident to all who deal with suicide attempters that these patients are heterogeneous, spanning a range of severity of attempt, apparent motivation, previous history and other phenomena. Some authors have sought to subdivide them using theoretical classifications or single key variables, such as age and sex, to derive useful subgroups (Beck and Greenberg, 1971; Wold and Tabachnik, 1974; Kreitman, 1976.) Relatively few studies have sought to use the newer statistical cluster-analytic techniques for deriving classificatory groups, the notable exceptions being Katschnig and Sint (1974), Kiev (1976) and Henderson *et al.* (1977). Such methods have their pitfalls (Everitt, 1974), but they may be particularly useful in situations where there is apparent diversity but clear-cut separations between distinct groups do not obviously emerge. The investigator measures his sample on appropriate ratings and then allows the data to produce their own groups. Elaine Rassaby and I therefore sought to apply these methods to descriptive data on a moderately large sample of suicide attempters obtained in the New Haven studies (Paykel and Rassaby, 1978).

Methods

Data Collection

The subjects were 236 patients derived from a study of suicide attempters presenting at an emergency room (casualty department) in the main hospital for the city (Paykel *et al.*, 1974). The study included all patients aged 16 years or over presenting with a suicide attempt, including a suicidal gesture. A suicidal attempt was defined as any intentionally self-inflicted injury (including by ingestion), unless there was good evidence that there was no self-destructive intent, such as in attempted abortion by pill ingestion, or cases of compulsive minor self-mutilation. For suicidal gestures to be included, there had to be not just suicidal feelings or threats, but some kind of act of potentially self-destructive nature even though without risk of significant personal injury, e.g. climbing on to a bridge or railing, toying with a gun, announcing intent and starting to ingest pills without actually taking more than one or two.

During a period of 25 weeks in 1970 and 1971, 274 consecutive patients were studied. Among these, 38 had more than 25 per cent of ratings missing and were omitted from the analyses. The subjects omitted included some who were seriously ill or unconscious, so that ratings based on interview could not be made initially, and were missed later. As a result, the most serious suicide attempters were under-represented. Like most attempters, the subjects were predominantly young, female, overdosers. The medical consequences of most attempts were relatively mild.

Information was collected by the junior psychiatrist responsible for initial clinical assessment and was recorded immediately after the assessment. Almost all suicidal patients were seen by a psychiatrist on presentation. For patients who were too physically ill or drowsy at the time of presentation, information was obtained later, omitting variables such as mental state that could only be rated at the time of admission.

A precoded data recording form was used. It contained 101 items covering demographic status, previous history, details of the attempt, judged and acknowledged motivations, mental state, social circumstances, treatment instituted and psychiatrist's feelings towards the patient. Definitions and anchor points for items were given in detail. Items were adapted from a variety of sources, particularly the Los Angeles Suicide Prevention Center Assessment of Suicidal Potentiality (Tabachnik and Farberow, 1961).

Further information was obtained by a research assistant on approximately one in every four patients. Within one week of initial presentation she interviewed the patient, either in hospital or at home, covering more extensively similar areas to those assessed by the psychiatrist. One month later, she also re-interviewed these patients to obtain information regarding intervening treatment.

From the pool of ratings by the psychiatrist, 14 were selected as especially relevant to classification and were used in the cluster analyses. Some of the variables were composite. Two — age and sex — were demographic. Two involved previous history: the number of previous suicide attempts and the number of previous suicidal gestures. Eight concerned the details of the recent suicidal behaviour, including method, severity and consequences; social circumstances of the attempt, and the rater's judgements of the detailed motivation of the suicidal behaviour condensed into two over-all dimensions: interpersonal motivation, and self-directed motivation. The last two items concerned mental state on presentation: severity of depression (mean of depressive

symptom ratings on clinical interview for depression), and hostility
(mean of ratings for reported irritability to others and overt hostility
manifested at interview).

Cluster-analytic Procedures

Cluster-analytic procedures are complex, and need not be laboured in
this report. They are sophisticated mathematical procedures aimed at
forming groups of individuals so as to maximise a particular statistical
clustering criterion. After preliminary principal component analysis
our data were analysed using the CLUSTAN group of programs
(Wishart, 1969; Everitt, 1974) available on the IBM 360 computer at
University College, London.

This incorporates a number of alternative methods, of which four
were used. Two of these methods failed to produce adequate clustering.
The most satisfactory clustering was produced by Ward's method,
which employs the sum of squared distances of individuals from
centroids of their clusters as the clustering criterion (Ward, 1963). This
was also the method employed by Katschnig and Sint (1974). An
iterative relocation procedure was also employed to optimise clusters.

Results

Classification Hierarchy

Figure 10.1 shows the classification dendrogram obtained using Ward's
method fusing from 20 clusters to one. This is a hierarchical
agglomerative method. It starts with all the individuals separate, and
first fuses the two closest together on the criterion to form a group.
It does this in successive steps until it finishes with a single group of
the whole sample. The figure shows the last 20 steps working upwards
in this family tree. The length of the vertical line indicates the range of
fusions over which the cluster was stable. At the right hand side of the
diagram was a cluster which remained stable over a great range of
fusions. The remaining groups were less stable, but the two-three- and
six-group levels persisted over moderate ranges. Four- and five-group
levels were only briefly stable. Three groups appeared to be the most
that could be obtained with stability, although the six-group level
merited inspection.

Iterative Relocation

One way of investigating stability of these groups was by the iterative
relocation procedure, which tried to re-assign individuals to other

Figure 10.1: Dendrogram From 20 to 1 Cluster

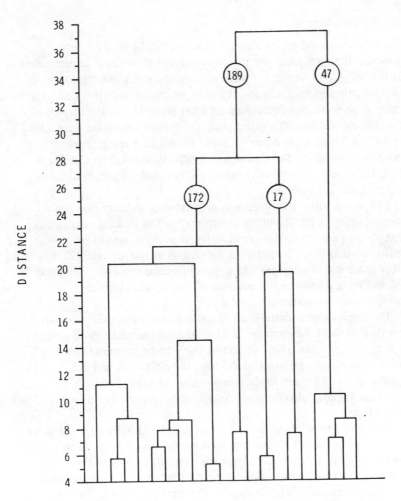

(CIRCLED FIGURES ON VERTICAL LINES INDICATE NUMBERS OF SUBJECTS IN GROUPS)

Source: Paykel and Rassaby, 1978.

groups where they might better fit. In fact, at two- and three-group levels the groups were almost completely unchanged after relocation, only 3 per cent and 2.5 per cent of subjects respectively changing groups. At the six-group level, 8.5 per cent moved, still a relatively small proportion.

Group Characteristics

When we examined group characteristics on the 14 classification variables, the two-group and three-group levels were easily interpretable. At the two-group level there was a striking and complete split by method between drug overdosers and those employing other methods. There were also some differences on other variables. At the three-group level the overdosers split further, but on iterative relocation were joined by a few patients using other methods. Figure 10.1 summarises characteristics of the three groups as finally obtained. The significant differences were on previous history, method, risk to life, motivation and hostility at interview.

The group with 51 subjects was that showing stability over the greatest range of fusions in the dendrograms. The striking feature was that all the patients used methods other than overdose (28 cut their wrists or other areas, 5 used guns, 18 various mixed methods). They made more severe attempts which were judged as producing the greatest risk to life, and showed less evidence of the various kinds of interpersonal motivation.

The largest group contained 172 patients; the most salient feature was that all had taken overdoses. They had the least history of previous attempts or gestures. They were most likely to be judged as showing interpersonal motivations, and although the difference was not significant, they tended to show less evidence of self-directed motivations. They also showed least evidence of overt hostility and irritability.

The third and smallest group contained only 13 individuals. Methods were mixed, although 77 per cent took overdoses. Risk to life was lowest. The most striking feature was a previous history of much repetition, with a mean of three previous attempts and eight previous gestures per patient. Patients showed the most evidence of hostility. Subsequent examination of individual ratings showed this mainly to be hostility and uncooperative behaviour at interview. This combination of chronicity, mild attempts and overt hostility made a striking constellation.

We also examined group characteristics of the groupings lower in the

Table 10.1: Characteristics of Groups

Classification variable	Non-overdosers n = 51	Overdosers n = 172	Recurrent n = 13
Previous history	2 attempts/ gestures	1.5 attempts/ gestures	mean of 3 attempts and 8 gestures
Method	100% non-overdose	100% overdose	mixed
Risk to life	higher	lower	lowest
Judged interpersonal motivation	moderate	highest	moderate
Hostility at interview	lower	lowest	high
Additional differences		admission least likely	psychiatrist's reaction shows least warmth and understanding, greater annoyance

Classification variables showing no differences include age, sex, rapidity of onset, social circumstances, self-directed motivation, depression at interview.

hierachy, but they did not seem meaningful. A number of variables, including age and sex, failed to differentiate groups. At the four-group level, the overdosers were split by sex, but without any other striking correlates. New groups appearing at five- and six-group levels were not readily interpretable. Three groups appeared to be the maximum the data could usefully provide.

Additional Differences

We also examined the wider pool of variables not used for classification. Many closely related to the classification variables, and on the whole they confirmed the findings on these. On demographic variables, there were no differences by race, social class or marital status. Overdosers gave less history of alcohol abuse than the two other groups.

A further group of variables covered treatment (Paykel *et al.*, 1974). Overdosers were least likely to require admission to hospital (43 per cent as opposed to 61 per cent and 62 per cent of the other groups) and, if admitted, were also likely to be admitted voluntarily rather than compulsorily (79 per cent as opposed to 42 per cent and 40 per cent of the other groups).

A checklist was used to record psychiatrists' attitudes to the patients

(Dressler *et al.*, 1975). Scores were derived on three factors. On two of these the recurrent group were regarded significantly less favourably. They received the lowest scores for attitudes reflecting warmth and understanding and the highest for those of annoyance. On the third factor (anxious and discouraged), this group also scored highest, but the difference did not reach significance.

Group Separation

One way in which to examine the success of the classifications is to see how well separated and internally compact the groups are. In order to do so, the three groups were subjected to a discriminant function analysis, using scores on the 12 principal components involved in the classification analyses. Figure 10.2 displays the groups on the two discriminant function axes. There was good separation between groups. The overdoser and non-overdoser groups were quite discrete, the recurrent group less so, with three aberrant individuals who differed from the rest in that in their recent attempt they had used non-drug methods.

The findings suggest that suicide attempters can be classified into three groups. The largest group comprises patients taking overdoses, with less risk to life and a predominance of interpersonal motivations. A second, smaller group is distinguished by the use of more violent methods with higher risk to life. A third and very striking group comprises recurrent attempters with previous histories of many attempts, relatively low risk to life, and overtly hostile behaviour which generates reciprocal hostility in the treating psychiatrist.

One aspect in our findings was surprising: age and sex did not emerge as differentiating features. This may partly be due to the fact that most of our sample were young, and also the omission from analyses, because of the method of data collection, of the most severe or deeply unconscious attempters, who could not be interviewed when first admitted, and therefore had too much missing data on the initial assessment.

A lengthy review of other studies is not possible here. However, I would draw attention briefly to two other cluster-analytic studies with some overlap. Katschnig and Sint (1974) subjected 276 suicide attempters to cluster analysis. They reported seven clusters, but five of these successively coalesced with a large cluster of younger female patients making attempts by overdose, and with predominantly 'conflict' motives. This resembles our overdoser group. The remaining group which did not coalesce until the final fusion, consisted of 35 older persons who had retired and showed 'unhappiness' motives. This

Figure 10.2: Plot of Individuals on Two Discriminant Functions

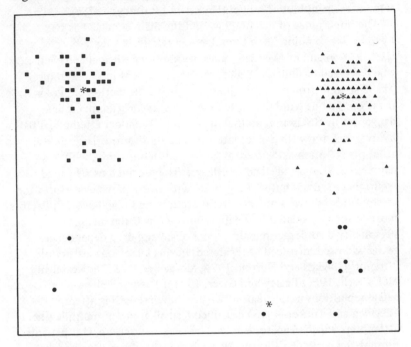

▲ = OVERDOSERS   ■ = NON-OVERDOSERS   ● = RECURRENT   * = CENTROIDS

Source: Paykel and Rassaby, 1978.

much smaller group bears some resemblance to our more severe group.

Henderson *et al.* (1977) reported three groups. One group was non-specific; a second group was depressed and alienated, with high risk to life; the third group showed low depression and low risk to life, and motivation particularly directed to an operant effect on others. The last two groups resemble our two larger groups and, as in our study, there was no relation to demographic variables such as age and sex. In a later analysis (Henderson and Lance, in preparation), three additional groups were delineated: repeaters, wrist-cutters, and an operant non-alienated group. The repeaters also appear to resemble those of the present study. Wrist-cutters are a group which most would want to separate, but has not emerged clearly from other studies, perhaps because they show few other specific characteristics (Weissman, 1975). Many other studies have described subgroups on clinical descriptive or theoretical grounds. Some are complex, although there is some overlap with our findings (Paykel and Rassaby, 1978).

The importance of our findings, and the main conclusions to which I would like to point, lie in the value of a relatively simple classification and of two major axes based on the suicidal behaviour, which seemed to underly it, and are also prominent in the literature. The first, and strongest in the literature, is the distinction between those on the one hand who make the more severe attempts, using dangerous methods and, on the other hand, the milder attempts, usually by overdose and with greater interpersonal motivation. The milder attempts are often associated, although not in our study, with less depression, younger age and female sex. The second axis we found was recurrence. A small but striking group with many previous gestures and attempts also shows a milder current attempt and high hostility. Factors most commonly related in the literature to repetition include personality disorder, criminality, alcoholism and drug dependence, being widowed, divorced or separated, having a previous history of attempts (Buglass and Horton, 1974; Morgan *et al.*, 1976; Kessel and McCulloch, 1966; Bagley and Greer, 1971). These mainly concern single repetitions in the year or two after the presenting attempt. Maxmen and Tucker (1973) described a small group of multiple suicide attempters which bears some resemblances to our group. Our patients presented a particular therapeutic problem: there was clear evidence that their own hostility engendered a reciprocal hostility in the treating psychiatrist.

Cluster-analytic methods present some difficulties (Everitt, 1974; Strauss *et al.*, 1973). Findings may not be stable, and require replication and validation. In any case, such methods are best regarded as exploratory rather than definitive. They can lend support to old classifications, or suggest new ones which may have heueristic or clinical utility. We would not claim that the present findings provide a definitive classification. A good deal of further work would be required. However, they do suggest that two axes — severity of method, and chronicity — are particularly important in that a number of other differences are associated with them. The threefold classification so derived at least has the virtue of simplicity and may be of utility.

References

Bagley, C. and Greer, S. (1971). Clinical and social predictors of repeated

Classification by Cluster Analysis 153

attempted suicide: a multivariate analysis. *British Journal of Psychiatry*, vol. 119, pp. 515-21.

Beck, A.T. and Greenberg, R. (1971). The nosology of suicidal phenomena: past and future perspectives. *Bulletin of Suicidology*, vol. 8, pp. 29-38.

Buglass, D. and Horton, J. (1974). A scale for predicting subsequent suicidal behaviour. *British Journal of Psychiatry*, vol. 124, pp. 573-78.

Dressler, D.M. *et al.* (1975). Clinician attitudes towards the suicide attempter. *Journal of Nervous and Mental Disease*, vol. 160, pp. 146-55.

Everitt, B.S. (1974). *Cluster Analysis*. Heinemann Educational Books, London.

Henderson, A.S., Hartigan, J., Davidson, J., Lance, G.N., Duncan-Jones, P., Koller, K.M., Ritchie, K., McAuley, H., Williams, C.L. and Slaughuis, W. (1977). A typology of parasuicide. *British Journal of Psychiatry*, vol. 131, pp. 631-41.

Katschnig, H. and Sint, P. (1974). Are there different types of attempted suicide? A cluster analytic approach. In *Proceedings of the Seventh International Conference for Suicide Prevention*, Amsterdam, 1973, Eds. N. Speyer, R. Diekstra and K. Van der Loo, Swets and Zeitlinger BV, Amsterdam.

Kessel, N. and McCulloch, W. (1966). Repeated acts of self-poisoning and self-injury. *Proceedings of the Royal Society of Medicine*, vol. 59, pp. 89-92.

Kiev, A. (1976). Cluster analysis profiles of suicide attempters. *American Journal of Psychiatry*, vol. 133, pp. 150-53.

Kreitman, N. (1976). Age and parasuicide ('attempted suicide'). *Psychological Medicine*, vol. 6, pp. 113-21.

Maxmen, J.S. and Tucker, G.J. (1973). No exit: the persistently suicidal patient. *Comprehensive Psychiatry*, vol. 14, pp. 71-79.

Morgan, H.G., Barton, J., Pottle, S., Pocock, H. and Burns-Cox, C.J. (1976). Deliberate self-harm: a follow-up study of 279 patients. *British Journal of Psychiatry*, vol. 128, pp. 361-68.

Paykel, E.S. and Rassaby, E. (1978). Classification of suicide attempters by cluster analysis. *British Journal of Psychiatry*, vol. 133, pp. 45-52.

Paykel, E.S., Hallowell, C., Dressler, D.M., Shapiro, D.L. and Weissman, M.M. (1974). Treatment of suicide attempters: a descriptive study. *Archives of General Psychiatry*, vol. 31, pp. 487-91.

Strauss, J.S., Bartko, J.J. and Carpenter, W.T. (1973). The use of clustering techniques for the classification of psychiatric patients. *British Journal of Psychiatry*, vol. 122, pp. 531-40.

Tabachnik, N.D. and Farberow, N.L. (1961). The assessment of self-destructive potentiality. In *The Cry for Help*, eds. N.L. Farberow and E.S. Shneidman, McGraw Hill, New York.

Ward, J.H. Jun. (1963). Hierarchical grouping to optimize an objective function. *Journal of the American Statistical Association*, vol. 58, pp. 236-44.

Weissman, M.M. (1975). Wrist cutting. *Archives of General Psychiatry*, vol. 32, pp. 1166-71.

Wishart, D. (1969). *CLUSTAN User Manual*. University College, London.

Wold, C.I. and Tabachnik, N. (1974). Depression as an indicator of lethality in suicidal patients. In *The Psychology of Depression: Contemporary Theory and Research*, eds. Friedman and Katz, John Wiley, New York.

11 SUICIDE AND PARASUICIDE: IDENTIFICATION OF HIGH- AND LOW-RISK GROUPS BY CLUSTER ANALYSIS WITH A 5-YEAR FOLLOW-UP

H. Katschnig, P. Sint and G. Fuchs-Robetin

There are two models of suicidal behaviour currently much used, the single syndrome model and the multiple syndrome model (Figure 11.1). In the *single syndrome approach* the various forms of suicidal behaviour — announcing or threatening suicide, attempting suicide for the first or a repeated time, finally committing suicide — are thought of as being manifestations of one and the same suicidal tendency, part of one and the same wish to die. In some cases this wish is regarded as being so strong that, if the means are available, it leads to a completed suicide, whereas in other instances, when the wish to live dominates the wish to die, more or less severe self-harming behaviour results. According to this single syndrome point of view differences between different forms of suicidal behaviour are simply differences in the *degree* of suicidal intent. If this were true we could adopt the public health concept of primary, secondary and tertiary prevention usually applied to chronic diseases. If attempting suicide is a less severe form of a completed suicide, we could identify people at risk for suicide in a similar way as we identify those in the early stages of diabetes. Such early identification is the crucial step in secondary prevention. Inherent in this approach is the concept of suicide as a disease.

If, however, we adopt a multiple syndrome approach, and think of each form of suicidal behaviour as a phenomenon on its own, having its own cause, purpose, course and outcome, we can no longer use the public health model of primary, secondary and tertiary prevention, but can only speak of actions taken before, during or after the self harming behaviour (prevention, intervention, 'postvention'). For example, we might ask what can we do to prevent attempted suicide, which might be a different problem from that of trying to prevent a completed suicide; or we might ask how to intervene when someone threatens suicide, which may be different from the necessary action to be taken when someone attempts suicide (Katschnig, 1977).

The purpose of this chapter is not to go into theoretical details of the speculative subclassifications of suicidal behaviour, like the strict separation between completed suicide and what different authors have

Figure 11.1: The Relationship Between the 'Single Syndrome Model' of Suicidal Behaviour and Primary, Secondary and Tertiary Prevention

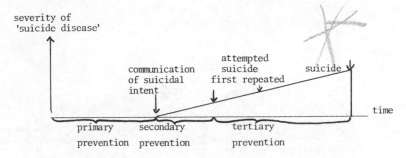

Source: From Katschnig, 1977:

Figure 11.2: The Relationship Between Observable Suicidal Behaviour and the Action Taken Before, During and After Specific Types of Suicidal Behaviour

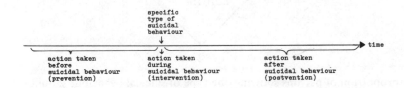

Source: From Katschnig, 1977.

called self-poisoning (Kessel, 1965), parasuicide (Kreitman *et al.*, 1969) or even pseudocide (Lennard-Jones and Asher, 1959); but to examine the question as to whether two forms of suicidal behaviour, attempted and completed suicide, conform to the single or the multiple syndrome model. To try and clarify the situation, we have introduced the concept of *transition probability* from one form of suicidal behaviour to another: that is the probability that after one type of suicidal behaviour has occurred another type of suicidal behaviour will ensue.

If the single syndrome model is pertinent, then a substantial

Figure 11.3: Transition Probabilities for Suicidal Behaviours

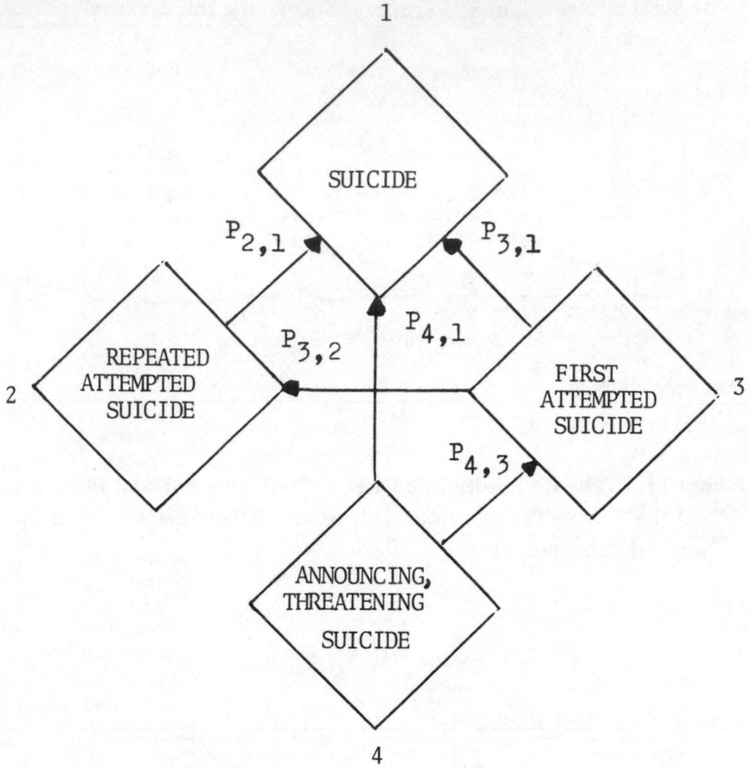

proportion of persons showing one type of suicidal behaviour should —
after a time — show one of the next forms of suicidal behaviour in the
postulated suicidal career. The proportion of people moving from one
type of suicidal behaviour — say threatening suicide — to another type
of suicidal behaviour — say committing suicide — would be the
respective transition probability, i.e. $p_{4,1}$. If the single syndrome
model is correct, at least some of these transition probabilities should
be high; if there are two or more types of suicidal behaviour, the
transition probabilities should be low.

We are concentrating in this study on one specific transition
probability, that from attempted to completed suicide. This subject
has been studied frequently and one review of the literature
incorporating a large number of studies lists the results shown in
Table 11.1 (taken from a paper by Wilkins, 1967). The results are
astonishing, ranging from 69 per cent committing suicide by one year

Table 11.1: **Percentages of Attempters Who Subsequently Commit Suicide**

Reference	Percentage	Follow-up period
Farberow and Shneidman	69	1 year
Moss and Hamilton	22	up to 20 years
O'Neal and Robbins	10.5	2 years
Schneider	12	18 years
	9	10 years
	4	1 year
Ettlinger	9	10 years
Ekblom and Frisk	8.7	6-8 years
Moto	8	5 years
Dahlgren	6	12 years
Hove	5	2-3 years
Pokorny	4	1 month to 14 years
Ettlinger and Flordh	3.6	8-24 months
Forssman	3	1 year
Stengel II	3	5 years
McCarthy	3	2 months to 2 years
Bachelor and Napier	2	1 year
Gardner, Bahn and Mack	2	1 year
Tuckman and Youngman	2	1 year
Schmidt, *et al.*	2	8 months
Jansson	1.3	1 year
Forssman and Jansson	1.1	1 year
Stengel I	1	5 years
Ringel	0.3	up to 3.5 years
Kiorbo	0.2	9 years

Source: From Wilkins, 1967, p. 291.

after the attempt, to 0.2 per cent committing suicide by nine years later. Possible interpretations of these discrepancies are a difference in methodological standards, different drop out rates (which are not given), or differences between the different cultures where the studies took place. All these may be relevant, but we would like to suggest an additional explanation for the variability of the results. If there are different types of attempted suicides (e.g. A, B and C), each one having its own risk (i.e. transition probability) for leading to a completed suicide after a certain time, it might be that the different transition probabilities encountered in the studies summarised here may simply reflect the different composition of the populations studied in respect to these subtypes of at risk populations (see Figure 11.4).

To test this interpretation we first tried to identify homogeneous subgroups of patients who had attempted suicide. In the second stage of our study we tried to establish the specific transition probabilities

Figure 11.4: Transition Probabilities from Attempted Suicide to Suicide

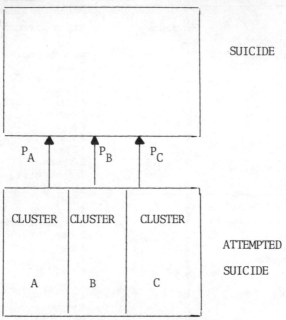

from attempted to completed suicide for each of the subgroups.

In our first study (Katschnig and Sint, 1974) we showed that it is possible to identify homogeneous and meaningful subpopulations in a random sample of attempted suicides being admitted to a detoxification centre. We used eight simple and clearcut variables to perform a cluster analysis (Ward's method) on 276 patients; a one in four sample of all patients with attempted suicide, admitted during the year 1971 to the Psychiatric Clinic of the University of Vienna, which at that time was also the central detoxification unit for Vienna. The eight variables were chosen so that any health worker should be able to obtain the relevant information. If certain combinations of variables were typical for subgroups of these attempted suicides, in the sense that a substantial number of persons showed this pattern, cluster analysis should be able to identify these persons and put them into homogenous groups.

The characteristics of our patients — roughly in accordance with what others have found — are shown in the left column of Table 11.2. The mean age of our 276 patients was 38 years; the age group between 20 and 29 comprising about a third of all the men and a quarter of all the women. Nearly two thirds of the total were women. Thirteen per

Table 11.2: Characteristics of Patients in Clusters II, III and IV

	All patients n = 276 (n = 262)*	Cluster II n = 92 (n = 91)*	Cluster III n = 34 (n = 30)*	Cluster IV n = 21 (n = 20)*
Mean age (years)	38	30	46	36
% Female	63	77	71	52
% Retired	13	0	0	0
% First admission	76	100	100	81
% Conflict motive	67	100	0	95
% Alcohol before attempted suicide	16	0	0	100
Drugs	85	100	100	100
% Unconscious on admission	11	0	0	0
% Dead after 5 years (all causes)	13	1	20	5
Expected	5	1	10	2
% Dead after 5 years (suicide)	4.2	0	3.3	0
Expected	0.1	0.1	0.1	0.1
		43 times		9 times
	As many suicides as expected			

*Numbers in parentheses correspond to the 262 patients followed up for five years. Percentages of deaths after 5 years are calculated with these figures.

cent of our patients were retired, one third of them being early pensioners; 76 per cent were first admissions. Two-thirds reported what we call a 'conflict motive' (cf. Katschnig and Sint, 1974), whereas 24 per cent reported a so-called 'unhappiness motive' (such as death of a loved one, financial difficulties, severe illness in a close person, etc.), 16 per cent had taken alcohol before the attempt and 85 per cent had used drugs. Eleven per cent were semi-conscious or unconscious on admission.

The cluster method used in this study first allocated the individuals into many small groups (clusters). In further steps these are combined into larger clusters. The stage with seven clusters allowed the most meaningful interpretation for the purposes of our study. The seven clusters identified in this way were remarkably homogeneous, a very high proportion of all persons belonging to a certain cluster were similar to each other in respect of our eight variables.

Cluster II with 92 patients, the largest cluster, comprised one-third of the population studied and was completely homogeneous in six of our eight variables (values 0 or 100 per cent in Table 11.2, second column): *no one* in this cluster was retired, *all* were first admissions, *all* admitted a conflict motive only, *no one* had taken alcohol before the attempted suicide, 100 per cent had taken drugs, they were all responsive, none had impaired consciousness (which suggests the amount of drugs ingested was low). The average age was the lowest, the percentage of women the highest among all clusters.

Hypothetically one could interpret this subpopulation as those who use attempted suicide as a strategy for ameliorating and re-establishing their interpersonal relationships. The use of drugs in small quantities together with the low average age may be indicative of the fact that there exist social contacts for which it is still worth while to struggle. We called this the 'cry for help' cluster, assuming a low risk of subsequent suicide. Our follow-up study will show whether this interpretation was right.

Cluster I comprised 35 patients and had characteristics significantly different from the previous cluster (see Table 11.3). The mean age was the highest of all clusters, 100 per cent of the patients belonging to this cluster were retired. Only 26 per cent reported a 'conflict motive', three-quarters reported an 'unhappiness motive', which was significantly above the average of the total sample. Methods of committing suicide and the sex of the patients did not deviate from the average significantly. Given the older average age and the predominance of the 'unhappiness-motive' we hypothetically assumed that this cluster comprised persons who were most at risk. In old age social contacts are frequently threatened by illness or death of near relatives, and loss of social contacts may result in an increased suicide risk. We concluded that these patients seem to be those who have really tried to commit suicide but survived. We call this cluster the 'failed suicide' cluster.

Details about the five other clusters, which may be regarded as clinically meaningful, are presented in Tables 11.2 and 11.3 but will not be discussed here.

The high degree of homogeneity in respect to some of the variables leads to the surprising fact that we were able to allocate each of our 276 patients into one of our seven clusters by means of a decision tree model (Figure 11.5). We do not expect to achieve this clearcut separation in a replication of the study, but could not resist the temptation to draw this decision tree. As can be seen from the figure this clearcut allocation was only possible when we took into account

Table 11.3: Characteristics of Patients in Clusters I, V, VI, VII

	All patients n = 276 (N = 262)*	Cluster I n = 35 (N = 28)*	Cluster V n = 37 (N = 37)*	Cluster VI n = 24 (N = 23)*	Cluster VII n = 33 (N = 33)*
Mean age (years)	38	66	35	34	30
% Female	63	60	65	54	33
% Retired	13	100	0	0	0
% First admission	76	66	0	71	82
% Conflict motive	67	26	62	75	64
% Alcohol before attempted suicide	16	9	0	29	27
Drugs	85	88	89	100	0
% Unconscious on admission	11	11	0	100	0
% Dead after 5 years (all causes)	13	50	14	17	12
Expected	5	16	4	2	3
% Dead after 5 years (suicide)	4.2	11	8	9	6
Expected	0.1	0.2	0.1	0.1	0.1
	43 times	As many suicides as expected	70 times		

* See note to Table 11.2.

Figure 11.5: Decision Tree

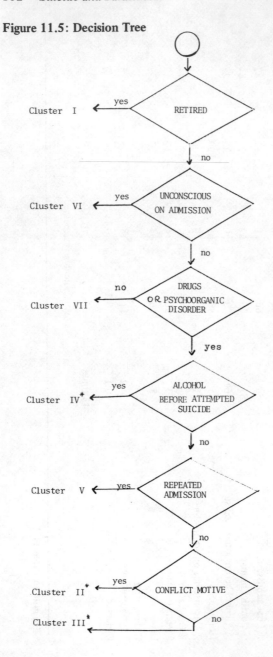

*Belongs to Cluster A in Figure 11.7.

diagnosis in addition to the eight variables used for cluster analysis.

We may conclude at this stage of our analysis that it is possible to separate our population of attempted suicides into homogeneous subgroups, and that the method was applicable, if not reproducible for other samples elsewhere. But are these subgroups of any clinical significance? We decided to test the relevance of our classification by a follow-up study checking for subsequent death. We were able to trace 95 per cent of our patients five years after the attempted suicide. We found out if they were still alive or, if they had died, what the cause of their death was. For the analysis presented here we omitted the 14 patients who had died within 8 days after admission (who by definition had become completed suicides). Out of the remaining 262 persons 35, i.e. 13 per cent were dead five years after admission for attempted suicide. We then calculated the expected death rate for all causes according to available life tables and found a rate of 5 per cent, which means a two-and-a-half-fold excess mortality for our patient sample, compared to an age and sex matched sample of the general population. The suicide rate was 4.2 per cent (11 cases), as opposed to 0.1 per cent for the expected suicide rate (as calculated from the published suicide rates for our study period for the city of Vienna). Our first conclusion from the follow-up study is that deaths from all causes, and deaths from suicide, were significantly more frequent in our population of attempted suicides, than would be expected for an age and sex matched sample of the general population.

The central question of our follow-up study is concerned with the mortality distribution in our seven homogeneous subpopulations identified by cluster analysis.

Our calculations revealed a very uneven distribution (see Tables 11.2 and 11.3). In cluster II, the 'cry for help' cluster (our biggest cluster), both mortality from all causes and mortality from suicide were equal to or even lower than in the general population. In fact, there was no single suicide in this cluster during the five-year period. Cluster I, however, the 'failed suicide' cluster, had an over-all mortality of 50 per cent, which was three times higher than predicted. (The expected value of 16 per cent is high because of the high average age of this subpopulation.) Eleven per cent, i.e. four persons in this cluster had committed suicide in the follow-up period (the predicted value: 0.2 per cent).

At the seven cluster stage, analysed so far, some of the clusters are small. However, the number of clusters is reduced step by step by fusing small clusters into bigger ones which provide a better basis for

Figure 11.6: Cluster Analysis : Dendrogram Showing Five Fusion Steps

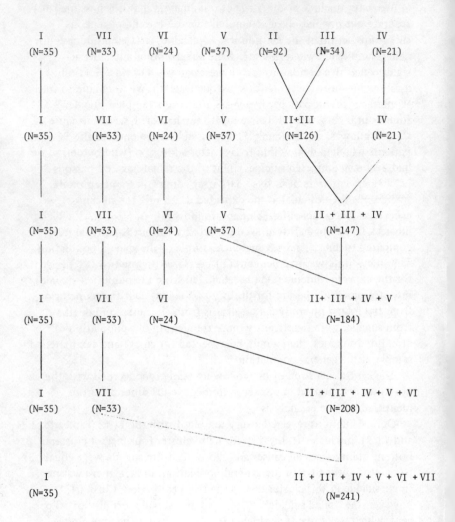

statistical analysis, though they are less homogeneous. As can be seen in Figure 11.6, clusters II, III and IV are thus fused into a big cluster of 147 persons after two fusion steps.

Looking at the suicide risk in this big cluster, we found it was still nine times higher than expected in the general population but we realised that this value was much lower than the 43-fold risk for the total sample (see bottom of Table 11.2). On the other hand, looking at the remaining group, comprising cluster I (the 'failed suicide' cluster), clusters V, VI and VII (Table 11.3), we found an increased suicide risk for this group of 129 patients: 70 times as many patients in this group died by suicide than would have been expected from available data for the general population (see bottom of Table 11.3).

Conclusion

We come back to our original formulation of the problem: are there subgroups of people with different transition probabilities from attempted suicide to suicide? We can now conclude that such subgroups do exist and that — at least in our study — they can be identified easily.

Figure 11.7: Transition Probabilities from Attempted Suicide to Suicide in Five Years for Two Subpopulations

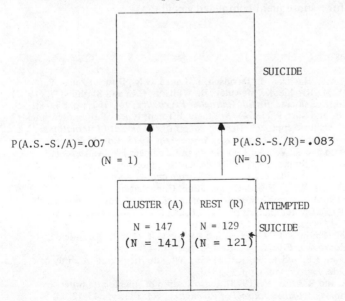

*See note to Table 11.2.

We were able to divide our sample into two clearcut groups (see Figure 11.7), one (Cluster A) comprising more than 50 per cent of our population and having a transition probability from attempted to completed suicide in five years of only 0.7 per cent. The remaining group had a much higher risk (8.3 per cent). Obviously in this second group the proportion of suicidal patients corresponding to the 'disease model' was much higher than in the first group and it could be suggested that it is this group which needs most of our therapeutic attention. Thus we can conclude that the analysis of our data favours the multiple sundrome model rather than the single syndrome model.

It remains to be seen in further studies, whether the classification found is consistent. If this is the case — and studies by Paykel and Rassaby (1978), Kiev (1976), Henderson *et al.* (1977) hint at this possibility — we would be in a better position to allocate our scarce resources to high-risk populations having identified them. However, we must not forget that attempted suicides who are low-risk suicides may nevertheless require help because of emotional distress. Using attempted suicide as a 'strategy' for getting out of emotionally troublesome situations (Katschnig and Steinert, 1975) must be regarded as a pathological form of 'problem solving', which may need therapeutic attention as well as those attempted suicides who have a high risk for a subsequent completed suicide.

References

Henderson, A.S., Hartigan, J., Davidson, J., Lance, G.N., Duncan-Jones, P., Koller, K.M., Ritchie, K., McAuley, H., Williams, C.L. and Slaghuis, W. (1977). A typology of suicide, *British Journal of Psychiatry*, vol. 131, pp. 631-41.

Katschnig, H. and Sint, P. (1974). Are there different types of attempted suicide? A cluster analytic approach. In *Proceedings of the Seventh International Conference for Suicide Prevention*, Amsterdam, 1973. Eds. N. Speyer, R. Diekstra and K. Van der Loo. Swets and Zeitinger BV, Amsterdam.

Katschnig, H. and Steinert, H. (1977). Prevention, intervention and postvention in suicidal behaviour. In *Suicide and Attempted Suicide in Young People*. World Health Organization, Copenhagen.

Kessel, N. (1965). Self-poisoning. *British Medical Journal*, vol. 2, pp. 1265-70.

Kiev, A. (1976). Cluster analysis profiles of suicide attempters. *American Journal of Psychiatry*, vol. 133, no. 2, pp. 150-3.

Kreitman, N., Philip, A.E., Greer, S. and Bagley, C.R. (1969). Parasuicide. *British Journal of Psychiatry*, vol. 155, pp. 746-47.

Lennard-Jones, J.E. and Asher, R.C. (1959). Why do they do it? A study of pseudocide. *Lancet*, vol. i, pp. 1138-40.

Paykel, E.S. and Rassaby, E. (1978). Classification of suicide attempters by cluster analysis. *British Journal of Psychiatry*, vol. 133, pp. 45-52.

Wilkins, J. (1967). Suicidal behaviour. *American Sociological Review*, vol. 32, pp. 286-98.

12 A FOLLOW-UP INVESTIGATION OF PATIENTS AFTER ATTEMPTED SUICIDE

R. Ettlinger

This chapter describes an outcome evaluation of a suicide prevention scheme working within the tradition of clinical psychiatry but with a social psychiatric orientation. It deals with persons from the city of Stockholm who had attempted suicide by poisoning and were taken care of in a medical intensive care unit. Most of them were in deep coma on admission and accordingly in need of intensive medical care in the form of life support of the vital functions — cardiac as well as respiratory. The scheme was staffed by two physicians (my assistant and myself), two social workers, one part-time psychologist and one secretary. Thus the study deals with an attempt at secondary prevention in a high-risk population. We also looked at various criteria of physical, mental and social handicaps. The variables and measurements were taken from official registers of different types; as such they were independent of the judgement and evaluation of the investigators.

The material consists of two groups of patients. The study group (Group S) comprises 670 patients treated in the period 1964-66. They were offered psychiatric, social and psychological help in connection with the attempted suicide. This offer was repeated after one month, six months and twelve months. If considered necessary, the patient was able to return frequently during the year after the suicidal attempt. After that the case was shelved, unless the clinical assessment contraindicated this, in which case contact with the scheme was maintained.

To evaluate the effect of the preventive scheme it was necessary to have a control group and the only one acceptable for ethical reasons were Group C, the 681 persons admitted to the same psychiatric ward under the same circumstances during the preceding three-year-period 1961-63. This control group had been cared for in a routine manner at the hospital. The additional facilities provided by the suicide prevention scheme, mainly after-care, were not available at that time.

Within Group S, the 202 patients admitted during 1965 were submitted to a more detailed examination. This subgroup (Group Sd) was compared with a subgroup of 233 patients in Group C, whose suicidal attempts occurred in 1962 (Group Cd).

167

Comparisons were made between the study group and the control group to make sure that the control group was well matched to the study group and could be used for its purpose. The groups were largely similar with regard to distribution by sex, age, marital status, socioeconomic group, employment, health insurance class, registered sickness, social assistance, criminality and abuse of alcohol, and the women for their number of pregnancies and abortions. In addition, the 1965 and 1962 subgroups were broadly similar in terms of 'burdening factors' at the time of the attempted suicide, factors such as somatic and psychiatric diagnoses, social inadequacy and the patient's intention to commit suicide.

We found there were about 40 per cent men and 60 per cent women in both groups. Women were over-represented in the study compared with the population of Stockholm at that time. The same distribution of socioeconomic grouping as found in an official investigation about living conditions were found in the two groups. Dividing the total male population of Stockholm into three socioeconomic groups, the lowest (III), was over-represented and socioeconomic group II was under-represented among men; no differences were found among women.

The age distribution, in accordance with most findings in the literature on attempted suicide, differed significantly from that of the total Stockholm population. As expected there was also an over-representation of divorced persons of both sexes and of single women in Group S.

In the small groups, which were examined more intensively than the others, we found some differences with regard to what we called 'burdening factors' at the time of the suicidal attempt. The differences show no specific pattern and can all be regarded as dependent on the differing depth of the investigation into the two groups. The same was found comparing the somatic diagnoses. In the study we included a judgement of the communicative function of the suicide attempt and a judgement of the intention to die. These showed no specific pattern either.

Each of the patients in the small groups were psychiatrically diagnosed on the basis of a review of all the available records and personal assessments. It is open to dispute as to whether a psychiatric diagnosis should have been attempted in every case. In my opinion the suicidal attempt — the nonverbal expression of crisis that cannot be communicated in any other way — is an exceptional state which can justifiably be given a psychiatric diagnosis. The disease classification used is the international classification of diseases code found in the 7th and 8th Revisions (of which the psychiatric section has been criticised a good deal). However the ICD code is still the only terminology which can be used for international comparisons.

It is noteworthy that in the study, psychoses occurred relatively infrequently, 15-16 per cent in both groups among the women, and 6-7 per cent among the men. The frequency of depressive psychoses was also low according to international standards. In contrast to this the proportion of depressive neuroses was very high. However, when the diagnoses of depression – neuroses plus psychoses – were summed, the figures were 44 per cent and 63 per cent of the women in the two groups and for 23 per cent and 25 per cent of the men. This agrees somewhat better with international statistics, suggesting that the deviations from international findings as to psychosis rates are largely attributable to differences in the classification of psychosis.

We also made a multidimensional classification of the patients according to Ottoson-Perris's model and used his dimensions 'symptomatology', 'personality disturbances' and 'aetiology'. Not very surprisingly we found that the predominant symptoms were anxiety and affective symptoms. It was also clear that abuse of alcohol was heavily involved. The assessment of personality disturbances, which have a subjective foundation in clinical psychiatry, lead to overdiagnosing and difficulties in distinguishing the basic personality from modifications caused by the environment in a wide sense. We were unable to resolve this conflict.

The groups were compared after 5-6 years using the same criteria, i.e. registered sickness spells, disability pensions and retirement, criminality, alcoholism and social assistance. In addition we also compared the total mortality, the suicide mortality and the frequency of known repeated attempted suicide. The total mortality rates within 5-6 years in the two groups were similar: male Group S 22 per cent and Group C 23 per cent, female Group S 15 per cent and Group C 13 per cant. The cause of death was taken from death certificates in the form of figures supplied by the Central Bureau of Statistics.

The suicide mortality rate was also taken from death certificates. We mostly accepted the 'official' cause of death, but in some cases changed those classified as non-suicide to suicidal death. This was because some cases were classified as non-suicidal when it was very doubtful as to whether it was a suicide or not. This opens the question as to whether suicide statistics should be based on 'official' cause of death classification or on other data. We suggest on the basis of our findings that the suicide mortality may be even higher than the official figures show.

The suicide mortality was about the same for both groups and much higher compared with studies from other countries. The suicide mortality (for men, Group S 12 per cent and Group C 16 per cent; women, Group S 11 per cent and Group C 9 per cent) was also higher than in other studies from Sweden and Scandinavia.

The proportion of known repeated attempted suicides was similar in the two groups. A comparison after 3-4 years showed similar results with regard to registered sickness spells, criminality, abuse of alcohol and social assistance. The only apparent effect of the preventive scheme was that the men in Group S who had a record of crime and drunken behaviour, had a significantly lower suicide mortality than those without such record.

It is necessary to discuss why we did not achieve a lowering in suicide mortality and why we did not find marked differences between the groups. First there was an increase in suicide mortality in Stockholm during the three years separating the two groups. This general rise was 16 per cent for men and 22 per cent for women. The rise also affected our selected groups and meant that the preventive work was given in an atmosphere of an increasing propensity to commit suicide, so that an unchanged rate between the groups could be said to represent some degree of success. Secondly, the change in the Swedish society during the period between the selection of the two groups included increased drug addiction, changing patterns of alcoholism with the abolition of rationing of wines and spirits and increased unemployment etc. All these factors may have influenced and masked any positive effect of the suicide prevention activities. Thirdly, as the data about the two groups were extracted from registers compiled over two different time periods, it is likely that coding practices varied, comparisons between the two periods may have been distorted by this and other factors. As previously mentioned, data from registers were used in order to be as objective as possible. Fourthly, there may be problems concerning the representativeness of the groups when we try to draw general conclusions from the study or to compare our findings with other studies. All the patients in this study came from a designated area of a big city. We have not had access to sufficient population data for the big catchment area of the hospital in order to standardise for differences. Fifthly, all the patients in the study were unconscious when admitted to hospital and in need of intensive medical care. In other words, they were all 'very severe cases' from the somatic point of view.

This does not necessarily mean that they were also 'severe cases' psychiatrically, though in fact, the high mortality rate in both groups is an indication of a biased selection of psychiatrically severe cases.

But even with all these explanations it is still a fact that the study — with its admitted defects in design — failed to show any marked effect of prevention as measured by the criteria chosen. It does not mean that the scheme did not help individual patients who undoubtedly gained support to try and lead a more satisfactory life. But this effect was not enough to counteract the over-all tendency to failure in the whole group. In fact there has been discussion in Sweden as to whether suicide prevention in this form is truly worthwhile, on the basis of the results of this study.

I think such conclusions are superficial and show very little knowledge of the problems of suicidology. Obviously our scheme was inadequate for the needs of the patients, although it was generously designed by Swedish standards. We were inexperienced in preventive work, and had no knowledge of the theory and practice of crisis therapy. We work in a municipal hospital without the support of a university clinic with all its facilities. The two most relevant explanations, however, seem to me to be the following:

(1) Suicidal acts are mostly not impulsive. Long before the attempted suicide a large proportion of the patients in both groups had already had frequent and lengthy periods of registered sickness for sundry complaints. We found, working through their problems with the patients, that the psychological attitude was formed long before the suicidal attempt. My point is that our suicide prevention scheme may have been offered much too late. Maybe one should consider intervening with some sort of support when faced with patients with vague patterns of illness. This involves difficulties in practice, because of the need to respect a person's independence and integrity. A society without willingness to be involved cannot solve this problem.

(2) The help available to the patients included detailed social investigation and social follow-up combined with psychiatric after-care, social medicine combined with a classical model of medical psychiatry. Maybe this model was more relevant for deviant personalities and those diagnosed as being severely mentally disordered. This possibility is borne out by the finding that an effect in terms of decreased mortality was obtained only in the group of men registered with the authorities for crime and drunken behaviour. But the problems of attempted

suicide are more complicated; and it is possible that the suicide prevention scheme described did not get to the roots of suicidal behaviour of all patients.

Two syndromes of suicide have been identified by Ovenstone and Kreitman. It is possible that to be effective two different preventive models are necessary, one basically psychiatric and the other socially orientated.

Reference

Ettlinger, Ruth (1975). Evaluation of suicide prevention after attempted suicide. *Acta Psychiatrica Scandinavica*, Supplement 260.

13 THE USE OF HEALTH SERVICES PRIOR TO NON-FATAL DELIBERATE SELF-HARM

R.J. Turner

Introduction

The increasing incidence of non-fatal deliberate self-harm has been a source of concern for a number of years (Smith and Davison, 1971; Kennedy *et al.*, 1974, Bancroft *et al.*, 1975 and Morgan *et al.*, 1975a). The increase is particularly disturbing because it has occurred in spite of the fact that there are now more health and social agencies to which a person can turn for help than ever existed in the past. Kreitman and Chowdhury (1973b) found that though 85 per cent of their series of 'first ever' admissions because of this form of behaviour were aware of the helping agencies to whom they could have taken their problem, only a third of this group had sought recent assistance.

A complex web of psychological and social forces surrounds each episode. It is unlikely that one style of help will suit all individuals who deliberately but non-fatally harm themselves. In planning, a preventive service assessment of the way patients make use of help which is offered, is an essential prerequisite. The study described in this chapter aimed to delineate the patterns of health care during the period of distress leading up to non-fatal deliberate self-harm, in turn relating this to the way patients used help which was subsequently offered.

Method

During the eighteen-month period June 1974 to November 1975, I was responsible for the psychiatric assessment of all cases of non-fatal deliberate self-harm admitted to the Bristol Royal Infirmary during one 24-hour period each week.

The operational definition for cases included in this study was that the patient had inflicted a non-fatal act of deliberate self-poisoning or self-injury with the knowledge that it was potentially harmful and that it had resulted in his admission to hospital. This form of behaviour is referred to here as 'DSH'.

The casualty and medical notes of each case were scrutinised, the nature of the act was noted and confirmed with the patient at interview and, where possible, with relatives as well. Each patient was interviewed in the normal way and a full history taken. At the same

173

time a semi-structured questionnaire was administered. Spontaneous discussion was encouraged, direct questioning being employed where appropriate. Particular attention was paid to establishing the agencies from which help had been sought during the period of recent distress. In each case the patient's view concerning the kind of help which would have been most acceptable was also obtained. A diagnosis according to the *Glossary of Mental Disorders* (HMSO, 1968) was made in each case. Arrangements were then made for the patient's further care.

Following the assessment the case was discussed with the relevant general practitioner and interview data collated with his records. Previous hospital medical notes were also scrutinised. Those patients whose place of residence was normally in the Bristol area were followed up via the psychiatric outpatient clinic at the Bristol Royal Infirmary. The ways in which they used this facility and the use they made of their general practitioner's surgery were monitored over a period of four months.

Results

Eighty-two cases of DSH were seen over the eighteen-month period. Two patients had to be excluded because they refused to cooperate.

Help Seeking Prior to DSH

Three main patterns of health care were delineated. Thirty-four 'non help-seekers' (non-HS) had made no known contact with their general practitioner or a psychiatric service for help with emotional or social problems over the time of their distress. Twenty-nine 'general practitioner help-seekers' (GPHS) had attended their general practitioner for relief of psychiatric symptoms, prescription of psychotropic medication, or for help with emotional or social difficulties over the time of their distress. They had not consulted psychiatric agencies. Seventeen 'psychiatric help-seekers' (PsyHS) had been in attendance at a psychiatric out-patient or in-patient unit during the time of their distress. There was no significant age or sex difference between the groups. However, significantly fewer single patients were found in the GPHS group ($p < 0.05$, see Table 13.1).

Fifty-one per cent of the whole series had received some previous psychiatric help. All those within the PsyHS group had been in treatment prior to their present series of out-patient appointments. In the GPHS and non-HS groups, fewer patients had received psychiatric care in the past, though in each group these still represented over a third of patients. Fifty-three per cent of the PsyHS group had

Table 13.1: Age, Sex and Civil Status

	Non-help seekers n = 34	GP help seekers n = 29	Psychiatric help seekers n = 17	Total n = 80	χ^2 Test and significance level between groups
Age 15-25 years	12 (35%)	6 (21%)	2 (12%)	20 (25%)	Not significant
Over 25 years	22 (65%)	23 (79%)	15 (88%)	60 (75%)	
Male	11 (32%)	8 (24%)	6 (35%)	25 (31%)	Not significant
Female	23 (68%)	21 (76%)	11 (65%)	55 (69%)	
Ever married	20 (59%)	26 (90%)	11 (65%)	57 (71%)	$\chi^2 = 7.174$ df = 2 p $<$ 0.05
Single	14 (41%)	3 (10%)	6 (35%)	23 (29%)	

Table 13.2: Previous Psychiatric Care

	Non-help seekers n = 34	GP help seekers n = 29	Psychiatric help seekers n = 17	Total n = 80	χ^2 Test and significance level between groups
Previous care	12 (35%)	12 (38%)	17 (100%)	41 (51%)	$\chi^2 = 21.468$ df = 2 p $<$ 0.001
Previous non-fatal deliberate self-harm act	7 (21%)	7 (24%)	9 (53%)	23 (29%)	$\chi^2 = 4.76$ df = 2 p $<$ 0.05

deliberately harmed themselves previously compared with 29 per cent
of the whole series (Table 13.2).

In 59 per cent of all cases the underlying cause of distress was an
interpersonal difficulty, which included marital problems and
disturbances in other key relationships. There was no significant
difference between the groups in this respect (Table 13.3).

The length of distress varied considerably. Forty-five per cent of
the non-HS group, 73 per cent of the GPHS group and 94 per cent of
the PsyHS group had been distressed for longer than a month. By
definition the patients in the non-HS group had not consulted their
general practitioner for emotional disorder over the time of their
distress; they had attended him somewhat less frequently than the
remainder of the series for symptoms associated with physical disorder,
though the difference between the two was not statistically significant.
Only 16 had consulted other agencies such as the social services or the
Samaritans and there was no significant difference between groups in
this respect.

Eighty-three per cent of the GPHS group and 76 per cent of the
PsyHS group had been treated with psychotropic drugs over the time
of their distress. Eighty-eight per cent of those patients who were
prescribed these drugs used them as the chosen agent for self-harm.
The majority of the non-HS group used non-prescribed drugs, which
for the most part were obtained at the point of crisis from the family
medicine cupboard (Table 13.4).

Sixty-six per cent of the GPHS group described some degree of
depressive symptoms prior to the episode of DSH (Table 13.5). A
transient situational disturbance was the commonest diagnostic category
found in the non-HS group (35 per cent). Such a disturbance had not
been associated with any psychiatric symptoms outside the crisis
situation and had at least in part been resolved by the time the
assessment was made. Personality disorder was the commonest
diagnosis in the PsyHS group (41 per cent), in which longstanding
difficulties in personal relationships and alcohol abuse were more
common than in the remainder of the series.

Only 12 per cent of the non-HS group thought that their general
practitioner possessed the skills appropriate to their particular crisis,
significantly less often than did the remainder of the series. Though
69 per cent of all patients knew of the Samaritans and 54 per cent of
the social services, only 20 per cent had actually consulted one of these
agencies over the time of their distress. Eighty-three per cent of the
GPHS group felt that they needed further help. This was a significantly

Table 13.3: Distress Prior to Act of Deliberate Self-harm

	Non-help seekers n = 34	GP help seekers n = 29	Psychiatric help seekers n = 17	Total n = 80	χ^2 test and significance level between groups
Cause of distress:					
Interpersonal difficulties	22 (65%)	17 (59%)	8 (53%)	47 (59%)	Not significant
Other difficulties	12	12	9		
Length of distress:					
Less than one month	19 (55%)	8 (27%)	1 (6%)	28 (35%)	$\chi^2 = 13.53$ df = 2 p < 0.05
Greater than one month	15 (45%)	21 (73%)	16 (94%)	52 (65%)	
GP consulted for: physical symptoms over time of distress	10 (29%)	13 (45%)	9 (53%)	32 (40%)	Not significant
Other agency consulted over time of distress: e.g. Samaritans, social services	7 (21%)	3 (10%)	6 (35%)	16 (20%)	Not significant

Table 13.4: Method of Self-harm

	Non-help seekers n = 34	GP help seekers n = 29	Psychiatric help seekers n = 17	Total n = 80	χ^2 test and significance level between groups
Psychotropic drug prescribed for patient	7 (21%)	18 (62%)	12 (71%)	37 (46%)	$\chi^2 = 15.98$ df = 2 p < 0.001
Non-prescribed drug	19 (56%)	5 (17%)	2 (12%)	26 (33%)	$\chi^2 = 14.88$ df = 2 p < 0.001

Table 13.5: Diagnosis

	Non-help seekers n = 34	GP help seekers n = 29	Psychiatric help seekers n = 17	Total n = 80	χ^2 test and significance level between groups
Depression	7 (21%)	19 (66%)	3 (18%)	29 (36%)	$\chi^2 = 13.06$ df = 2 p < 0.01
Transient situational disturbance	12 (35%)	7 (24%)	nil	19 (24%)	$\chi^2 = 10.46$ df = 1 p < 0.01
Personality disorder	9 (26%)	1 (3%)	7 (41%)	17 (21%)	$\chi^2 = 10.08$ df = 2 p < 0.01
Alcoholism	3 (9%)	2 (7%)	4 (23%)	9 (11%)	
Psychosis	nil	nil	3 (18%)	3 (4%)	
Anxiety state	2 (6%)	nil	nil	2 (3%)	
No psychiatric disorder	1 (3%)	nil	nil	1 (1%)	

Table 13.6: Attitudes to Further Help

	Non-help seekers n = 34	GP help seekers n = 29	Psychiatric help seekers n = 17	Total n = 80	χ^2 test and significance level between groups
GP seen as a helper	4 (12%)	9 (31%)	7 (41%)	20 (25%)	$\chi^2 = 6.11$ df = 2 p < 0.05
Knew of:					
Samaritans	23 (76%)	17 (58%)	15 (88%)	52 (69%)	Not significant
Social services	16 (41%)	15 (52%)	12 (71%)	43 (54%)	Not significant
Further help requested	20 (59%)	24 (83%)	10 (59%)	54 (77%)	$\chi^2 = 6.70$ df = 2 p < 0.05

Table 13.7: Follow-up Data: Utilisation of Help Which Was Offered

	Non-help seekers n = 29	GP help seekers n = 26	Psychiatric help seekers n = 15	Total n = 70	χ^2 test and significance level between groups
Psychiatric Clinic:					
Non-attenders – declined help	9 (31%)	2 (8%)	2 (13%)	13 (19%)	
accepted help but did not attend	6 (21%)	3 (10%)	6 (40%)	15 (21%)	
total non-attenders	15 (52%)	5 (18%)	8 (53%)	28 (40%)	$\chi^2 = 7.44$ df = 2 p < 0.05
Attenders – defaulted after commencing attendance	4 (14%)	8 (31%)	2 (12%)	14 (20%)	$\chi^2 = 11.33$ df = 2 p < 0.01
continued until discharged	10 (34%)	13 (50%)	5 (33%)	28 (40%)	$\chi^2 = 7.44$ df = 2 p < 0.05
General Practitioner: Consulted for emotional difficulties	7 (24%)	17 (65%)	nil	24 (34%)	$\chi^2 = 16.44$ df = 1 p < 0.01

greater proportion than in the other groups (Table 13.6).

Follow-up Data

Of the 80 cases seen for assessment six were normally domiciled outside the Bristol area and were therefore referred for further care, either to their general practitioner or to the hospital psychiatric service in their own area. Four patients in the non-HS group were already in regular contact with the probation service and as no specific psychiatric treatment seemed indicated, these were re-referred to their respective probation officers. Thus a total of 70 cases (88 per cent of the original series) were offered follow-up by psychiatric agencies in Bristol (Table 13.7). I personally gave follow-up appointments to 56 patients. The remaining 14 were referred to other psychiatric teams working within the city as the patients were already under their care.

A total of 28 patients (40 per cent) did not avail themselves of the offer of further help; 19 per cent declined the offer of an appointment at the psychiatric clinic; a further 21 per cent whilst accepting and apparently welcoming an opportunity to talk further, in fact never kept their first appointment, they did not telephone to cancel it, nor did they subsequently contact the clinic to give any reason for their non-attendance. Such inconsistency was most common amongst the PsyHS patients (40 per cent). It was least common in the GPHS (10 per cent) who were also more likely than others to utilise offers of subsequent help, only 18 per cent failing to do so. A further 14 patients (20 per cent) failed to complete their outpatient treatment programme in spite of attending initially. Twenty-eight patients (40 per cent) completed their attendance at the clinic and were formally discharged (GPHS 50 per cent, PsyHS 33 per cent, non-HS 34 per cent, $\chi^2 = 7.44$, df = 2, p < 0.05).

Discussion

Secondary prevention in non-fatal deliberate self-harm has proved disappointing. Although an earlier study reported that psychiatric intervention is beneficial (Greer and Bagley, 1971), others have not been so optimistic, particularly with regard to prevention of repetition (Chowdhury *et al.*, 1973; Gibbons *et al.*, 1978). It is clearly important to explore methods of primary prevention whereby effective intervention can be achieved before DSH occurs. The findings of the present study show that there are three distinct patterns of help-seeking in persons who proceed to resort to DSH.

The non-help-seekers may be described as those whose episodes of

distress have been of acute onset and whose lives have been acutely
disrupted, often due to interpersonal difficulties (Ovenstone and
Kreitman, 1974). They are commonly single and have been relatively
infrequent attenders at their general practitioner's surgery. They do not
perceive him as being the person best able to help them with their
emotional problems, perhaps because they do not know him well.
Neither do they perceive the Samaritans or Social Service agencies as
being particularly relevant to their difficulties. Such patients are
therefore unlikely to look for and persist with a formal treatment
programme which requires an appointment to be made some days or
weeks before an assessment is made and a treatment contract offered.
Their need would appear to be at the point of crisis.

Those we describe as general practitioner help-seekers (36 per cent)
see their doctor as the ideal confidant (Kreitman and Chowdhury,
1973a). Certainly consultation rates for minor emotional illness have
increased dramatically in the last 20 years, and it would seem that
general practitioners are increasingly willing to treat such cases.
Family habits, customs and traditions make it easier for some patients
than others to consult their general practitioners on such problems
(Kessel and Shepherd, 1965). Those who are married and perhaps in
their late 20s or early 30s have commonly had some reason to consult
their general practitioners before the point of crisis. Thus in their
distress they find it relatively easy to turn to him. However, in this
study it was found that they commonly presented with symptoms of
depression and were often treated with psychotropic medication which
was later used in the deliberate self-harm episode. Many patients who
present in this way are helped effectively and do not turn to deliberate
self-harm, but for a proportion this kind of help is not enough. The
motivation behind deliberate self-harm in such individuals is not clear,
but it would seem that having found that this kind of help has failed to
meet their needs they do not know where to turn next. The subsequent
deliberate self-harm act may be explicable, in some degree, as a
challenge to the patient's general practitioner to provide a different
solution to his problem.

In a high proportion of these cases the patient knows that the real
cause for his distress has not been brought out into the open and
discussed. This may be because he is unable to speak about himself
fully and the general practitioner may appear disinterested. If six
minutes is, on the average, all that is available for such consultations
(Royal College of General Practitioners, 1973) it is understandable that
psychotropic medication is prescribed as the quick solution to such

problems. However, it must be said that many general practitioners do feel frustrated by a system of consultations that demands so much of them and wish that they could spend more time with their patients. When further help is offered in the out-patient clinic these particular patients are willing to accept the offer and a high proportion make a treatment contract and complete it. They therefore seem to do well.

The group we describe as 'psychiatric help-seekers' (21 per cent) are those who harm themselves despite help from their general practitioner, a psychiatric clinic team and often after other social services have been involved. In terms of previous psychiatric care and self-harm episodes this group is significantly more disturbed. They are those whom Ovenstone and Kreitman (1974) describe as the 'chronically disorganised'. They have had more days in hospital than the normal psychiatric patient (Pallis, 1975) and have had a great amount of help from numerous agencies. They often turn to hospital staff for support but usually, through repeated episodes of self-harm, succeed in alienating themselves with unreasonable demands for special attention. By these means, however, they force themselves back into a treatment setting with which they are unable to cooperate. It seems they attend poorly and apparently gain little.

If we are to make any progress with regard to primary prevention of deliberate self-harm then the various ways in which patients perceive the help that they need and its optimal form of presentation must obviously be taken into account. Those who are clearly reluctant to seek any help at all constituted 43 per cent of our series and pose a particular challenge to the development of new styles of helping such individuals in crisis. Those who are already in contact with various forms of help through the psychiatric agencies, about one-fifth of our series, also constitute a major problem because they continue to resort to DSH in spite of a great deal of help and support. The remaining third of our series had consulted a general practitioner because of emotional and personal difficulties prior to resorting to DSH and it seems that we need to review the problems which such patients present to the primary health care team. The precise role of psychotropic drug prescription needs particular scrutiny; very little is known about the rate at which prescription of these drugs is complicated by DSH, even less how this varies with social conditions and personal characteristics of the recipients. It seems clear that nowhere more than in the prevention of non-fatal deliberate self-harm are new styles of primary prevention urgently required.

Acknowledgements

I am greatly indebted to Dr H.G. Morgan, Senior Lecturer in Psychiatry in the Department of Mental Health, Bristol University, who inspired and guided me in this research whilst I worked with him as a lecturer in that department. I am most grateful to the general practitioners who cooperated with this study. I would also like to thank Mr Alan Hayward, Principal Clinical Psychologist, Glenside Hospital, Bristol, for his statistical advice, and Mrs Sylvia Denning, Mrs Noreen Iles and Mrs Rita Tapley for their help with the organisational and secretarial aspects of the work. This paper is based on material submitted for an MD thesis.

References

Aitken, R.C.B., Buglass, D. and Kreitman, N. (1969). The changing pattern of attempted suicide in Edinburgh 1962-67. *British Journal of Preventive and Social Medicine*, vol. 23, pp. 111-15.

Bancroft, J.H.J., Skrimshire, A.M., Reynolds, P., Simkin, S. and Smith, J. (1975). Self-poisoning and self-injury in the Oxford Area: epidemiological aspects. *British Journal of Preventive and Social Medicine*, vol. 29, pp. 170-77.

Buglass, D. and Horton, J. (1974). A scale for predicting subsequent suicidal behaviour. *British Journal of Psychiatry*, vol. 124, pp. 573-78.

Chowdhury, N., Hicks, R.A. and Kreitman, N. (1973). The evaluation of an after-care service for parasuicide (attempted suicide) patients. *Social Psychiatry*, vol. 8, pp. 67-81.

Gibbons, J.S., Butler, J., Urwin, P. and Gibbons, J.L. (1978). Evaluation of a social work service for self-poisoning patients. *British Journal of Psychiatry*, vol. 133, pp. 111-18.

Greer, S. and Bagley, C. (1971). Effects of psychiatric intervention on attempted suicide: a controlled study. *British Medical Journal*, vol. 1, pp. 310-12.

Kennedy, P., Kreitman, N. and Ovenstone, I.M. (1974). The prevalence of suicide and parasuicide (attempted suicide) in Edinburgh. *British Journal of Psychiatry*, vol. 124, pp. 36-41.

Kessel, N. and Shepherd, M. (1965). The health and attitudes of people who seldom consult a doctor. *Medical Care*, vol. 3, pp. 6-10.

Kreitman, N. and Chowdhury, N. (1973a). Distress behaviour: a study of selected Samaritan clients and parasuicides (attempted suicide patients). Part 1. General aspects. *British Journal of Psychiatry*, vol. 123, pp. 1-8.

Kreitman, N. and Chowdhury, N. (1973b). Distress behaviour: a study of selected Samaritan clients and parasuicides (attempted suicides). Part II. Attitudes and choice of action. *British Journal of Psychiatry*, vol. 123, pp. 9-14.

Morgan, H.G. Pocock, H. and Pottle, S. (1975a). The urban distribution of non-fatal deliberate self-harm. *British Journal of Psychiatry*, vol. 126, pp. 319-28.

Morgan, H.G., Pocock, H., Burns-Cox, C.J. and Pottle, S. (1975b). Deliberate self-harm: clinical and socioeconomic characteristics of 368 patients. *British*

Journal of Psychiatry, vol. 127, pp. 564-74.
Morgan, H.G., Barton, J., Pottle, S., Pocock, H. and Burns-Cox, C.J. (1976).
   Deliberate self-harm: a follow-up study of 279 patients. *British Journal of
   Psychiatry*, vol. 128, pp. 362-8.
Ovenstone, I.H.K. and Kreitman, N. (1974). Two syndromes of suicide.
   British Journal of Psychiatry, vol. 124, pp. 336-45.
Pallis, D.J., Langley, H. and Birtchnell, J. (1975). Excessive use of psychiatric
   services by suicidal patients. *British Medical Journal*, vol. 3, pp. 216-18.
Royal College of General Practitioners (1973). Present state and future needs of
   general practice. *Report from General Practice*, 16.
Smith, J.S. and Davison, K. (1971). Changes in the pattern of admissions for
   attempted suicide in Newcastle-upon-Tyne during the 1960s. *British Medical
   Journal*, vol. 4, pp. 412-19.

14 THE DIFFERENCES BETWEEN THOSE WHO REPEAT AND THOSE WHO DO NOT

R.D.T. Farmer

Introduction

The substantial increase in the annual numbers of hospital admissions for self-poisoning over the past twenty years has been widely reported and commented upon. The spectacular trend is enough in itself to justify an energetic search for methods of prevention. An essential step in designing a preventive programme is to identify those factors that enhance an individual's susceptibility to the disease or condition to be prevented: that is, the isolation of 'risk factors'. It is also important to discover the circumstances that precipitate episodes. Intervention may be directed towards reducing the individual's susceptibility or towards reducing the prevalence of those adverse circumstances that are likely to precipitate an episode. Both courses may be adopted concurrently. In the case of self-poisoning, which is not necessarily fatal, indeed is rarely fatal, two types of study are required; one is of individuals from whom 'risk factors' may be deduced, and the other is of episodes, from which precipitating factors can be deduced.

Because an individual may have more than one episode of self-poisoning in his life, it is necessary to use a different sampling frame to investigate *individuals* from that which would be adopted for the investigation of *episodes*. The identification of the characteristics of individuals, and thus the isolation of risk factors, requires a slightly different study design to that which would be used to investigate the precipitating events associated with episodes. If the proportion of individuals who have more than one episode is small then the difference between the sample frames may be so small as to make no real difference.

In this chapter, two studies are presented. The first is concerned with the secular trends in repeat admissions for self-poisoning at a central London hospital. From that study it is concluded that the tendency towards repetition has increased during the five years studied. Next the findings from a sample of self-poisoning patients (as opposed to episodes) who were admitted to one of two hospitals in the centre of London (St Stephens, Chelsea and the Westminster) between February and August 1976, are presented. The particular aspects of the study that are reported here concern the identification of the ways in which the family backgrounds and childhood experiences of self-poisoning patients differ from the general population.

Secular Trends in Repeat Admissions

Method

As no special record system for self-poisoning patients existed at the hospital used for this investigation it was necessary to identify the self-poisoning episodes from routine hospital records. The day books of the accident and emergency department covering the five years 1972-76 were scrutinised by a research worker. All attendances that had been diagnosed and recorded as self-poisoning by drugs were identified. Poisoning by alcohol alone and poisoning in drug addicts classified as such were excluded. The name, age, sex and address of patients were abstracted and sorted using a computer in order to identify people who had appeared more than once. The matching criteria were the same name, sex and age within two years. They were then allocated a unique identity number. The proportion of patients each year who re-attended within three months, six months, and one year was calculated.

Results

Table 14.1 shows the re-attendance rate for two age groups. The results for the final year are incomplete as a further year's data would need to be examined to determine all repeat admissions within 12 months. In all three time periods examined there has been a consistent year by year increase in the rate of repetition amongst people aged 15-29 years. In the older age group the increase in the percentage who repeat is less clear.

Table 14.1: Percentage of Patients in Each Age Group Who Were Re-admitted Within Time Shown

Year when first admitted	Age 15-29 years at first admission			Age 30-44 years at first admission		
	3 months	6 months	12 months	3 months	6 months	12 months
1972	5.9	8.1	10.7	7.0	10.5	12.6
1973	7.6	10.1	10.8	10.5	13.3	17.5
1974	9.9	13.7	16.1	6.0	9.0	13.9
1975	11.0	14.2	16.7	10.0	13.9	20.6
1976	11.6[a]	15.1[a]		6.4[a]	10.6[a]	

a. Incomplete data.

The Characteristics of Self-poisoning Patients

Method

It is relatively simple to ensure that a sample of self-poisoning patients does not include the same individual more than once. It is more difficult to ensure that the probability of a patient's being included in the sample is not affected by the number of episodes he has suffered or will suffer in his life. If the study design takes the form of random sampling of episodes then an individual who has ten episodes in a given period has ten times the chance of being sampled than the person who has but one episode during the same period. The simplest way of overcoming this problem, if a representative sample of individuals not episodes is sought, is to sample only first ever episodes. People who are having their first ever episode are representative of that fraction of the total population who poison themselves on at least one occasion. (People having a second episode are a subset of those who have had one episode.) In the course of time some of the individuals selected on this basis will undergo further episodes and so distribute themselves across the range of numbers of episodes in a way that is representative of the population of self-poisoners from which they were drawn. A sample such as this should include all people who die as a result of their first ever episode of self-poisoning. Clearly if the research method involves interview, it would be impossible to include them. However, the proportion of episodes of self-poisoning that are fatal is so small (about 6 per cent) that they can be ignored.

People whose sampled episode is of any particular rank (N) may be compared with the 'first ever episode' group and conclusions may be drawn about people who have at least N episodes. The size of the sample required to produce adequate numbers within many different ranks is high. In this investigation all people admitted for a non-first episode were grouped together.

All patients aged between 15 and 30 years who were admitted in the period February to August to one of the two hospitals for the treatment of self-poisoning were identified as soon as possible after their admission. An attempt was made to interview them all. The same structure questionnaire was used in all cases; one of the questions asked was how many episodes they had ever had in the past. During the six-month period, 195 different individuals were identified and interviewed. A further 20 were identified but were not interviewed. They were not seen either because they had been discharged, or discharged themselves, before the research interviewer arrived at the hospital or because they refused to cooperate. For 76 (21 males and 55 females) of the 193 patients with known episode rank recruited to the study the index episode was their first ever. This group is called the EI group. The remaining 117 (34 males and 83 females) had a previous history of self-poisoning; this group is referred to as the EN group.

The characteristics of the 76 patients in the EI group were compared with those of a 'control' group. Subjects for the 'control' group were recruited whilst waiting to consult their general practitioner for any reason other than self-poisoning. Any patient who gave a history of self-poisoning was excluded from further consideration. They were interviewed using the same structured questionnaire as was used with the index patients. For each of the EI patients, two controls, matched for age (within one year), sex, whether they had ever married, and their father's social class, were identified. Thus, the 'control' group comprised 152 persons. The age and sex distribution of the three groups (control, EI, EN) is given in Table 14.2.

The frequency of occurrence of various factors relating to the family background was compared between groups. The particular aspects of childhood and family life that were explored were: maternal age at birth of subject; position of family; size of sibship; experience of sibling loss by death; parental separation or death.

Table 14.2: Age and Sex Distribution of the Three Groups

Group		Male			Female		Total
Age	15-19	20-24	25-30	15-19	20-24	25-30	
Control	6 (4)	22 (14)	14 (9)	36 (24)	40 (26)	34 (22)	152 (100)
EI	5 (7)	9 (12)	7 (9)	19 (25)	19 (25)	17 (22)	76 (100)
EN	5 (4)	18 (15)	11 (9)	23 (20)	36 (31)	24 (21)	117 (100)

Figures given in parenthesis are the percentage of the group total.

Results

The ages of the mothers of the subjects at the time of the subject's birth are shown in Table 14.3. Clearly there is no difference between the distribution of maternal ages in group EI and the control group. The distribution of maternal ages of patients in the EI and EN groups were significantly different, ($\chi_2^2 = 6.02$, $p < 0.05$), the EN group being more likely to have young mothers than the EI group. A relatively large proportion of the patients were unable to give information about their father's age and, therefore, detailed analysis of paternal age is not given

Table 14.3: **Maternal Age in Year of Subject's Birth**

Group	<20	20-29	>29	Not known	Total known
Control	6 (4%)	84 (56%)	61 (40%)	1	151 (100)
EI	3 (4%)	40 (55%)	30 (41%)	3	73 (100)
EN	15 (14%)	63 (57%)	32 (29%)	7	110 (100)

Table 14.4: **Mean Sibship Sizes and Position Within Sibship**

Group	Number of subjects for whom the size of sibships and position in sibship is known	Sibship size		Mean position in sibship	
		Mean	sd*	Observed	Expected
Control	152	3.1	1.65	2.05	2.04
EI	75	3.7	2.29	2.35	2.33
EN	115	4.1	2.70	2.14	2.53

* Standard deviation.

here.

The relevance of the position of subjects within sibships was investigated using a randomisation test. It is assumed that the position of the subjects within their sibship is random with each position having an equal chance of selection, thus in a sibship of size N the mean position within the sibship of the individual selected is $\frac{(N+1)}{2}$. The 'expected score' for mean family position within the group = $\frac{(\text{mean sibship size} + 1)}{2}$. Table 14.4 shows the mean sibship sizes of subjects in each group, the mean position within the sibship and the expected mean position within the sibship.

The mean sibship sizes of the EI group was significantly greater than that of the control group ($t = 2.24$, $p < 0.05$); however, there was no difference in the mean sibship sizes of group EI and EN ($t = 1.04$, $p < 0.1$). The mean position within the sibship of 'control' and EI subjects did not differ from their expected positions (using the randomisation test for control subjects $t = 0.13$, and for EI, $t = 0.10$).

Table 14.5 shows the number in each group whose parents had died or separated before the subject reached the age of 15 years. When the subjects who were unable to give information about parental separation are excluded, the difference between the control group and EI group in the proportions whose parents had died or separated is not significant ($\chi_1^2 = 1.24$), nor is the difference between the group EI and group EN

Table 14.5: Separation and Death of Subject's Parents

Group	Parents living together at age 15	One or both parents dead or parents separated	Not known
Control	122 (80%)	29 (19%)	1
EI	55 (72%)	19 (25%)	2
EN	73 (62%)	40 (34%)	4

Table 14.6: Death of Siblings of Subjects

Group	One or more dead siblings reported	No dead siblings reported	Total known	Not known
Control	7 (5%)	144 (95%)	151	1
EI	18 (24%)	57 (76%)	75	1
EN	26 (23%)	89 (77%)	115	2

(χ^2_1 = 1.96). However, a χ^2 test for trend of proportion with parents together from control to EN group is significant. (χ^2_2 = 8.73, p < 0.05.)

A remarkably high proportion of the EN patients reported the loss of a sibling by death (Table 14.6). Even after standardisation for variations in family size in the self-poisoning groups there remained an excessive number in both groups who reported sibling loss.

Discussion

The first study reported here appears to indicate that the proportion of patients who repeat is high and that the proportion repeating has tended to increase each year. In drawing conclusions from these data their limitations must be understood. They only take account of repeat admissions to the same hospital and are, therefore, an underestimate of the proportion who repeat. The changes seen here could be due to changes in the mobility of the local population but there is no evidence from the community that such a change has occurred. As there is good reason to suppose that non-first episodes constitute a large and increasing proportion of the total episodes their effect on the sampling of self-poisoning patients cannot be ignored. Consequently, a sample of individuals rather than of episodes must be used to make inferences about the characteristics of individuals.

The second study indicates that in many respects individuals who poison themselves do not differ from the general population but that people who have more than one episode do. This being so, it is likely that there will be difficulty in identifying the 'at risk' population with great precision thus making primary prevention difficult. On the other hand, those likely to have a second episode should be identifiable with greater precision thereby offering greater scope for the prevention of non-first episodes.

Acknowledgement

This research was funded by the Small Grants Committee of the DHSS, London.

15 THE EFFECTIVENESS OF THE SAMARITANS IN THE PREVENTION OF SUICIDE

C. Jennings and B.M. Barraclough

Introduction

Since 1963 the suicide rate in England and Wales has fallen by a third from 12 to 7·8 per 100,000. No other European country has had a comparable fall and to identify its cause would be a major contribution to suicide prevention. A number of theories have been proposed to explain this fall, including safer domestic gas, improved psychiatric care of the mentally ill, improved medical care of the poisoned, a shift in the criteria used by coroners for returning suicide verdicts, social changes in British society and the work of the Samaritans. The present study is concerned with the effect of the Samaritans on the completed suicide rate. We did not investigate their effect on parasuicide nor the value of their contribution in providing contact and comfort and relieving distress.

The Samaritans Incorporated is an independent national organisation which aims to provide a confidential listening and 'befriending' service to troubled people. By appropriate national and local advertising the despairing and suicidal are invited to visit or telephone their local Samaritan branch for help. Branches are staffed by carefully selected and trained volunteers.

There is a prima facie case that the Samaritans are responsible for the fall in the suicide rate in England and Wales. The rapid growth of the organisation through the 1960s parallels the decline in the suicide rate and both the Samaritans and the fall in the suicide rate are said to be unique to England and Wales (Fox, 1975).

The scientific case was made by Bagley (1968) who compared suicide rate trends in towns with Samaritan branches and control towns without branches. Bagley used two methods to select controls, the first was a measure of the 'ecological' similarity of the towns, the second used predictors of the future suicide rate.

The ecological method used the results of a study by Moser and Scott (1961) which examined the variation of 57 social, demographic, health and economic variables among the larger towns and cities of England and Wales. They derived four principal components which summarised the differences between towns. The components were given

194

the following interpretations: (1) social class, (2) population change 1931-51, (3) population change 1951-58 and (4) overcrowding. Each town was given a score on each component. Bagley chose as controls the closest non-Samaritan county boroughs to each of the first 15 county boroughs with Samaritan branches.

Bagley's second method was to choose three predictor variables, viz.: the percentage of the population aged 65 or over, the number of females per 1,000 males and a social class index. Towns were ranked on these variables and the non-Samaritan county boroughs with the least average difference of rank from each of the first 15 Samaritan county boroughs were chosen as controls. Bagley found that the suicide rate of the Samaritan towns fell while the rate in both sets of control towns rose and that this difference was statistically significant.

We decided to re-examine the relationship between Samaritan activities and suicide prevention. Bagley's finding has become widely accepted as proving that the Samaritans are responsible for the fall in the national suicide rate. If this is true there are profound implications for the planning of suicide prevention services. Yet the national suicide rate has not declined as steeply since 1970 despite the continued increase of Samaritan activities. Suicide rates per 100,000 from 1970 were 8.1, 8.1, 7.7, 7.8, and for 1974, 7.9. Over the same period the number of Samaritan branches in the British Isles grew from 115 to 154 and the number of new clients per year from 70,000 to 190,000. In retesting Bagley's hypothesis that Samaritan services are associated with a reduction in suicide we have improved on his method for selecting controls and have looked at a larger number of towns.

Method and Results

We used four methods of selecting controls, the first two based on ecological similarity, the others on predictor variables. Our first method used Bagley's 15 Samaritan towns to provide a direct comparison with his study, but we chose controls for their closeness to Samaritan towns on all four components which accounted for more of the variance between the towns than did two components.

Our second method paired together county boroughs most similar on the four components regardless of whether or not they were Samaritan towns, and then excluded those pairs where neither town had a Samaritan branch or where both had one. This left 23 pairs of Samaritan and control towns, a larger sample than the first method and including a wider range of branch opening dates.

Our third method used as a predictor variable the suicide rate of the town before the branch opened. By matching on suicide rate we would be controlling for the factors which caused that rate. The non-Samaritan towns with a suicide rate closest to that of each of the first 33 Samaritan towns were chosen as controls.

Our fourth method used the proportion of single person households as a predictor variable. The proportion living alone has long been known to correlate highly with the suicide rate. We found pairs of towns most similar on this variable regardless of whether or not they had Samaritan branches and then excluded those pairs where neither town had a Samaritan branch or where they both had one. This left 35 pairs of Samaritan and control towns.

To summarise. Four sets of control towns were chosen by these methods:

I.   Matching on four components, using Bagley's 15 Samaritan towns.
II.   Matching on four components but choosing pairs from all county boroughs.
III.   Matching on the pre-opening suicide rate.
IV.   Matching on the percentage of single person households.

Crude suicide rates were calculated from the numbers of suicides and the estimated populates for county boroughs in the Registrar General's Statistical Reviews for the years 1957-73. Three-year average suicide rates were used in all analyses to reduce the influence of any extreme variation in annual rates. For each town we found the average suicide rate for the three-year period before the Samaritan branch opened and the three-year period after the branch opened and then found the percentage change between these two rates. For the control towns we took the three-year periods before and after the opening of the Samaritan branch in the town with which the control was matched. We carried out Wilcoxon matched-pairs signed-ranks tests to determine whether there were statistically significant differences between the percentage changes in the Samaritan compared with the control towns. A full description of our methods can be found in Jennings *et al.* (1978).

Our results can be seen in Table 15.1. The four Wilcoxon tests revealed no significant differences at the 0.05 level between the Samaritan and control towns, so all four methods failed to demonstrate that towns with a Samaritan branch show a significantly greater

Table 15.1: Results of Comparing Samaritan and Control Towns

Method of choosing controls	n	Mean % change Samaritan	Control	Wilcoxon test (one-tailed) p
I Matching on 4 components. Bagley's towns only	15	0.0	−2.6	0.19
II Matching on 4 components. Towns chosen from all county boroughs	23	−9.2	−9.6	0.42
III Matching on pre-opening suicide rate	33	3.0	−5.0	0.24
IV Matching on single-person households	35	−3.5	−2.5	0.23

reduction in suicide rate than towns without a branch.

An alternative analysis is shown in Figure 15.1, where are plotted the mean suicide rates for the Samaritan towns and their matched control towns (chosen by method III), for the six years before and the six years after the opening of each Samaritan branch. Without labels it would be impossible to decide which curve is which.

Discussion

In this type of study the way controls are chosen is crucial. Our methods of choosing controls were better than Bagley's because they resulted in closer similarity between Samaritan and control towns. We achieved this by using four components in methods I and II which accounted for 60 per cent of the variance between the towns. Bagley used two components which accounted for only 43 per cent of the variance. In methods III and IV our predictor variables were more highly correlated with the subsequent suicide rate than were Bagley's predictor variables. In addition we used larger samples of towns and a wider range of branch opening dates. (Bagley only had data available to 1964 while we used branches which opened between 1960 and 1970.)

Our study has been criticised by Bagley (1977) and by Lawton (1977) on the grounds that the suicide rate in the control town might be reduced by the effect of a Samaritan branch in a nearby town and so no difference should be expected between Samaritan and control towns. This argument was strengthened by Lawton's observation that many of our control towns were within 20 miles of a Samaritan branch.

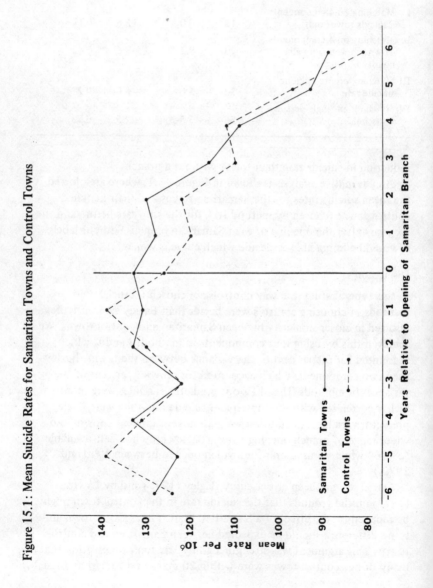

Figure 15.1: Mean Suicide Rates for Samaritan Towns and Control Towns

It is, however, most unlikely that our results can be explained in this way. First, an examination of the percentage changes of individual towns' suicide rates shows that a total of 48 per cent of the Samaritan towns showed a rise in their suicide rate after the branch opened and 36 per cent of the control towns showed a rise despite many of them being within 20 miles of a Samaritan centre. So it seems that Samaritan branches have little effect on the suicide rates of the nearby control towns and indeed in many cases they do not reduce the suicide rates in their own towns. Secondly, most of Bagley's control towns were within 20 miles of a Samaritan centre and so, if Bagley's and Lawton's argument is valid, one would have expected suicide rates in his control towns to have fallen to the same extent as in his Samaritan towns and no significant difference to have emerged between Samaritan and control towns. In fact the reverse happened, the suicide rate of most of Bagley's control towns rose and a significant difference between ‾ Samaritan and control towns was found. Thirdly, we found controls for 14 of the 15 Samaritan towns used in method I by matching on four components but ensuring that each control town was more than twenty miles from a Samaritan centre for the full comparison period. No control could be found for Oxford. No significant difference was found between Samaritan and control town suicide rates. These points cast doubts on Bagley's and Lawton's arguments by showing that there is no evidence that a Samaritan branch reduces the suicide rate in nearby towns without branches.

Other studies evaluating suicide prevention centres tend to support our findings. We searched the medical literature from 1965 and found only two controlled studies, apart from Bagley's, of the effectiveness of suicide prevention centres. Bridge *et al.* (1977) carried out a multiple regression analysis which concluded that suicide prevention centres in North Carolina had little or no effect on the suicide rate. Lester (1974) took 24 American cities, 16 with suicide prevention centres and 8 without, and controlling for population size found that the centres had no statistically significant effect on suicide rates. However, suicide prevention centres in America may differ from the Samaritans in a number of ways including confidentiality, independence from psychiatric services, use of volunteers and level and accuracy of public knowledge so perhaps we should be cautious in drawing conclusions from these studies. Holding (1975) looked at the short term effect on the suicide rate in Edinburgh of the BBC TV series 'The Befrienders'. He found that the suicide rate did not decrease although the number of contacts with the Samaritans more than doubled. Bagley's is therefore the only controlled study to have demonstrated a significant relative fall in the suicide rate in towns which have a suicide prevention service.

In conclusion then, we have failed to corroborate Bagley's findings despite using improved methods of selecting controls. When taken together with the lack of evidence from other controlled studies that suicide prevention centres reduce the suicide rate, our findings seriously undermine the scientific case for the Samaritans' effectiveness in reducing the suicide rate.

References

Bagley, C. (1968). The evaluation of a suicide prevention scheme by an ecological method. *Social Science and Medicine*, vol. 2, pp. 1-14.

Bagley, C. (1977). Suicide prevention by the Samaritans. *Lancet*, vol. ii, pp. 348-49.

Bridge, T.P., Potkin, S.G., Zung, W.W.K. and Soldo, B.J. (1977). Suicide prevention centers: ecological study of effectiveness. *Journal of Nervous and Mental Disease*, vol. 164, pp. 18-24.

Fox, R. (1975). The suicide drop — why? *Royal Society of Health Journal*, vol. 95, pp. 9-14.

Holding, T.A. (1975). Suicide and 'The Befrienders'. *British Medical Journal*, vol. 3, pp. 751-52.

Jennings, C., Barraclough, B.M. and Moss, J.R. (1978). Have the Samaritans lowered the suicide rate? A controlled study. *Psychological Medicine*, vol. 8, pp. 413-22.

Lawton, A. (1977). Suicide prevention by the Samaritans. *Lancet*, vol. ii, p. 706.

Lester, D. (1974). Effect of suicide prevention centers on suicide rates in the United States. *Health Services Reports*, vol. 89, pp. 37-39.

Moser, C.A. and Scott, W. (1961). *British Towns*. Oliver and Boyd, Edinburgh.

Registrar-General. *Statistical Reviews of England and Wales* (1957 to 1973). HMSO, London.

PART FOUR

Assessment — Who Should Do It?

16 THE ASSESSMENT OF PATIENTS FOLLOWING SELF-POISONING: A COMPARISON OF DOCTORS AND NURSES

J. Catalan

Introduction

The continuing pressure which self-poisoning patients place on general hospitals, their casualty departments and busy psychiatrists (Bancroft *et al.*, 1975; Holding *et al.*, 1977; Wexler *et al.*, 1978), together with the problem of repetition, has led to the exploration of forms of management of the self-poisoning patient which depart in varying degrees from the recommendations of the Hill Report. Thus, the role of house physicians (Gardner *et al.*, 1977) and social workers (Newson-Smith and Hirsch, 1977) in assessment of self-poisoning patients and the involvement of social workers in their aftercare (Gibbons *et al.*, 1978) have been investigated.

This chapter describes the role of nurses in the assessment of self-poisoning patients referred to a psychiatric unit in a district general hospital and discusses the preliminary results of a study comparing the nurses' assessments with those carried out by doctors working in the same unit.

The Clinical Setting

The Psychiatric Consultation Service is a 10-bedded unit located in a district general hospital. The unit is the responsibility of one consultant psychiatrist and has strong links with the Oxford University Department of Psychiatry, members of which provide clinical cover. The permanent staff includes nurses, a social worker and occupational therapist. General practice and psychiatric trainees are attached to the service for four and six months respectively. The Psychiatric Consultation Service deals with all psychiatric referrals within the general hospital, the majority of which are cases of self-poisoning and self-injury.

Self-poisoning patients referred by the casualty officers or house physicians are assessed by the doctors or nurses on duty as soon as the patient is fit to be interviewed. After assessment, referrals are discussed with other members of the team and a senior psychiatrist before further management is arranged. The senior psychiatrist is available to

203

see patients if necessary. In practice, self-poisoning patients whose physical condition is satisfactory vacate their medical beds within hours of the assessment interview.

Doctors and nurses introduce themselves to the patients as 'counsellors' from the psychiatric unit and give details of their status if further information is requested (see Figure 16.1).

Figure 16.1: The Clinical Setting

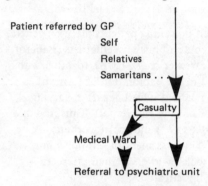

Patient referred by GP
Self
Relatives
Samaritans . .

Casualty

Medical Ward

Referral to psychiatric unit

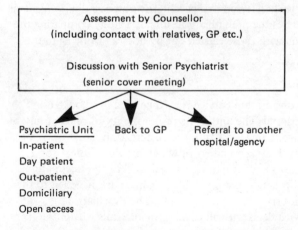

Assessment by Counsellor
(including contact with relatives, GP etc.)

Discussion with Senior Psychiatrist
(senior cover meeting)

Psychiatric Unit   Back to GP   Referral to another
In-patient   hospital/agency
Day patient
Out-patient
Domiciliary
Open access

Training of Counsellors

Prior to the start of the study the nurses and doctors concerned were given instruction in the assessment of patients. The principles and general aims of the initial interview are described in an assessment manual especially compiled for the investigation (Bancroft and Catalan,

1977) and based on research carried out by members of the Oxford University Department of Psychiatry (Bancroft *et al.*, 1977). In addition to discussion of the material contained in the manual, the training included development of interviewing skills using audio-recordings of interviews and supervision through a one-way mirror, together with seminars on relevant topics, such as mental state examination, alcoholism, effects of drugs, etc. The nurses' training lasted five weeks and the doctors' three weeks. The difference was due to the doctors' previous experience in carrying out individual interviews. Table 16.1 summarises the main points covered in the assessment manual and Table 16.2 gives details of the training of nurses.

Table 16.1: Main Points in Assessment Manual

General Aims of Assessment Interview

1. Evaluate continuing suicidal risk
2. Gain understanding of why the person took the overdose
3. Establish what help is needed
4. Influence the patient to use alternative ways of coping

Stages of the Interview:

1. Establish rapport
2. Clarify circumstances of the act, including degree of suicidal intent
3. Assess mental state
4. Clarify current problems and duration: problem list
5. Assess coping resources: personal; external; previous ways of coping with problems
6. Establish what help the patient wants or is prepared to accept
7. Reach a negotiated contract for further action

Table 16.2: Training of Nurses (duration five weeks)

1. Discussion of Manual of Assessment
2. Attendance at interviews carried out by trainer or experienced counsellors
3. Trainees' own interviews under supervision:
   - audiorecording
   - one-way mirror
4. Discussion of trainees' audiorecordings in group with other trainees
5. Seminars on mental state examination, alcoholism, depressive illness, problem orientated approach, psychopharmacology, etc.

The Assessment Study

Aims

The purpose of the investigation was to answer the following questions:

(a) Are there differences in the adequacy of the assessment interviews carried out by doctors and nurses?

(b) If there are differences, what is their nature and extent?

(c) Is the nurses' role acceptable to, firstly the patients and, secondly, their general practitioners?

Counsellors

Eight doctors and eight nurses were included in the study. Table 16.3 shows details of their sex and professional background. It is important to stress that although some of the nurses had previous psychiatric experience, none of them had been involved in assessment of self-poisoning patients prior to the start of the study.

Table 16.3: Counsellors (n = 16)

Doctors (n = 8)	5 Psychiatric trainees (4 males, 1 female) 3 GP trainees (2 males, 1 female)		
Nurses (n = 8)	5 RMN (1 Sister, 4 Staff Nurses) 2 SRN (Staff Nurse grade) 1 SEN (Staff Nurse grade)	without previous psychiatric experience	All female

Patients

Patients were included in the study if they had been admitted following self-poisoning, were aged 16 years or over and were not in current in-patient or day-patient psychiatric care.

Procedure

Suitable patients were randomly allocated for assessment to the counsellors. Each counsellor saw a minimum of five patients and the interviews with patients number one, three and five were, with the patient's permission, tape-recorded. Patients whose interviews had been recorded were also seen after assessment by a senior psychiatrist who carried out an independent evaluation. All patients and counsellors were interviewed after the assessment interview by a research assistant for collection of further information. In addition, the patients' general practitioners were contacted after assessment and again six months later.

Measures

Several criteria were used to evaluate the assessments:

(1) Adequacy of the Assessment Interview. For this, full transcripts of the 48 tape-recorded interviews were rated by three senior psychiatrists, blind to the identity of the counsellors, using a rating scale based on the assessment manual. In the first part of the rating scale the psychiatrists rated whether the counsellor had clarified the circumstances surrounding the overdose, examined the patient's mental state, explored the patient's problems and coping resources and made plans for further action. In the second part of the scale, the psychiatrists rated the degree of correspondence between the information obtained by the counsellor and that gathered by the independent psychiatrist. There was a total of 36 items and their reliability proved to be satisfactory (Catalan *et al.*, in preparation).

(2) Consumers' Views. The patients' rapport with the counsellors was investigated by means of interview and self-report, including semantic differential measures. The general practitioners' satisfaction with the assessments and their views on the involvement of nurses were obtained by telephone interview.

In all cases, the final aftercare arrangements as well as changes suggested after the Senior Cover meeting were noted and the repetition of self-poisoning or self-injury up to six months after the assessment was investigated by contacting the general practitioners and through the Unit's monitoring system. However, repetition was not regarded as an important measure of the adequacy of the original assessment, as it was felt that subsequent management is likely to be just as, or more important in modifying repetition rates. On the other hand, repetition rate could be seen as an indirect measure of the efficacy of assessments. Table 16.5 summarises the measures.

Results

One hundred and twenty patients were included in the study. Demographically, the patients were comparable to the total population of self-poisoners referred to the Psychiatric Consultation Service during

Table 16.4: Rating Scale

Part One = Items to be Covered by Counsellor

1. Clarification of circumstances of overdose:
       Events leading up to the act
       Drugs taken and quantity
       Degree of isolation
       Precautions against discovery
       Suicide note
       Actions to gain help after the act
       Alcohol at the time
       Previous S/P or S/I
       Reasons for the overdose
2. Mental state:
       Suicidal ideas at time of act
       Suicidal ideas at time of assessment
       Mood
       Appetite
       Sleep
       Weight
3. Problem areas:
       Marital/partner
       Parents
       Children
       Siblings
       Alcohol
       Job
       Housing
       Law
       Social isolation
4. Coping resources:
       External supports
       Personal resources
5. Further action:
       What the patient wants
       Specific suggestions for further help

Part Two = Comparison with Independent Assessment

   Degree of correspondence of first 5 items of the Problem List
   Adequacy of problem list as summary of the interview findings
   Whether mental illness or serious suicidal risk have been missed

the study period. There were no differences between the patients assessed by doctors and nurses according to demographic data and scores on the risk of repetition scale (Buglass and Horton, 1974).

Table 16.5: Assessment Study — Measures

1. Adequacy of the Assessment Interview: (n = 48)
   Transcripts of tape-recorded interviews rated by blind judges using
   Rating Scale

2. Consumers' Views: (n = 120)
   Patients: Rapport with counsellor (interview)
              View of counsellor (semantic differential)

   General Practitioners:
              Adequacy of plans and communication
              with GP   } interview
              Satisfaction with role of nurses

3. Process Study: (n = 120)
   Changes in problem list and plans following Senior Cover meeting
   Patients seen by Senior Cover psychiatrist
   Final aftercare arrangements

4. Repetition of Self-poisoning Self-injury (up to $^6/_{12}$) (n = 120)
   From GP and hospital records

(1) Adequacy of the Assessment Interview: Judges' Ratings. No
statistically significant differences were found between doctors and
nurses for the 'clarification of circumstances surrounding the overdose',
'coverage of problem areas', 'coping resources' and 'further action'. In
'exploration of personal resources' the nurses obtained higher scores
than the psychiatrists but the difference just failed to reach statistical
significance.

In the section on 'mental state examination', the nurses obtained
consistently higher scores than the doctors, but the differences failed
to reach statistical significance. The nurses covered the item 'impaired
appetite' more often than the psychiatrists and the difference was
statistically significant ($p < 0.05$). The GP trainees also scored
significantly higher than the psychiatrists on this item ($p < 0.05$).

No significant differences were found between the subgroups of
counsellors in terms of the correspondence between their ratings of
the first five problems listed and those of the independent assessor, and
the over-all adequacy of the problem lists, but there was a consistent
trend in favour of the psychiatrists compared with the GP trainees, and
in favour of the nurses compared with the GP trainees.

No statistically significant differences were found between the
counsellors according to the judges' ratings of whether mental illness
or serious suicidal risk had been missed, but the differences found are
of interest: in two cases the judges thought that mental illness had been
missed and the assessors in both cases were nurses. In the first case, the

nurse had known the patient in another hospital and this may explain the apparent incompleteness of the assessment. In the second instance the senior cover psychiatrist recognised the problem during the discussion and carried out a further assessment with the nurse concerned.

(2) Consumers' Views. No significant differences were found between doctors and nurses in relation to the patients' rating of the rapport they felt the counsellor had established with them. The results are shown in Table 16.6. Analysis of the semantic differential measures using the Mann-Whitney U-test showed that the doctors were seen as more capable of helping ($p < 0.05$) and the nurses as kinder ($p < 0.05$). No differences were found between subgroups.

No significant differences were found between doctors and nurses in relation to the general practitioners' satisfaction with the assessments, as shown in Table 16.7. The majority of general practitioners appeared to have no objections to the involvement of nurses provided they were trained, supervised, did not prescribe medication and the consultant took final responsibility for the patients.

No significant differences were found in relation to changes in problem list and further plans after the counsellors had discussed their cases with the senior cover psychiatrist, and although more patients assessed by nurses were seen by the senior psychiatrist, the difference was not significant (see Table 16.8). The only difference in after-care arrangements was that the nurses more often than other counsellors offered patients 'open access' to the service ($p < 0.001$).

Table 16.6: Consumers' Views — The Patient

Did you find X easy to talk to?			
	Yes	No	Other
Doctor	97.8%	0.0%	2.2%
Nurse	94.5%	2.7%	2.7%

Did you feel X understood you?			
	Yes	No	Other
Doctor	80.0%	11.1%	8.9%
Nurse	75.3%	11.0%	13.7%

Could you confide in X?			
	Yes	No	Other
Doctor	91.1%	2.2%	6.7%
Nurse	76.7%	9.6%	13.7%

Table 16.7: Consumers' Views – The General Practitioner

(a) GPs' View of Immediate Plans Following Assessment

Patients seen by:	Agreed	Disagreed	Other
Doctors	37 (97.4%)	0 (0.0%)	1 (2.6%)
Nurses	65 (95.6%)	1 1.5%)	2 (2.9%)
Total	102 (96.2%)	1 (0.9%)	3 (2.8%)

(b) GPs' Views of Involvement of Nurses in Assessments

Patients seen by:	Wholly in favour	In favour provided some conditions were met	No objection	Doubtful reservations
Doctors	18 (47.4%)	11 (28.9%)	7 (18.4%)	2 (5.3%)
Nurses	21 (30.9%)	20 (29.4%)	22 (32.4%)	5 (7.4%)
Total	39 (36.8%)	31 (29.2%)	29 (27.4%)	7 (6.6%)

Table 16.8: Effect of Senior Cover Discussion

	Assessed by doctor (n = 45)	Assessed by nurse (n = 75)	
Changes in 'problem list'	1 (2.2%)	3 (4.0%)	NS
Changes in 'plans for further action'	7 (15.5%)	16 (21.3%)	NS
Patient seen by senior psychiatrist	2 (4.4%)	13 (17.3%)	NS

As regards repetition, 4 (9.1per cent) of the patients assessed by doctors had a further episode while 8 (10.9 per cent) repeated amongst those seen by the nurses. The difference is not statistically significant and the figures are in keeping with previous repetition rates found in the same unit prior to the large scale involvement of nurses in assessments (Bancroft and Marsack, 1977).

Table 16.9: Aftercare

	Assessed by doctors (n = 45)	Assessed by nurses (n = 75)	
Discharged	10 (22.2%)	21 (28.1%)	NS
Refused help	1 (2.2%)	3 (4.0%)	NS
Psychiatric Unit			
I/P	9 (20%)	16 21.3%)	NS
D/P	– –	4 (5.3%)	NS
O/P	19 (42.2%)	21 (28%)	NS
Total	28 (62.2%)	41 (54.6%)	NS
Referred to other psychiatric hospitals	6 (13.2%)	10 13.4%)	NS
	Assessed by doctors	Assessed by nurses	
Offered 'open access'	4 (8.8%)	29 (38.6%)	p < 0.001

Table 16.10: Repetition – Six-month Follow-up

Assessed by:	New episode of self-poisoning or self-injury
Doctor	4 (9.1%)
Nurse	8 (10.9%)

Discussion and Conclusions

The results reported show that, within the context of the study, no major differences between doctors and nurses can be found. In relation to the possibility of mental illness being missed by the nurses, the results give support to the model described and the supervisory role of the psychiatrist. Other differences, such as those found in the semantic differential measures, are likely to relate to the counsellor's sex rather than professional background.

We are aware of the theoretical problem of showing that there are no differences between the two groups, but the fact that multiple measures fail to show significant differences gives strong support to the idea that the nurses do not perform any less well than the doctors.

The results indicate that nurses can be used for the assessment of patients following self-poisoning when such nurses have been trained and supervision is available. A model similar to the one described here could be implemented elsewhere by training two or three nurses working alongside the psychiatrist. The nurses could carry out the majority of the assessments and discuss them with the psychiatrist. This procedure would relieve the pressure on the latter without detriment to patients and would still be in keeping with the recommendations of the Hill Report.

Acknowledgements

This research was funded by the Department of Health and Social Security and was part of a wider research programme which included J.H.J. Bancroft, K.E. Hawton, D. Whitwell, P. Marsack and J. Fagg. Thanks are given to D.H. Gath, Professor M. Gelder and D. Johnston for their help and advice.

References

Bancroft, J.H.J., Skrimshire, A.M., Reynolds, F., Simkin, S. and Smith, J. (1975). Self-poisoning and self-injury in the Oxford area: epidemiological aspects 1969-73. *British Journal of Preventive and Social Medicine*, vol. 29, pp. 170-77.

Bancroft, J.H.J., Skrimshire, A.M., Casson, J., Harvard-Watts, O. and Reynolds, F. (1977). People who deliberately poison or injure themselves: their problems and their contact with helping agencies. *Psychological Medicine*, vol. 7, pp. 289-303.

Bancroft, J.H.J. and Marsack, P. (1977). The repetitiveness of self-poisoning and self-injury. *British Journal of Psychiatry*, vol. 131, pp. 394-9.

Bancroft, J.H.J. and Catalan, J. (1977). Assessment procedure following self-poisoning or self-injury. Oxford University Department of Psychiatry.

Buglass, D. and Horton, J. (1974). A scale for predicting subsequent suicidal behaviour. *British Journal of Psychiatry*, vol. 124, pp. 573-8.

Catalan, J., Marsack, P,, Hawton, K.E., Bancroft, J.H.J. and Whitwell, D. Assessment of patients following self-poisoning: a comparison of doctors and nurses. In preparation.

Gardner, R., Hanka, R., O'Brien, V.C., Page, A.J.F. and Rees, R. (1977). Psychological and social evaluation in cases of deliberate self-poisoning admitted to a general hospital. *British Medical Journal*, vol. 2, pp. 1567-70.

Gibbons, J.S., Butler, J., Urwin, P. and Gibbons, J.L. (1978). Evaluation of a social work service for self-poisoning patients. *British Journal of Psychiatry*, vol. 133, pp. 111-18.

Hill Report (1968). *Hospital Treatment of Acute Poisoning*. Report of the Joint Subcommittee of the Standing Medical Advisory Committee, HMSO, London.

Holding, T.A., Buglass, D., Duffy, J.C., Kreitman, N. (1977). Parasuicide in

Edinburgh: a seven-year review 1968-1974. *British Journal of Psychiatry*, vol. 130, pp. 534-43.

Newson-Smith, J.G.B. and Hirsch, S.R. (1977). The social worker's assessment versus the psychiatrist's. Paper read at meeting of the Social and Community Psychiatry Group, Royal College of Psychiatrists, 30 November, 1977.

Wexler, L., Weissman, M.M. and Kasl, S.V. (1978). Suicide attempts 1970-1975: updating a United States study and comparison with international trends. *British Journal of Psychiatry*, vol. 132, pp. 180-85.

17 THE USE OF SOCIAL WORKERS AS ALTERNATIVES TO PSYCHIATRISTS IN ASSESSING PARASUICIDE

J.G.B. Newson-Smith

Introduction

This study was carried out to investigate the role of social workers in the assessment of parasuicide patients. Official guidelines on the management of these patients have not considered social workers as alternatives to psychiatrists. However, the Hill Report on the hospital treatment of acute poisoning (1968) does recommend social evaluation in addition to psychiatric evaluation.

Recent work has attributed increasing importance to social and personal factors both in understanding and treatment of parasuicide (Paykel *et al.*, 1975; Kiev, 1976). This suggests that social workers can have a fundamental role in the assessment and management of parasuicides, yet as long as official guidelines are adhered to social workers may not do the initial assessment interview single-handed. This means social workers may be used in the following ways: (1) In conjunction with psychiatrists on each patient. This involves unnecessary duplication of work and is wasteful of resources. (2) On receipt of a specific request for their help. This referral may be made by the medical team or the psychiatrist and often on the direct request of the patient. (3) Not at all.

It must be remembered that our present management is not particularly effective. Psychiatrists, particularly those in training grades, may be unfamiliar with the alternatives available to deal with patients' social and interpersonal problems. Social workers' skills may in fact be at least as relevant as those of psychiatrists in dealing with the general problems of parasuicides. Harris (1976), a social worker, made a plea for this role stating their training is well suited to dealing with the types of problems encountered and that job satisfaction will increase by using skills acquired during training.

The unanswered question to which this study addresses itself, is whether social workers can reliably and dependably carry out the initial assessments or whether a psychiatric assessment is in fact necessary. First, one must show that social workers are capable of detecting the presence of severe mental illness. The present study was designed to

215

test whether social workers can assess parasuicide patients who have been admitted to hospital as effectively as psychiatrists charged with this responsibility in every day practice. Particular emphasis is placed on the safety and reliability of diagnostic and management decisions.

Method

Seven social workers volunteered to join the study and agreed to carry out the assessments in addition to their normal work. It was considered important to use a group of social workers with varying experience rather than test the skills of any one individual. Four worked in the general medical department and of these four two had one or more year's experience of psychiatric social work and two had none; the remaining three worked in the psychiatric department and had at least one year's experience. All junior psychiatrists agreed to participate in the study (four registrars and one senior house officer). At this time, 1976, referrals for a psychiatric opinion on parasuicide patients went to the duty junior psychiatrist and consultant psychiatrists were not routinely involved. Twenty patients were seen during a pilot study and a rating schedule to compare assessments was tested and modified. During this time a series of six seminars was held between the research psychiatrist and the social workers to discuss mental illness in general and parasuicide and suicide in particular.

Selection of Subjects and Methods

Each morning parasuicide admissions listed in the casualty book for the past 24 hours (72 hours after weekends) were visited by the research psychiatrist in order of admission. The first two fit for assessment entered the study, those not ready for assessment were carried forward to the next day. Numbers of admitted patients varied from 0 to 5. The patient was asked to cooperate with interviews by the research psychiatrist and social worker for the purpose of developing better understanding of attempted suicide and to improve the help offered. It was stressed that interviews were confidential and for research purposes only. Only the regular psychiatrist (i.e. duty psychiatrist) would be offering help and making decisions about their care. Social workers undertook not to communicate about patients they had seen nor to enquire about subsequent management, as this could influence subsequent assessments.

Referrals to the duty psychiatrist by the medical firm proceeded as usual. If the duty psychiatrist saw the patient before the social worker the patient was excluded from the series in order to avoid contamination of the patient's response to the social worker, i.e. if the patient already knew he was to go home with a clinic appointment and communicated this to the assessing social worker this could affect her judgement. Both the social worker and the duty psychiatrist were asked to carry out a routine clinical assessment and fill out the rating schedule at the end of the interview.

Role of Research Psychiatrist

The research psychiatrist obtained a standardised mental state assessment in order to compare judgements on the mental state by the two disciplines. The patient was interviewed on the day of initial interviews using the ninth edition of the present state examination (PSE) (Wing *et al.*, 1974), and the patient also completed the 60-item version of the general health questionnaire (GHQ) (Goldberg, 1972). These were repeated at three-month follow-up when information was also obtained about subsequent parasuicide acts, and any treatment received.

Analysis of Rating Schedule Responses

This was done in two ways: (1) Frequency counts which show the percentage of patients given each rating by the two disciplines. This therefore reflects the bias of each discipline in assessing these patients. It does not compare ratings on individual patients. (2) Agreement between the two groups was analysed by cross tabulation. Agreement on an item was calculated as the number of cases in which the two disciplines agreed expressed as a percentage of the total number of patients rated on this item. Significance of agreement was tested using the Kappa statistics.

Results

Sixty-five entered the study in order to obtain full assessments of 60 patients. One patient refused additional interviews, three discharged themselves before being seen by the duty psychiatrist and one was discharged directly to psychiatric out-patients thus precluding in-patient assessment. Sixty-two per cent were female and 38 per cent male. The mean age was 34 years (range 15-87). The reasons for admission from casualty were self-poisoning (59 patients) and lacerated wrists (one patient). Information was obtained on 87 per cent at three-month follow-up.

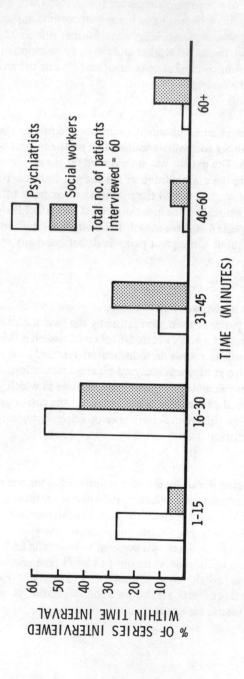

Figure 17.1: Interview Times for Psychiatrists and Social Workers

Length of Interviews

The time spent on each interview was recorded (Figure 17.1). Psychiatrists carried out 27 per cent of their assessments in 15 minutes or less (social workers 7 per cent). Psychiatrists did the majority of their interviews in times between 16-30 minutes. (Psychiatrists 56 per cent, social workers 42 per cent.) Correspondingly, social workers carried out a greater number of longer interviews. Psychiatrists spent more than one hour on only three per cent of the series and social workers on 14 per cent of the series.

Mental Illness

This was investigated on the rating schedule with the question: do you consider this parasuicidal act is part of a longer standing depressive/ psychotic/organic mental disorder? Psychiatrists indicated illness was possibly/definitely present in 43 per cent of the series, and social workers 65 per cent of the series. Agreement on this item was low at 60 per cent (not significant), i.e. the two disciplines agreed in 60 per cent of the series on the possible/definite presence or absence of mental illness, and correspondingly disagreed in 40 per cent. The standardised mental state assessments were used to examine why agreement was so low.

The patients were divided into three groups on the basis of their GHQ score (Table 17.1). Both disciplines rated only a minority as ill in the low range, and both rated 77 per cent as ill in the high range. However, there was considerable disagreement in the middle score range, where social workers rated illness in 79 per cent and psychiatrists in only 35 per cent. There were 24 patients where the two disciplines disagreed about the presence of mental illness. The index of definition level (see note at end of chapter) derived from the PSE interview was used as a standardised measure to determine whether mental illness was present in these patients. This was felt to be of particular significance in a study where screening for severe psychiatric illness was of prime importance.

Table 17.1: Mental Illness (Percent of patients in 3 GHQ scores ranges judged as ill)

GHQ score range	0-20	21-40	41-60
Psychiatrists	22	35	77
Social workers	33	79	77

There was definite PSE evidence of mental illness (at levels 5-8) in five of the six patients (83 per cent) where only psychiatrists rated mental illness. However, there was corresponding evidence in only ten of the eighteen patients (56 per cent) where only social workers had rated mental illness. This and the GHQ evidence confirms psychiatrists are better at applying their rules for identifying mental illness than social workers. It leaves open the question, however, as to whether these patients should be regarded as ill.

When judgements for the more severely ill patients (levels 7 and 8) were examined separately it was found both disciplines had correctly identified as ill all four patients. Both disciplines also correctly rated as ill the two patients in the study who did not fall into the depressive category but were diagnosed as 'phobic' and 'paranoid' respectively on the PSE Catego system.

Personality Assessment

This item was included to examine the bias shown by the two disciplines in rating personality for a population of patients which includes many with major personality problems and others with poor coping mechanisms. However, results are similar. Psychiatrists rated 55 per cent to have abnormal or disordered personalities and social workers similarly rated 63 per cent. Agreement on this item is 68 per cent ($p < 0.01$).

The Need for a Psychiatrist and the Role of the Psychiatrist

The psychiatrists indicated that a psychiatrist is needed in some role in addition to the assessing social worker for 73 per cent of patients and social workers indicated this is necessary for 82 per cent of patients. These figures are initially very disappointing in a study looking at alternatives to a mandatory psychiatric assessment. However, this disappointment is modified in that the psychiatrist is only needed as the main therapist in 39 per cent of the psychiatrists' ratings and 30 per cent of the social workers' ratings, i.e. both disciplines showed a similar tendency in seeing the psychiatrist as an adjunct rather than the main therapist. Predictably it was found the social workers' ratings for whether a psychiatrist was necessary varied with the type of social work experience. An experienced psychiatric social worker indicated a psychiatrist was necessary in 13 per cent of her ratings, whereas a medical social worker with no psychiatric experience indicated a 100 per cent need for a psychiatrist.

Urgency for a Psychiatric Opinion

Similar indications were given for an urgent psychiatric opinion before discharge (psychiatrists 58 per cent of the series, social workers 53 per cent). Similar use was shown for urgent out-patient appointments (psychiatrists 10 per cent of the series, social workers 12 per cent). Social workers made more indications for non-urgent out-patient appointments.

The most important practical issue is whether a psychiatric opinion is required before discharge. Agreement for this is low at 62 per cent ($p < .05$) and for 23 patients disagreement occurred on this decision.

The presence of mental illness on PSE evidence does not help in examining this low agreement. Seventy-seven per cent and 80 per cent respectively of the patients, where only the psychiatrists or only the social workers indicated this opinion was necessary before discharge, reached threshold and above index of definition levels.

If we postulate a psychiatrist is only required before discharge where his specific skills are demanded urgently, e.g. (1) immediate prescriptions of physical treatment; (2) compulsory or immediate admission; (3) diagnostic confusion, then we can consider the reliability of social workers making this judgement as compared to psychiatrists. On these criteria we looked at subsequent events in these twenty-three patients where disagreement occurred and we found over-all follow-up results have upheld the social workers' original judgements as being at least equally valid as those of psychiatrists.

Immediate Management

Both disciplines opted for discharge offering psychiatric and/or social help as the most useful choice (psychiatrists 65 per cent of their ratings, social workers 52 per cent). Social workers were more cautious about discharging patients from in-patient care. They chose to keep in more patients either on a medical or a psychiatric ward (psychiatrists 27 per cent of their ratings, social workers 45 per cent). Agreement on whether to prolong hospitalisation or discharge is 72 per cent ($p < 0.01$).

At follow-up the research psychiatrist found that three patients who were discharged after psychiatric assessment required emergency admission within the following three weeks for the same psychiatric disorder as was apparent after the overdose. A further two patients were re-referred by the medical team who were worried about discharging them. The more cautious social workers had opted to prolong hospitalisation on these five patients.

Compulsory Detention

This item had to be rated in a rather hypothetical way as only the psychiatrists were in a position of offering and discussing management plans with the patients. However, both disciplines gave a low recommendation for compulsory detention (psychiatrists 12 per cent of their ratings, social workers 7 per cent). Agreement was 88 per cent. One patient was detained and the social worker agreed with the psychiatrist over the need for this.

Further Help

The most popular category for further help was psychiatrist plus social worker (psychiatrists 58 per cent of their ratings, social workers 67 per cent). There were low rates for psychiatrists and social workers as exclusive helpers.

Type of Social Worker Help

Social workers showed a preference for hospital social work help and psychiatrists for local authority based help. Indications for other organisations, e.g. Probation Service and Prisoners Aid Society, were low.

Suicidal Intent, Motive and Future Risk

Suicidal intent of some degree was present more often in the social workers' assessment (psychiatrists 45 per cent of their ratings, social workers 67 per cent). The motive most frequently attributed to the patients by both disciplines was temporary escape from an unbearable situation (psychiatrists 42 per cent of their ratings, social workers 32 per cent). The will to die as a main motive was rated present infrequently (psychiatrists 12 per cent of their ratings, social workers 20 per cent).

The possibility of further suicidal behaviour in the near future was predicted at high rates (psychiatrists 65 per cent of their ratings, social workers 70 per cent). Eight patients repeated the overdose during the three-month follow-up period; one died. Both disciplines had predicted the likelihood of a further attempt and had recommended out-patient help for this patient who committed suicide. Psychiatrists failed to predict two patients and social workers one patient of the others who repeated the overdose.

Interview Factors

Both disciplines indicated that the interviewing of a third party, i.e. relative or friend, would be useful or essential for the majority of patients (psychiatrists 63 per cent of their ratings, social workers 67 per cent). Ratings on whether the patient was totally unreliable or dubious as a historian are similar (psychiatrists 30 per cent of their ratings, social workers 23 per cent). One patient proved at follow-up to have given a totally fallacious history. The duty psychiatrist had rated him as a reliable historian and the social worker as a dubious historian.

Personal and Situational Factors

The presence or absence of 17 items was examined. The first section involved physical and psychological factors, e.g. alcohol abuse and physical illness. The second involved interpersonal factors, e.g. social isolation and marital problems. The third section involved more material factors, e.g. housing and financial problems. Psychiatrists rated all items less frequently, but only three differences in frequencies reached statistical significance: (1) Forced separation (psychiatrists 15 per cent of their ratings, social workers 35 per cent) ($p < .05$). (2) General relationship problems (psychiatrists 40 per cent of their ratings, social workers 65 per cent) ($p < .05$). (3) Family problems (psychiatrists 28 per cent of their ratings, social workers 55 per cent) ($p < .01$).

They agreed on presence of physical illness in seven patients. Patients where disagreement occurred were examined against further information obtained by the research psychiatrist and it was found social workers were usually correct. There were ten patients where only the social workers had rated physical illness present (disabling arthritis (2), Parkinson's disease (1), hypochondriasis (1), hypochondriacal delusions (1), post-influenza depression (1), gynaecological disorders (2) and alcoholism with physical symptoms (2). In contrast only one patient was rated as ill just by the psychiatrist (alcoholism with physical symptoms). Two epileptics, misdiagnosed on admission as overdoses and referred as such for psychiatric opinion, were rated by both disciplines as physically and not mentally ill.

Discussion

The study has shown that social workers are capable of carrying out initial assessment interviews on parasuicide patients. At this stage it was not possible for ethical reasons to carry out a randomised trial between psychiatrists and social workers. The design of the study therefore does not provide results on what would have happened if the social workers management, here different, had been followed.

Social workers tended to use slightly longer interview times. They wanted more psychiatric opinions and they wanted to keep patients in hospitals more often. They diagnosed mental illness more frequently in patients with a moderate number of depressive and neurotic symptoms. Over-all they were more cautious — a bias towards caution amongst persons inexperienced in dealing with parasuicide patients is understandable if not commendable.

It would seem that social workers have much to contribute over selection of appropriate help. Various points arose at discussion meetings which were held between the research psychiatrist and the social workers after the series had been completed including all follow-up interviews. Each patient was discussed in detail. The social workers' relatively frequent recommendations for hospital social worker help depended on the assumption a hospital social worker would interview the patient before discharge and they attached therapeutic importance to this interview. They felt patients were more likely to use help at a time of high risk from a worker they had already encountered. They were aware of the great pressures under which local authority-based social workers work. Perhaps more realistically they did not generally consider them as an alternative to hospital workers to follow up the patient. The social workers were asked to rate for each patient they had originally assessed, whether they considered available social work resources had been used satisfactorily. They were satisfied for 54 per cent of the 60 patients.

The social workers' training would appear to be an advantage in recognising interpersonal problems, and choosing the most appropriate type of social or counselling help. Some trainee psychiatrists have little experience yet on these aspects of diagnosis and management.

Conclusion

We suggest from our findings an alternative assessment procedure for these patients. Social workers, depending on availability, could undertake to deal with a proportion of referrals. It would be of paramount importance to have a back-up service from an experienced psychiatrist. The psychiatrist would need to be available for consultation with the social workers about urgent problems. A psychiatric interview with the patient must be possible wherever necessary, either as an in-patient or as an out-patient. It is envisaged the need for a psychiatric consultation would drop as the expertise and confidence of the social worker increased. It is emphasised that regular meetings would be necessary, e.g. weekly between the psychiatrists and social workers. This would provide a forum where difficult cases could be discussed and decisions about further management taken. It would also give to each discipline an opportunity to learn more about the other discipline's expertise.

Acknowledgements

We wish to thank the following at Charing Cross Hospital: Professor S.R. Hirsch under whose guidance and supervision the study was undertaken; the Clinical Research Committee who awarded the research fellowship; and the psychiatrists and social workers who took part in the study, S. Abovich, F. Al-Sudani, A. Lisei, P. Taraba and R. Wilkie (doctors) and M. Billing, P. Blunt, C. Court, A. Forest, J. George, A. Marwaha and T. Mitchell (social workers).

Note

The index of definition level is the degree of certainty whereby symptoms present can be classified into one of the conventional functional psychiatric diagnoses. Levels 1 to 4 are below threshold and no diagnosis is reached. Levels 5 to 8 are at threshold and above and the diagnosis is reached with increasing degrees of certainty.

References

Goldberg, D.P. (1972). *The Detection of Psychiatric Illness by Questionnaire.* Oxford University Press, London.
Harris, B. (1976). Communication in attempted suicide. *Social Work Today*, vol. 6, pp. 722-24.
Hill Report (1968). *Hospital Treatment of Acute Poisoning.* Report of the Joint Subcommittee of the Standing Medical Advisory Committee. HMSO, London.
Kiev, A. (1976). Crisis intervention and suicide prevention. In *Suicidology: Contemporary Developments*, ed. E.S. Shneidman. Grune and Stratton, New York, pp. 445-78.
Paykel, E.S., Prusoff, M.P.H. and Myers, J.K. (1975). Suicide attempts and recent life events. A controlled comparison. *Archives of General Psychiatry*, vol. 32, pp. 327-33.
Wing, J.K., Cooper, J.E. and Sartorius, N. (1974). *The Measurement and Management of Psychiatric Symptoms.* Cambridge University Press, Cambridge.
Wing, J.K. (1976). A technique for studying psychiatric morbidity in in-patient and out-patient series and in general population samples. *Psychological Medicine*, vol. 6, pp. 665-71.
Wing, J.K., Mann, S.A., Leff, J.P. and Nixon, J.M. (1978). The concept of a 'case' in psychiatric population surveys. *Psychological Medicine*, vol. 8, pp. 203-17.

18 MEDICAL-PSYCHIATRIC CONSULTATION AND LIAISON: AN EVALUATION OF ITS EFFECTIVENESS

R. Gardner

Introduction

When attempted suicide ceased to be an indictable offence, the Ministry of Health advised all hospitals to see that patients admitted for such an attempt received psychiatric attention. The Hill Report (1968) recommended that in all cases of deliberate self-poisoning, patients should be referred to designated treatment centres in district general hospitals and seen by psychiatrists. This advice is not always followed. General practitioners do not send all such patients to hospital (Kennedy and Kreitman, 1973). Arrangements for assessing them vary and many self-poisoned patients are not seen by psychiatrists (Greer and Bagley, 1971; Collier et al., 1976). Ten years after the Hill Report there are few special treatment centres for poisoning and most of our district general hospitals lack psychiatric units.

But if these resources were to become available would we choose to keep the Department of Health's recommendation in the Hill Report? In the case of any other clinical condition, however life threatening, medical practitioners are free to decide whether specialist advice is necessary. One of the aims of their training is to equip them to handle the common medical emergencies. Stengel (1968) regarded the management of attempted suicides in the general hospital as of crucial importance in medical education. He pointed out that in treating these patients, trainee doctors and nurses can be made to realise the importance of their patients' psychological and social problems. There is also a preventive aspect. Better training in evaluating suicidal risk and patients' psychosocial difficulties might lead doctors to prescribe with greater care.

At Addenbrooke's Hospital Gardner et al. (1977) have shown that if junior doctors and nurses are suitably taught, medical teams can assess suicide risk and identify patients who require psychiatric treatment, help from social workers or both. Physicians now exercise full clinical responsibility for the self-poisoned patients admitted under their care. Since November, 1977, they have undertaken the initial psychiatric assessment of all such patients, requesting specialist psychiatric advice or help from the unit social worker when necessary. This chapter describes what has been taught and evaluates the effectiveness of the medical-psychiatric consultation and liaison during the clinical trial and after it.

Patients and Methods

Between October 1974 and May 1975, self-poisoned patients admitted to Old Addenbrooke's Hospital, were randomly allocated to seven medical teams (M) or to twelve duty psychiatrists (P) for an initial psychiatric assessment and decision as to 'disposal' (Gardner *et al.*, 1977). All the consultant physicians and consultant psychiatrists who customarily treated such patients at Addenbrooke's took part. Both groups of assessors asked for help from social workers when necessary. Once the medical teams had completed their assessments, psychiatrists provided most (90 per cent) of the hospital treatment. From the 1 June 1975 when entries to the trial ceased, we continued the randomisation and the same assessment procedure while awaiting the outcome.

In July 1975, six beds were designated for cases of self-poisoning in one of the medical wards in New Addenbrooke's Hospital. Only about half of the patients have since been admitted to this ward, most of the others going to three other medical wards and a few to surgical ones. I remain responsible for the teaching of junior staff, share consultations with the other psychiatrists and have an out-patient clinic on the same site to facilitate referrals from the wards and accident department.

Teaching Junior Doctors

When pre-registration house physicians and medical registrars take up their posts they are taught the principles of a psychiatric assessment by me; told about the subgroups of patients who commonly poison themselves; the possible outcome in terms of suicide and repetition of self-poisoning, and the proportion of admissions who are likely to be offered psychiatric treatment and aftercare; the local arrangements for transferring patients to psychiatric wards, making out-patient appointments and obtaining help from social workers; they are asked to see that appointments for clinics and with general practitioners are made before the patients are discharged and within a few days of their leaving hospital; that any medication is given into the care of a relative or friend and, if possible, that patients come accompanied to clinics or surgeries.

At the time of each ward consultation, the unit social worker and I ask the views of the junior doctor and nursing staff when making our own assessment. Afterwards, we discuss the management of the patient with them.

Teaching the Nurses

Nurses are encouraged to listen and talk to patients and their relatives; to contribute to the medical teams' assessments; and to make the necessary arrangements for the patients' subsequent treatment and aftercare.

During the clinical trial, the unit social worker and I met nurses on the ward every few weeks to discuss their work and difficulties with these patients, to give them some of the facts about suicide and attempted suicide and to explain the local system for arranging psychiatric treatment and aftercare. Since 1975 we have held a weekly meeting to which nurses from any of the wards taking self-poisoned patients may come along.

Results

There were 312 consecutive admissions (276 patients) to the trial. Allowing for withdrawals, 246 patients were admitted to it for the first time. Of these, 126 were allocated to M and 120 to P. During the 13-month post-trial period there were 510 admissions, or 453 patients. After withdrawals there were 392 patients, of whom 192 were allocated to M and 200 to P. (For each period, one admission only, the first for a patient in that period, has been included in the following analyses unless stated otherwise. Figures in parentheses refer to the post-trial period.) The trial and the post-trial period enabled us to answer a number of questions.

Accidental or Deliberate Self-poisoning

Were the medical teams capable of differentiating accidental from deliberate self-poisoning? Out of the 246 (392) admissions, the poisoning was considered accidental in eight (10) instances, uncertain in six (eight) and deliberate in the remainder. Since there were few cases of accidental poisoning and the distribution of the three types of poisoning was the same for M and P we conclude that the medical teams were capable of making this distinction.

Medical Risk and Suicidal Risk

Did the medical teams base their decisions about further psychiatric treatment on the physical condition of their patients? Table 18.1 shows the levels of consciousness of patients after admission to Addenbrooke's and the recommended treatment and aftercare. There is no significant difference between M and P. It can be seen that although the medical risk was low for the majority of patients in both groups, more than half of those who were conscious or drowsy only were recommended for psychiatric treatment. A similar number of patients in coma were so referred. Clearly the medical teams appreciated that the medical risk did not correlate with the need for further psychiatric care.

Table 18.1: Level of Consciousness of Self-poisoned Patients and Type of Treatment Recommended for Them by the Medical Teams and Psychiatrists (figures in parentheses refer to the post-trial patients)

Assessors	Treatment	Conscious or drowsy	Unconscious but responsive	Unconscious and unresponsive
Medical teams	In-patient	20 (36)	3 (5)	6 (4)
	Out-patient	49 (65)	5 (6)	1 (4)
	Social worker	10 (24)	5 (1)	0 (0)
	General practitioner	22 (34)	3 (6)	1 (2)
Psychiatrists	In-patient	18 (26)	4 (6)	2 (2)
	Out-patient	41 (74)	4 (9)	4 (6)
	Social worker	9 (24)	1 (3)	0 (2)
	General practitioner	28 (33)	7 (7)	2 (4)

Ten patients, one during trial and nine post-trial, for whom one of the variables was unrecorded have been excluded from this table.

Diagnosis

Were the medical teams able to make a psychiatric diagnosis? Tables 18.2 and 18.3 show the illness and personality diagnoses chosen by the two groups of assessors. There is some difference between M and P which lies within the first two categories of both tables. Altogether, 58 (97) patients, 32 (56) M and 26 (41) P were found to have no psychiatric disorder, i.e. they had a normal personality and a diagnosis of 'situational disturbance'.

Was the diagnosis of any practical value? In Table 18.4 it is apparent that the diagnosis influenced the decisions about future psychiatric treatment which were made not only by the psychiatrists, but also by the medical teams.

Consultation and Liaison

How often will physicians ask psychiatrists to see their self-poisoned patients if referral is no longer routine? In the clinical trial, the medical

Table 18.2: Illness Diagnoses Chosen by the Medical Teams and Psychiatrists for Self-poisoned Patients (figures in parentheses refer to the post-trial patients)

Illness diagnosis	M	P
No psychiatric illness	24 (22)	14 (11)
Situational disturbance	32 (62)	40 (72)
Depressive illness/reaction	63 (92)	57 (101)
Mania	0 (0)	1 (0)
Organic psychiatric disorder	2 (2)	0 (4)
Schizophrenia	1 (5)	2 (0)
Epilepsy	2 (3)	0 (1)
Other	2 (6)	6 (11)

Table 18.3: Personality Diagnoses Chosen by the Medical Teams and Psychiatrists for Self-poisoned Patients (figures in parentheses refer to the post-trial patients)

Personality diagnosis	M	P
Normal personality	68 (112)	47 (94)
Personality disorder	36 (61)	56 (86)
Subnormality	2 (2)	1 (2)
Drug dependence	4 (4)	5 (2)
Alcoholism	11 (5)	5 (6)
Other	5 (8)	6 (10)

Table 18.4: Diagnostic Categories of Self-poisoned Patients and the Types of Treatment Recommended for Them by the Medical Teams and Psychiatrists (figures in parentheses refer to the post-trial patients)

Assessors	Diagnostic category	Psychiatric treatment	Social work help	GP
	No psychiatric disorder	24 (35)	9 (17)	23 (30)
Medical	Depressive illness/reaction	55 (77)	6 (6)	2 (8)
teams	Other psychiatric disorder	6 (10)	0 (2)	1 (4)
	No psychiatric disorder	19 (39)	5 (16)	30 (25)
Psychiatrists	Depressive illness/reaction	47 (72)	5 (12)	5 (17)
	Other psychiatric disorder	7 (13)	0 (1)	2 (2)

Six post-trial patients, for whom one of the variables was unrecorded, have been excluded from this table.

Table 18.5: Types of Treatment Recommended for Self-poisoned Patients and Types of Treatment Received by Them (figures in parentheses refer to the post-trial patients)

Treatment	M	P
In-patient psychiatric	31/29 (40/47)	25/24 (32/34)
Out-patient psychiatric	42/56 (65/75)	37/49 (71/90)
Social worker[a]	15/15 (/25)	9/10 (/29)
General practitioner[b]	11/26 (/42)	16/37 (/44)

Ratios are: no. of patients receiving that treatment/no. of patients recommended for that treatment.

a. Post-trial numbers not available for treatment received.

b. Only patients who saw their GP within one month of discharge are included; post-trial numbers not available for treatment received.

Six post-trial patients, for whom the 'disposal' was not recorded, have been excluded from this table.

teams asked for psychiatric opinions for 14 per cent of their patients, and in the next 13 months, the proportion was 22 per cent. It might have been anticipated that the medical teams would 'play safe' by referring an unnecessary number of their patients to psychiatric wards and clinics. But this did not prove to be the case. They identified similar numbers for further psychiatric treatment as did the psychiatrists, not only during the clinical trial, but also in the 13 months after it (see Table 18.1).

Did patients actually receive the treatment recommended for them? From Table 18.5 it appears that this objective was achieved equally for M and P. There was also no difference between M and P in the number of patients who received ECT and the various psychotropic drugs. The medical teams might have been expected to select more unsuitable patients for treatment than the psychiatrists, but the duration of stay in psychiatric wards was the same for patients referred by M and P, as were the drop-out rates at out-patient clinics (Gardner *et al.*, 1978).

Outcome

Did the patients assessed by the medical teams fare less well than those assessed by psychiatrists? Patients who were admitted to hospital after entries to the trial ceased were not followed up. Table 18.6 gives details of outcome at one year for the 246 patients admitted for the first time into the trial. (By relapse is meant repetition of self-poisoning, or self-injury (or both), or suicide.) The differences in outcome between M and P are not significant. Figure 18.1 shows the proportion

Table 18.6: Outcome for Patients in the Clinical Trial

	M	P
No relapse	81	65
Relapsed	28	35
Suicide	0	1
Drop out[a]	17	19

a. Follow-up incomplete or impossible.

of patients surviving without relapse, corrected for drop-outs, plotted against time. The graph shows that a larger proportion of the medical teams' patients survived without relapse, but this difference is not significant at any point of the graph ($p > 0.05$). The proportions of patients surviving one year without relapse are 72.25 per cent (standard error (SE) 3.9 per cent) and 65 per cent (SE = 4.3 per cent) for M and P, respectively.

Discussion and Conclusions

The results of this study show that it is the effectiveness of the training of junior staff and of the consultation/liaison which matters, and not that psychiatrists should see all self-poisoned patients. At Addenbrooke's we are teaching this subject in greater detail. Student nurses are taught on the wards and during their general training programme. Every intake of medical students is given one session on 'poisoning' with contributions from a clinical biochemist, paediatrician, physician and psychiatrist. During their psychiatric attachments, each group of students has a seminar on suicide and attempted suicide. The rotation of junior staff enables more doctors and nurses to be trained in assessment methods and so helped to develop favourable attitudes towards self-poisoned patients.

Returning to the question: would we choose to keep the Department of Health's recommendation in the Hill Report? There is now a strong case for amending it and using a more selective approach in the management of deliberate self-poisoning. This would allow a variety of methods to be tried and tested. Psychiatrists should not withdraw from this work, but should teach junior staff how to carry out the psychological and social evaluation of such patients, as well as ensuring that psychiatric treatment and aftercare are available once patients have been assessed.

Figure 18.1: First Admissions to Trial Only

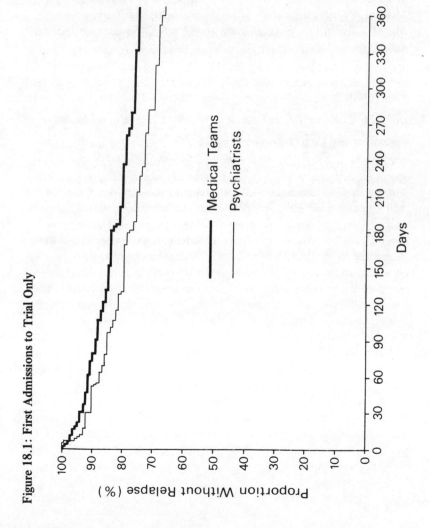

Acknowledgements

This project (No. 79/80) was financed by the East Anglian Regional Health Authority. We thank the consultant physicians at Addenbrooke's Hospital and the consultant psychiatrists at Fulbourn Hospital for permission to interview their patients; the medical and nursing staff at Addenbrooke's, particularly Sister P. Mountford; Mrs V. O'Brien, unit social worker, and the senior duty psychiatrists at Fulbourn Hospital for their participation; Mr R. Hanka and Miss S.J. Roberts for statistical advice and help; Mrs B. Evison and Mrs M. Gardner for data collection and Miss S.K. Gardner for secretarial assistance.

References

Collier, J., Cummins, T.A. and Hamilton, M. (1976). *Journal of the Royal College of Physicians*, vol. 10, no. 4, p. 381.
Gardner, R., Hanka, R. *et al.* (1977), *British Medical Journal*, vol. 2, p. 1567.
Gardner, R., Hanka, R., Evison, B., Mountford, P.M., O'Brien, V.C. and Roberts, S.R. (1978), *British Medical Journal*, vol. 2, p. 1392.
Greer, S. and Bagley, C. (1971), *British Medical Journal*, vol. 1, p. 310.
Hill Report (1968), *Hospital Treatment of Acute Poisoning*. HMSO, London.
Kennedy, P. and Kreitman, N. (1973), *British Journal of Psychiatry*, vol. 123, p. 23.
Ministry of Health, HM no. 61, p. 94.
Stengel, E. (1968). Attempted suicides. In *Suicidal Behaviours*, ed. H.L.P. Resnick. J. and A. Churchill, London.

PART FIVE

The Management of Survivors

19 MANAGEMENT OF SELF-POISONING: SOCIAL WORK INTERVENTION

J.S. Gibbons

Introduction

In 1975-76 the Department of Psychiatry at Southampton University provided an experimental social work service for patients who came to the casualty department after deliberately poisoning themselves. This chapter, written from the point of view of a social worker, describes the service in an attempt to evaluate it.

In Southampton, as elsewhere (Bancroft *et al.*, 1975; Buglass and Horton, 1974) self-poisoning was increasing in the period before the service was set up. There had been a rise in casualty attendances for self-poisoning of 11 per cent over a three-year period (Smith, 1972). Self-poisoners were routinely managed by a consulatation with a duty psychiatrist who referred the patient to specialised services where necessary. In 1972, under this routine service, 15 per cent of the total were immediately admitted to a psychiatric-hospital and 28 per cent were referred for psychiatric out-patient treatment. Six per cent were referred to social agencies. This routine service was thought unsatisfactory. It was inconsistent, since at least 20 psychiatrists were involved in consultations, and it appeared to be based on assumptions about the primarily psychiatric nature of self-poisoners' difficulties. There was evidence that self-poisoning was usually an impulsive answer to a temporarily unbearable social situation, often involving other family members (Lawson and Mitchell, 1972). Yet under the routine service 40 per cent were seen as needing psychiatric treatment compared to only 6 per cent seen as needing help with social problems.

The experimental social work service was planned to be crisis oriented, explicitly time limited and directed whenever possible at the patient in the context of his close relationships and in his home rather than the hospital. The particular social work method used, task-centred casework (Reid and Epstein, 1972), is based on an explicit contract of limited work which both worker and client agree to undertake during a defined time period (up to a maximum of 3 months in this trial). The method involves 4 stages of work: (1) The range of problems the client perceives in a number of life areas is explored in order to locate a *target*, the problem perceived as most salient by the client and which he is most motivated to reduce. (2) The goal of treatment is then defined in terms of one or more specific *tasks*, formulated collaboratively by client and worker. Agreement is reached about the time needed to complete the tasks. (3) The social worker's job is then to help the client complete the tasks. (4) At termination there is a formal *evaluation* when client and worker discuss what has been achieved and identify further tasks to be undertsken by the client alone.

This social work service was provided by two qualified and experienced social workers who were employed in the Department of Psychiatry.

Methods

Patients who were aged at least 17, lived in a defined geographical area and came to the casualty department between April 1975 and March 1976 after taking an overdose where considered for inclusion in a trial of the experimental social work service. A research psychiatrist interviewed patients on recovery of consciousness and obtained demographic, social and clinical information using structured instruments. Cases who needed immediate psychiatric admission (8 per cent) or were already in continuing treatment with a psychiatrist or social worker whom they had seen within two weeks (18 per cent) were excluded. The remainder were then randomly allocated to an experimental group receiving task-centred casework or to a control group, until there were 200 in each. The control group received routine service, similar, except for the more systematic initial consultation, to that usually offered: a third were referred for psychiatric treatment, 13 per cent to social agencies and the remainder back to their general practitioners. There were no significant differences in social or clinical characteristics between experimental and control groups.

Outcome Criteria Used

In evaluating service effectiveness neither clients' problems nor successful outcomes can be easily defined. Both are likely to have different meanings depending on whether they are viewed from the clients' or the service providers' perspective. Repetition of self-poisoning and use of psychiatric services during a follow-up year were criteria of successful outcome from the service providers' perspective; change in ratings of social problems and degree of satisfaction with service received, were criteria designed to take the clients' perspective into account.

To check on repeated admission for self-poisoning and use of psychiatric services, record searches were made covering general practitioners (90 per cent success), two general hospitals and three psychiatric hospitals servicing the area. General practitioner and hospital records of patients who were known to have moved were obtained. In order to assess immediate and longer-term improvement in social problems a random half of the 400 clients was interviewed four months after the index overdose and the other half eighteen months after it. Interviews were carried out by three experienced interviewers who had no connection with the service and knew nothing of the clients other than name, age and address. Seventy-eight per cent were reinterviewed.

Clients' satisfaction with service was assessed by using a short, structured questionnaire. Change in perceived social problems was assessed by a longer semi-structured questionnaire administered at baseline and follow-up. Information was gathered about the perceived severity of life problems in seven areas: (1) *Significant personal relationships*: difficulties in getting on with someone important to the client with whom he was in a continuing personal relationship. (2) *Social transitions:* problems arising from recent or impending changes such as bereavement, break-up of relationships. (3) *Social relations*: loneliness or unsatisfying social life. (4) *Emotional distress interfering with coping ability.* (5) *Practical difficulties*: work, money or housing. (6) *Problems with formal organisations.* (7) *Domestic difficulties*: ̣ problems in role performance as a parent or housewife.

Reliability studies were carried out at the baseline and follow-up stages and proved satisfactory for all areas except domestic difficulties, which was omitted as a change measure. After detailed questioning clients were asked to rate the severity of difficulties they mentioned under each heading on a scale ranging from 0 (no problem) to 4 (very considerable problem). Thus the questionnaire gave an estimate of clients' views on the severity of their problems at overdose and how these views had changed four months and eighteen months later.

The Sample

Two-thirds of the trial sample were women. The age range was from 17 to 81 with a peak in the twenties. In comparison with the local population more were divorced, more came from semi or unskilled manual occupations and more were out of work. Over a quarter had been previously admitted to hospital for self-poisoning; a fifth had previous in-patient psychiatric treatment and rather more had previous out-patient treatment. Sixty-nine per cent were judged by the research psychiatrist (who used the Present State Examination) to be suffering from a defined psychiatric disorder on their recovery from overdose — usually neurotic depression. Substantial minorities had problems with alcohol or drugs or had been in trouble with the police. The trial sample resembled the total population of self-poisoners, but an excess number of the highest risk cases was excluded because they were already receiving psychiatric treatment (Gibbons *et al.*, 1978b).

The social problems most commonly reported, and seen as most considerable at the time of overdose, were subjective feelings of distress, difficulties arising from recent or impending change, usually the break-up of a love relationship; and difficulties in personal relationships, usually with a spouse (Figure 19.1). Eighty-three per cent of all the married cases still living with a spouse reported marital problems. Over half were having more than one row a week and the majority of these involved violence. Younger, married women were most likely to complain of relationship problems. About half the sample reported practical problems to do with work, money or housing and these were more likely to be men. Nearly half complained of unsatisfying social relations, loneliness or isolation. Less than 20 per cent complained of problems with organisations, usually the police, or in carrying out domestic roles.

Results

Take-up of Experimental Service

About 90 per cent of the experimental group accepted some contact with the social workers immediately after the overdose (Table 19.1). About a quarter had a brief contact of two or three interviews which did not go beyond clarifying the problems. Over half completed a period of task-centred work with an average of nine interviews. However, about a fifth, usually those with multiple and long-standing problems, could not be contained within an agreed time limit and developed into longer-term cases.

Effects of Experimental Service

Repetition. Repetition of self-poisoning was measured by documented reattendance at a casualty department in the following year. There was no difference in outcome between experimental and control groups (13.5 per cent *v.* 14.5 per cent repeated).

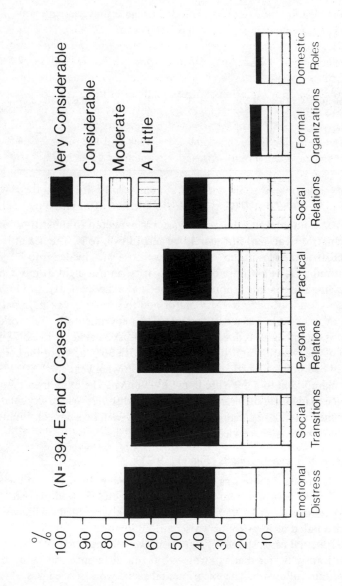

Figure 19.1: Proportions Reporting Social Problems in Different Life Areas at Time of Overdose

Table 19.1: Use by Clients of Task-centred Service

	n	Mean number of interviews	Mean number of weeks	Mean number of agencies contacted	Mean number significant others contacted	Mean number of target problems
Task-centred	105	8.9	9.9	2.7	1.1	1.3
Task-centred, over-ran time limit	33	24.2	25.9	5.1	2.3	2.1
Ended after problem search	49	2.5	3.7	1.1	0.6	–
Planned long term	2	75	50	8	2	4.5
No contact	11	–	–	–	–	–

Use of Psychiatric Services (Table 19.2)

The experimental social work service was expected to substitute for psychiatric treatment not merely be an addition to it. The use of psychiatric services in the year after overdose was divided into 'continuing' (five or more out-patient visits, and/or eight or more days as an in-patient and/or more than a week as a day-patient); and 'brief' (one to four out-patient visits and/or one to seven days as an in-patient and/or week or less as a day-patient). The experimental social work service significantly reduced clients' use of psychiatric services: 78 per cent of the experimental group compared with 66 per cent of the control group had no psychiatric contact in the following year ($p < .02$). This was mainly due to a decrease in use by women. The experimental service made little difference to male self-poisoners' use of psychiatric help but only half as many experimental women became continuing users of psychiatric services.

Change in Social Problems (Figure 19.2)

A total problem score was obtained by summing the scores on the six problem areas. About two-thirds of control cases showed over-all short-term and long-term improvement in social problems while about a third failed to improve or worsened. Eighty-one per cent of experimental cases showed short-term over-all improvement — significantly better than controls — but this difference was reduced at long-term follow-up. The experimental social work service was

Table 19.2: Use of Psychiatric Services in Year Following Overdose

Pattern of use	Experimental					
	Male	Female	Total	Male	Female	Total
Continuing	11	12	23	6	27	43
	(17%)	(9%)	(11%)	(11%)	(18%)	(21%)
Brief	6	15	21	13	22	35
	(10%)	(11%)	(11%)	(25%)	(14%)	(18%)
None	45	11	156	34	98	132
	(73%)	(80%)	(78%)	(64%)	(67%)	(66%)
Total	62	138	200	53	147	200
	(100%)	(100%)	(100%)	(100%)	(100%)	(100%)

Figure 19.2: Proportions Showing Improvement in Social Problems 4 Months and 18 Months After Overdose (n = 303)

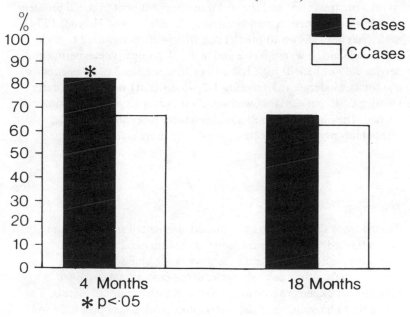

$* p < \cdot 05$

particularly successful with problems of personal relations and unsatisfying social relations, both in the short and long term.

Satisfaction with Services

At follow-up clients were asked how much help they had received following their overdose. Experimental clients felt they had received significantly more help (p < .02) in particular with leading a more satisfying social life and in feeling less upset and disturbed in themselves. They had also received more help in getting along better with someone important to them, getting needed services and with practical problems. Both groups felt equally helped in coping with some change or upheaval. Over 40 per cent of experimental clients but only 12 per cent of control clients were 'very satisfied' with the service received, while twice as many control as experimental clients were 'unsatisfied'.

Risk Category and Outcome

The effects of sex and of risk category upon outcomes were examined (Table 19.3). Men did no better with the experimental than with the routine service although they were significantly more satisfied with it. Experimental women not only preferred their service but also had less psychiatric treatment and showed more improvement in social problems than control women. A standardised scale (Buglass and Horton, 1974) which has been shown to predict risk of repetition was used to divide the sample into low, moderate and high risk groups. The experimental service did not benefit high risk cases (those scoring 3-6, 13 per cent of the total). Moderate risk (scoring 1-2, 45 per cent) and low risk cases (scoring 0, 42 per cent) showed significant gains from the experimental service. They improved their social problems more than controls, needed less psychiatric treatment and were more satisfied.

Discussion

The evidence therefore suggests that crisis-oriented social work services have a limited but useful part to play in the management of self-poisoning patients. Although such services are unlikely to affect repetition rates, they can substitute, in the case of many women patients, for expensive psychiatric services without any ill effects. They are likely to have an immediate effect on clients' social problems and be highly acceptable to them. Such services appear more likely to be useful to women with a moderate risk of repetition and to clients who want to improve an unhappy marriage or unsatisfying social life.

Acknowledgements

Members of the research team were: Mrs I. Bow, Miss J. Butler,

Table 19.3: Effects of Risk Category and Sex on Outcomes

Outcome	Low and Moderate (0-2)		High (3+)		Male		Female	
	Exp.	Cont.	Exp.	Cont.	Exp.	Cont.	Exp.	Cont.
% Repeating	10.7 (177)	12.3 (171)	34.8 (23)	24.2 (29)	16.1 (62)	15.1 (53)	12.3 (138)	13.6 (147)
% Psychiatric treatment	16.9 (177)	26.9* (171)	56.5 (23)	72.4 (29)	27.4 (62)	35.8 (53)	19.6 (138)	32.6** (147)
% Improved social problems short term	85.9 (71)	68.2** (63)	50 (10)	55.5 (9)	80 (25)	78.6 (14)	82.1 (56)	63.1 (58)
% Satisfied short and long term	62.3 (138)	34.8** (132)	41.2 (17)	22.2 (18)	68.1 (47)1	26.5*** (34)1	58.3 (108)	35.3*** (116)

Totals in brackets *p < .05   **p <.02   ***p < .01

Dr J. Elliott, Mrs C. Foster, Professor J.L. Gibbons (Director), Mrs G. Glastonbury, Mrs J. Powell, Mrs J. Riley, Dr P. Urwin; Mr A. Cotton provided computer services.

References

Bancroft, J.H.J., Skrimshire, A.M., Reynolds, F., Simkin, S. and Smith, J. (1975). Self-poisoning and self-injury in the Oxford area: epidemiological aspects, 1969-73. *British Journal of Preventive and Social Medicine*, vol. 29, pp. 170-77.
Buglass, D. and Horton, J. (1974). A scale for predicting subsequent suicidal behaviour. *British Journal of Psychiatry*, vol. 124, pp. 573-78.
Gibbons, J.S., Elliot, J., Urwin, P. and Gibbons, J.L. (1978a). The urban environment and deliberate self-poisoning: trends in Southampton, 1972-77. *Social Psychiatry*, vol. 13, pp. 159-66.
Gibbons, J.S., Butler, J., Urwin, P., Gibbons, J.L. (1978b). Evaluation of a social work service for self-poisoning patients. *British Journal of Psychiatry*, vol. 133, pp. 111-18.
Lawson and Mitchell (1972). Patients with acute poisoning seen in a general medical unit, 1961-71. *British Medical Journal*, vol. 4, pp. 153-56.
Smith, A.J. (1972). Self-poisoning with drugs: a worsening situation. *British Medical Journal*, vol. 4, pp. 157-59.
Reid, W. and Epstein, L. (1972). *Task-centered Casework*. Columbia University Press, New York.

20 DOMICILIARY AND OUT-PATIENT TREATMENT FOLLOWING DELIBERATE SELF-POISONING

K. Hawton

During the past five years in Oxford we have developed a multi-disciplinary approach to assessment and management of self-poisoning patients (described in Chapter 16). They are assessed by a member of the emergency team which includes junior psychiatrists, a GP trainee, psychiatric nurses and a social worker. A senior psychiatrist meets the team each day to discuss the patients who have been assessed. During 1977, of 896 referrals to the service, 29 per cent were assessed by doctors, 53 per cent by nurses and 9 per cent by the social worker. The rest were seen by personnel temporarily attached to the service for training purposes.

For a patient not requiring referral elsewhere, the team member who has assessed the patient will, where indicated, carry out the subsequent management. In addition to out-patient care by the team we have also developed home-based (domiciliary) treatment. Since the latter is likely to prove more expensive in terms of time and travelling we felt it important to evaluate this form of management.

Our treatment approach tends to be brief, flexible and focused on the patient's current problems. This approach is described in our treatment manual. An 'open access' telephone service is available.

In the research project to be described the relative efficacy of a flexible domiciliary regime was compared with once-a-week out-patient management. The weekly out-patient regime was chosen for comparison since this is the usual method of management for self-poisoning patients in most parts of the country. Several authors (Stanley, 1969; Paykel et al., 1974; Kreitman, 1977; Blake and Mitchell, 1978) have reported high drop-out rates occurring with out-patient care with approximately half the patients failing to keep their first appointments.

In addition we studied therapists from different professional groups, namely psychiatry, nursing and social work.

Rather than study large numbers of patients, which would have necessitated using only crude outcome measures, such as repetition of self-poisoning, we decided to study relatively small numbers which would allow detailed evaluation of changes in various aspects of social functioning, mood and problem resolution, as well as assessment of the patients' attitudes to their treatment.

Method

Treatment Regimes

Domiciliary. All treatment sessions occurred in the patient's home. They could be held as frequently as the therapist felt necessary but could only occur during the daytime on week days. The open access telephone service was made available to all patients in this regime.

Out-patients. All treatment sessions took place in an out-patient clinic in the general hospital, each therapist's sessions being held on a particular week-day afternoon. A patient could not be seen more than once per week. The open access telephone service was not made available but telephone messages could be left with a secretary.

The same basic treatment approach, as described in our treatment manual, was used in both treatment settings. Thus the main differences between the two treatments were in terms of the setting in which they occurred and the flexibility allowed. Individuals other than the presenting patient (e.g. spouse, boy/girlfriend, or other family members) were included in treatment sessions wherever indicated.

Sessions in both conditions could last up to, but not more than, one hour and treatment could continue for up to three months from the time of discharge from hospital. During the first two months the sessions could be held as frequently as allowed in each regime, but during the third month, if treatment continued this long, a maximum of two sessions could occur in either regime. If necessary, psychotropic drugs were prescribed by the general practitioner after recommendation from the therapist; this ensured that the medically unqualified therapists were not at a disadvantage. In our service drug prescribing is kept to a minimum.

If a patient failed to keep his initial appointment or dropped out of treatment he was offered one more appointment. It was left to each therapist to decide when treatment was completed.

Therapists

These were: two *psychiatrists*, one male with three years' experience of psychiatry, and one female with five years' experience; one *psychiatric nurse* with eight years' experience; one *social worker* who had spent three years in community social work.

All four therapists had worked as regular members of the emergency service and therefore had considerable experience in the assessment and

treatment of overdose patients. For the purpose of the study they all
underwent a special training procedure and took on pilot cases to
familiarise themselves with the research methodology.

Assessments

At the initial assessment a wide range of demographic information was
collected for each patient. In addition patients were scored on the
suicide intent scale (Beck *et al.*, 1973) and the risk of repetition scale
(Buglass and Horton, 1974). These were used to ensure comparability
of the two groups of patients, as well as for predictive purposes. In
Table 20.1 are shown the outcome measures and the times at which
each was used.

   Social adjustment was evaluated using the American Social
Adjustment Scale of Weissman and Paykel (1974) which is an observer
rating scale. The original form in which a two-month period is assessed
was modified to cover a one-month period, and minor changes in some
items made to suit a British population. The reliability of the new
version of the scale was checked. The scale covers the following role
areas: work, social and leisure activities, relationships with extended
family, marriage, parental function, relations with family unit and
economic independence. It includes an assessment of performance of
tasks, interpersonal relationships, friction and satisfaction in each role
area. Only the mean scores for each role area, rather than the scores on
the sub-items, will be reported here.

   Outcome on target problems was evaluated using a simple four-point
scale of the extent to which therapeutic goals set by the therapist were
achieved. *Mood* was assessed using an abbreviated 25-item version of
the self-rated Lorr-McNair Mood Scale (Lorr *et al.*, 1967) which yields
a total mood score and scores on five subscales. *Repetition* of self-
poisoning was also recorded and patients scored on a seven-point
Suicide Ideation Scale developed for the study. In addition all patients
were asked about their attitudes to the treatment received.

Treatment Design

Patients were included in the study if they had been admitted to
hospital following an overdose, were aged 16 or over, not in current
psychiatric treatment, not suffering from alcoholism or drug addiction,
and resided within the study area, which, with Oxford as its centre, had
an average radius of 15 miles. Patients found, after initial assessment, to
need psychiatric hospital in-patient or day-patient care were excluded,
as were those of no fixed abode.

Table 20.1: Assessment Procedures and Times of Assessments

Assessment Measure	Pre-treatment	Post-treatment	Six months	One year
		Times of assessments		
Social adjustment scale	✓	✓	✓	
Target problems (assessor)		✓	✓	
(therapist)		✓		
Mood scale (Lorr-McNair)	✓	✓	✓	
Repetition of self-poisoning			✓	✓
Suicide Ideation Scale		✓	✓	
Attitudes to treatment	✓			
General practitioner questionnaire				✓

Table 20.2: Treatment Design

	Treatment Group	
	Domiciliary	Out-patients
Therapist A (Psychiatrist)	8 patients	8 patients
Therapist B (psychiatrist)	12 patients	12 patients
Therapist C (psychiatric nurse)	16 patients	16 patients
Therapist D (social worker)	12 patients	12 patients
Total	48 patients	48 patients

There were 48 patients in each treatment condition, patients being randomly assigned to one or the other after initial assessment. In addition patients were randomly assigned to therapists. The patients were allocated as shown in Table 20.2.

Assessments were conducted by a senior psychiatrist, blind to the treatment regime but not to the therapist involved. They were carried out pre-treatment and at the end of treatment. Patients who did not complete treatment or failed to attend their first appointments were assessed after one month. All patients were assessed six months after their overdoses. The therapists also rated outcome on target problems at the end of treatment for those patients who had received at least one treatment session. A brief questionnaire was sent to all the patients' general practitioners after one year. In addition our routine monitoring service was used to detect any referrals to hospital following further self-poisoning.

Comparisons of groups of patients on the social adjustment and mood scale scores at the two follow-up assessments were by covariate analysis based on adjusted follow-up scores which controls for differences in pre-treatment scores.

Results

The two groups of patients were comparable on a wide range of characteristics except for a slight excess of those in the out-patient regime having received previous out-patient psychiatric treatment (χ^2 = 3.90, p < .05). The research subjects were representative of a complete four-month sample of patients fitting the research criteria.

Acceptability of the Two Treatment Regimes

As can be seen in Table 20.3 the domiciliary regime resulted in far greater compliance, with twice as many patients completing treatment than in the out-patient regime, and only three not keeping their initial appointment.

Patients completing treatment in the domiciliary regime received a mean of 4·30 treatment sessions (range 1-8) and those in the out-patient regime 4·95 sessions (range 1-10). The mean length of treatment sessions was 44 minutes in the domiciliary regime and 47 minutes in out-patients.

Follow-up Rates

Complete follow-up data were obtained for 92 per cent of patients at the end of treatment, for 85 per cent at six months and for 96 per cent through the general practitioners' questionnaire after one year.

Table 20.3: Acceptability of the Two Treatment Regimes

Outcome	Treatment group			
	Domiciliary (100% = 48)		Out-patients (100% = 48)	
	n	(%)	n	(%)
Completed treatment	40	(83)	20	(42)
Dropped out of treatment	5	(11)	15	(31)
Failed to keep initial appointment	3	(6)	13	(27)

χ^2 = 17.92, df = 2, p < .001.

Table 20.4: Improvements for the Total Patient Sample During Follow-up

Assessment measure	Post- *v.* pre-treatment	Six months *v.* post-treatment
Social Adjustment Scale		
Role areas:		
work	**	0
social and leisure	**	**
extended family	**	*
marital	*	0
parental	0	0
family unit	**	0
economic independence	0	0
Over-all score	**	**
Mood Scale		
Subscales:		
cheerfulness	**	0
anger	**	0
anxiety	**	0
depression	**	0
fatigue	**	0
Total score	**	0

**p < .001   *p < .05   0 no difference

Changes for the Total Patient Sample During Follow-up

Their Social Adjustment and Mood Scale scores are summarised in Table 20.4.

Social Adjustment. The over-all sample showed significant improvements in social adjustment between the pre- and post-treatment assessments for work, social and leisure, extended family, marital and family unit role areas, and in the over-all social adjustment score. Further significant improvements occurred between the post-treatment and six month assessments for social and leisure and extended family role areas, and in the over-all social adjustment score.

Mood. The total mood scale scores and the scores on the five subscales all showed highly significant improvement between the pre- and post-treatment assessments but no further significant improvements between the post-treatment and six month assessments.

Comparison of the Two Patient Groups

Repetition of Self-poisoning. Although an excess of patients repeated in the out-patient group the difference did not attain statistical significance at six months or one year as can be seen in Table 20.5.

The Risk of Repetition Scale proved to have good predictive value for repeats during the one-year follow-up period with 41 per cent of those patients with initial scores of three or more repeating compared with 8 per cent of those with scores of two or less ($x^2 = 7.70$, $p < .01$). The rest of the results comparing the two patient groups are summarised in Table 20.6.

No significant differences were found between the domiciliary and out-patient groups at either of the follow-up assessments on the Social Adjustment, Mood or Suicide Ideation Scales. Rather more of the target problems for the patients in the domiciliary group were rated by the assessor as resolved or improved at both the post-treatment and six-month assessments, and by the therapists at the end of treatment for patients attending any treatment sessions.

Comparison of Patients Completing Treatment in the Two Treatment Groups

In view of the substantial difference in the proportions of patients completing treatment in the domiciliary and out-patient groups it was important to compare the outcome of those completing in the two treatment groups. No difference was found for repetition of self-poisoning during the one-year follow-up with four (10 per cent) of the domiciliary group and three (15 per cent) of the out-patient group completers repeating. The rest of the results are summarised in Table 20.7.

No significant differences emerged between the two groups of completers on the Social Adjustment Scale but there was a marked trend for the out-patient group to have improved more in most role areas. More target problems were rated as resolved or improved for the out-patient completers by both the assessor and therapists at the post-treatment assessments, but the reverse was true for the assessor's ratings at six months. The mood scale scores showed a marked trend favouring the out-patient completers, the difference on the sub-scale of 'fatigue' being significant at six months. There were no differences in the suicide ideation scores.

Table 20.5: Repetition of Self-poisoning (or Self-injury) for Patients in the Two Treatment Groups (%)

Treatment group	Patients repeating during follow-up period		
	0-6 months	6-12 months	Whole year
Domiciliary (n = 47)	2 (4)	3 (6)	5 (11)
Out-patients (n = 48)	6 (13)	1 (2)	7 (15)

Table 20.6: Comparison of the Two Patient Groups

	Assessment			
	Post-treatment		Six months	
Treatment group	Domiciliary	Out-patients	Domiciliary	Out-patients
Assessment Measure				
Social Adjustment Scale	0		0	
Target Problems (rated resolved or improved)				
Assessor	63%	55%	66%	52%
Therapist (for those patients attending at least one treatment session)	73%	68%	–	–
Mood Scale	0		0	
Suicide Ideation Scale	0		0	

0 no difference

Out-patient Group: Comparison Between Patients Completing Treatment and Those Dropping Out

In order to see whether treatment was effective it was important to see whether those who completed treatment did better than those who had no treatment at all, or those who failed to complete. These comparisons could only be carried out for the out-patient group because such a large proportion of those in the domiciliary group completed treatment. The following results are therefore for the out-patient group only.

There was no difference for repetition of self-poisoning; two (15 per cent) of the out-patient non-attenders compared with three

Table 20.7: Comparison of Those Patients Completing Treatment in the Two Treatment Groups

| | Assessment | | | |
| | Post-treatment | | Six months | |
Treatment group	Domiciliary	Out-patients	Domiciliary	Out-patients
Assessment Measure				
Social Adjustment Scale		(+)		(+)
Target Problems (rated resolved/improved)				
Assessor	63%	66%	66%	57%
Therapist	74%	80%	–	–
Mood Scale		(+)		(+)
Subscale: fatigue		(+)		*
Suicide Ideation Scale	0		0	

* $p < .05$ (F ratio)   (+) favourable trend   0 no difference

Table 20.8: Out-patient Group: Comparison Between Patients Completing Treatment and Those Not Attending Their First Appointment

| | Assessment | | | |
| | Post-treatment | | Six months | |
Patient group	Completers	Non-attenders	Completers	Non-attenders
Assessment measure				
Social Adjustment Scale	(+)		(+)	
Role areas:				
work			*	
family unit			*	
Target Problems (rated resolved or improved by assessor)	66%	30%	57%	35%
Mood Scale	(+)		(+)	
Subscale: fatigue		0	*	
Suicide Ideation Scale		0		0

* $p < .05$ (F ratio)   (+) favourable trend   0 no difference

(15 per cent) of the attenders repeated. The rest of the results comparing those completing treatment with the non-attenders are summarised in Table 20.8.

The social adjustment scores showed a marked trend towards better outcome for those completing treatment, reaching statistical significance for work role and relations with family unit at the six-month assessment. Far more of their target problems were rated resolved or improved, and they generally had better mood scale scores with the subscale of 'fatigue' showing a significant difference at six months.

Patients keeping at least one out-patient appointment but subsequently dropping out of treatment were in general better off at follow-up than those having no treatment at all. Thus their social adjustment scores were in general more favourable, a significant difference being found for work role at six months, and they had made greater progress towards achievement of target problems with 52 per cent being rated by the assessor as resolved or improved at the post-treatment assessment, and 53 per cent at the six-month assessment.

One-year Follow-up

For the period between the six-month assessment and the one-year follow-up patient groups were compared on the number who visited the general practitioner for any reason, visited for 'psychiatric' reasons, received psychotropic drugs, or were referred to a psychiatrist. No major differences were found between the two treatment groups, nor between those completing treatment in the two treatment groups, and between the out-patient completers as compared with the non-attenders and non-completers.

Twelve patients referred themselves to the emergency service after the end of treatment; all had completed treatment. A further two made telephone contacts only, one having completed treatment and the other having dropped out. The proportions of patients making further contact with the service amongst those completing treatment (22 per cent) was significantly greater than among those not completing treatment (3 per cent; $\chi^2 = 9.62$; $p < .01$).

Attitudes to Treatment

Of the patients who attended any treatment sessions 78 per cent reported finding the treatment helpful. This applied to a greater proportion of those in the domiciliary group (81 per cent) than in the out-patient group (74 per cent) but the difference was not significant.

The most frequent reason given for the treatment being helpful by those completing treatment was that the therapist had specifically discussed their problems. This applied in 70 per cent of cases.

Considering all the patients there was a trend towards the out-patient group more often saying that, if faced with the same situation which led to the initial overdose, they would/might do the same thing again. Of patients completing treatment in either condition fewer said they would or might, take another overdose (21 per cent) than of those not completing (28 per cent) but the difference was not significant.

Only three of those patients who dropped out of treatment in either condition said this was because their therapist had proved unhelpful. Fifty-nine per cent of patients either not keeping their first appointment or dropping out of treatment said this was because the appointment had not been convenient, but 43 per cent said they regretted not having, or not completing, treatment. This applied more to those who had received some treatment (59 per cent) than to those who received none (23 per cent) but the difference did not quite attain significance ($\chi^2 = 2.52$).

Comparison of Therapists

As can be seen in Table 20.9 no major differences were found between the therapists in the extent to which their patients complied with treatment, took further overdoses or rated their therapist as helpful.

Table 20.9: Comparison of Psychiatrists, Nurse and Social Worker (%)

	Psychiatrists	Nurse	Social worker	
Completion of treatment				
Domiciliary group	19 (95)	11 (69)	10 (83)	NS
Out-patient	8 (40)	7 (44)	5 (42)	NS
Both groups	27 (68)	18 (56)	15 (63)	NS
Repetition of self-poisoning during one year	4 (10)	5 (16)	3 (13)	NS
Therapy rated as helpful (by patients attending any sessions)	27 (77)	16 (67)	17 (94)	NS

Conclusions

For the total sample, rapid improvement appeared to occur during the first few weeks after taking an overdose. Provision of treatment in the patients' homes led to much greater compliance. The results must be interpreted carefully since all patients were offered treatment, whereas in the normal clinical situation patients are selected for subsequent treatment according to suitability and compliance with out-patient treatment in our service is then considerably higher. However, comparison of the two groups of patients in this study revealed no major differences in outcome.

There was evidence that patients who completed treatment in the out-patient group were better off at follow-up than those completing in the domiciliary group. Since the out-patients had to make much greater effort to receive treatment than those offered home-based care it is likely that those who attended out-patient appointments were more highly motivated. Thus, it does not seem appropriate to suggest we should greatly revise our current treatment policy, especially as domiciliary treatment is more expensive both in terms of therapists' time and travelling. However, domiciliary care may be more appropriate for some patients. It was predicted that a greater proportion of patients who were primarily experiencing a problem of loss would complete treatment in the out-patient regime than those with dyadic problems or family problems and there was some support for this hypothesis. This might be expected since for treatment of a dyadic or family problem it would usually be necessary for two or more individuals to be motivated to attend hence reducing the likelihood of compliance with out-patient care.

Another factor that must be considered is therapist satisfaction; it is very demoralising to find that a large proportion of patients to whom out-patient care has been offered fail to turn up. For some patients it may be best to see them initially in their homes and subsequently in out-patients. Useful information can often be obtained by visiting the home and compliance with out-patient care may be increased once patients begin to see their problems improving.

Is treatment worth offering to self-poisoners not suffering from psychiatric illness? A trial including random allocation to treatment or no treatment would be necessary to really answer this question. However, in this study those completing or receiving at least some treatment in the out-patient group were better off at follow-up than those receiving no treatment at all, particularly in terms of improvement in target problems. Thus the results lend some support to the current policy of making treatment available for the majority of patients and are in keeping with previous findings from studies by Greer and Bagley (1971) and Kennedy (1972) although neither was a properly controlled study.

Our policy of having non-medical therapists providing treatment has been supported, with no important differences appearing between the doctors, nurse and social worker. These were all relatively experienced therapists and one cannot necessarily extrapolate from them to their professional groups in general. However, our clinical experience over the past six years lends further support to this policy. The crucial factors determining who should carry out treatment are probably not professional roles but the type of training received. A well-trained, enthusiastic therapist is likely to be at least as effective as one with little training, whatever his profession, or indeed a busy psychiatrist for whom the care of self-poisoning patients may represent an unwelcome extra clinical burden.

Acknowledgements

This study was supported by a grant from the Department of Health and Social Security. Dr John Bancroft collaborated in the design and provided encouragement throughout. Thanks are due to the four therapists, Pepe Catalan, Breda Kingston, Averil Stedeford and Nick Welch, and to Joan Fagg and Tamsin Humphries who acted as research assistants.

References

Beck, A.T., Schuyler, D. and Herman, I. (1973). Development of suicide intent scales. In *The Prediction of Suicide*, ed. by A.T. Beck, H.L.P. Resnik and D.J. Lettieri. Charles Press, New York.
Blake, D.R. and Mitchell, J.R.A. (1978). Self-poisoning: management of patients in Nottingham, 1976. *British Medical Journal*, vol. 1, pp. 1032-35.
Buglass, D. and Horton, J. (1974). A scale for predicting subsequent suicidal behaviour. *British Journal of Psychiatry*, vol. 124, pp. 573-78.
Greer, S. and Bagley, C. (1971). Effect of psychiatric intervention in attempted suicide: a controlled study. *British Medical Journal*, vol. 1, pp. 310-12.
Kennedy, P. (1972). Efficacy of a regional poisoning treatment centre in preventing further suicidal behaviour. *British Medical Journal*, vol. 4, pp. 255-57.
Kreitman, N. (1977). *Parasuicide*. John Wiley, New York.
Lorr, M., Daston, P. and Smith, I.R. (1967). An analysis of mood states. *Educational and Psychological Measurement*, vol. 27, pp. 89-96.
Paykel, E.S., Hallowell, C., Dressler, D.M., Shapiro, D.L. and Weissman, M.M. (1974). Treatment of suicide attempters. *Archives of General Psychiatry*, vol. 31, pp. 487-91.
Stanley, W.J. (1969). Attempted suicide and suicidal gestures. *British Journal of Preventive and Social Medicine*, vol. 23, pp. 190-95.
Weissman, M.M. and Paykel, E.S. (1974). *The Depressed Woman: A Study of Social Relationships*. University of Chicago Press, Chicago.

21 SERVICES FOR PARASUICIDE AND THE PLACE OF A POISONINGS UNIT

N. Kreitman

A whole series of problems arise when one attempts to devise a rational system of care for parasuicides. For many of these problems the data currently available are inadequate, so one is forced to fall back on clinical judgement. A further difficulty is that therapeutic outcome has to be judged by at least two sets of criteria. The first of these embraces relief of current distress, the treatment of mental illness associated with parasuicide, and the resolution of social crisis. The second group concerns prevention of repetition of parasuicide and of ultimate suicide.

With these in mind one can usefully review the actual or potential sequence of service contacts of parasuicides and consider what each stage has to contribute to the patient's well-being. The first link in the chain, logically speaking, should be the general practitioner, although, in Edinburgh at least, only a minority of patients entering care do so by this route. One can also note in passing that little is known about the number of parasuicides there are in the community who never come to the notice of their general practitioners; an unpublished study from Holland suggests that there may be three concealed cases for every one known (Diekstra, 1979). There is nothing to guide us as to whether making contact with the general practitioner is of any advantage from the psychiatric viewpoint, but since physical damage and toxic states obviously require medical assessment, it would seem prudent to recommend that any overdose or self-injury should be brought to the attention of a doctor.

Of those patients who do consult their general practitioners a proportion will be managed by him and the remainder referred on to hospitals or other agencies. The factors which influence this decision have been documented (Kennedy and Kreitman, 1973). The same study indicates that patients do benefit by being referred for psychiatric care.

Once a patient has reached hospital and received emergency physical care the next decision concerns whether additional attention is of any demonstrable benefit. For various reasons, of which ethical considerations are probably primary, no evidence on this point has ever been collected. A different question can be posed as to whether a psychiatrist as compared to a non-specialist offers the preferable next stage of management. Studies have recently appeared in which the clinical assessment of psychiatrists and non-psychiatrists are compared (e.g. Gardner, 1977, and chapter 17 of this book). These studies consider the feasibility of spreading the service load rather than evaluating relative efficacy, and all emphasise that however provision is organised, adequate psychiatric back-up must be always available. The fact that a substantial minority of parasuicides are suffering from diagnosable and treatable psychiatric disorders surely points to the need for the retention of psychiatric responsibility, although there is no reason why the psychiatrist should not be assisted with preliminary screening by suitably trained colleagues.

An allied question is whether patients seen at hospital should be routinely admitted and if so whether to a special unit or to a general ward. One can do little more here than set out personal views.

Routine admission of all poisoned or self-injured patients is an expensive policy but there are three grounds for advocating it. First, the assessment of a complex family crisis or of a bewildered and confused patient is a difficult exercise at the best of times. For it to be carried out in the middle of the bustling emergency department designed for quite other purposes is making a difficult task almost impossible. Admission does enable examination to be carried out when the effects of the drugs have worn off and when there is time for the systematic review of the problem and to interview relatives.

Secondly, admission provides the patient with a temporary respite from the setting in which the parasuicide occurred. It affords a brief period during which the patient and his circle are separated and during which each can reflect and make provisional plans for the future. Thirdly, admission serves to provide active and positive care at the time of the crisis, especially by means of appropriate nursing, for people at a high level of subjective distress, whether formally ill or not. Fourthly, the act of admission becomes part of the whole drama of the parasuicide. Some might argue that this heightening effect is not always desirable and might even encourage the patient to repeat the overdose when another crisis occurs. However, identifying the situations in which this might possibly be true requires extraordinary prescience unlikely to be achieved while working under pressure. Moreover, the patient's requirements for careful assessment would appear to be very much more important. Referral for out-patient interview fails on a massive scale.

The remaining question is whether admission should be to a special unit as compared to a general receiving ward as is commonly the case. Again it must be recognised that the provision of a special poisoning treatment centre as recommended by the Hill Report (1968) requires considerable resources, although these may be used for a number of wider purposes. Only one centre of the recommended kind has been established so far in the United Kingdom, but experience there suggests that the system has a number of substantial advantages.

The first of these, and the one which is of greatest importance from the patient's viewpoint is that it is possible to provide a 'ward culture' of acceptance. This is an extremely important aspect of the problem especially as the hostility manifested by general ward staff to the self-poisoning patient is so clearly documented (e.g. Ramon *et al.,* 1975). Secondly, it enables the receiving hospital to organise special toxicological skills and equipment, to enable interested physicians to develop experience in toxicology and to keep abreast of the bewildering variety of harmful substances which flood the drug market. Conversely the lack of such a centre often leads to a situation in which none of the physicians in a hospital has very much interest or expertise in the area. Thirdly, the importance of a poisoning centre as a base for undergraduate teaching ought to be emphasised. Parasuicide provides an excellent model for the approach which undergraduates are now encouraged to develop, giving equal attention to the somatic, psychological and social facets of the patient's problems. Fourthly, existence of such a centre also provides an invaluable source for postgraduate teaching and research. The operation of 100 per cent admission policy enables the accumulation of a systematic body of relatively unbiased data over a period of many years and can also provide a springboard for numerous, more focused studies. The cost in energy and time of carrying out such work without such a facility is extremely high.

References

Diekstra, R. (1979). Personal communication.
Gardner, R., Hanka, R., O'Brien, V.C., Page, A.J.F. and Rees, F. (1977). Psychological and social evaluation in cases of deliberate self-poisoning admitted to a general hospital. *British Medical Journal*, vol. 2, pp. 1567-70.
Hill Report (1968). *Hospital Treatment of Acute Poisoning*. HMSO, London.
Kennedy, P. and Kreitman, N. (1973). An epidemiological survey of parasuicide ('attempted suicide') in general practice. *British Journal of Psychiatry*, vol. 123, p. 23.
Ramon, S., Bancroft, J. and Skrimshire, A. (1975). Attitudes towards

self-poisoning among physicians and nurses in a general hospital. *British Journal of Psychiatry*, vol. 127, pp. 257-64.

NOTES ON CONTRIBUTORS

B.M. Barraclough, Consultant Psychiatrist, Graylingwell Hospital, Chichester.

J. Catalan, Honorary Senior Registrar in Psychiatry, University of Oxford.

M. Choquet, Psychologist, Attachée de Recherche à l'Institut National de la Santé et de la Recherche Médicale (INSERM), Le Vesinat, France.

F. Davidson, Division de la Recherche Médico-sociale, INSERM, Le Vesinat, France.

R. Ettlinger, Psychiatrist, Götgatan, Stockholm.

F. Facy, Equipe de Recherche sur les Sociopathies, INSERM, Le Vesinat, France.

R.D.T. Farmer, Senior Lecturer in Community Medicine, Westminster Medical School, London.

G. Fuchs-Robetin, Psychiatric Clinic, University of Vienna.

R. Gardner, Consultant Psychiatrist, Cambridge Health District (Teaching).

J. Gibbons, Lecturer in Applied Social Studies, Department of Sociology and Social Administration, University of Southampton.

K. Hawton, Clinical Lecturer in Psychiatry, University of Oxford.

S.R. Hirsch, Professor of Psychiatry, Charing Cross Hospital Medical School, London.

J. Jenkins, MRC Clinical Psychiatry Unit, Graylingwell Hospital, Chichester.

C. Jennings, Research Officer, MRC Clinical Psychiatry Unit, Graylingwell Hospital, Chichester.

H. Katschnig, Psychiatrist, Allgemeines Krankenhaus der Stadt Wien, University of Vienna.

N. Kreitman, Consultant Psychiatrist, MRC Unit for Epidemiological Studies in Psychiatry, Royal Edinburgh Hospital.

A. Levey, MRC Clinical Psychiatry Unit, Graylingwell Hospital, Chichester.

H.G. Morgan, Consultant Senior Lecturer in Mental Health, University of Bristol.

J. Newson-Smith, Senior Registrar, Atkinson Morley's Hospital, Wimbledon, London.

263

S.E.M. O'Brien, Research Lecturer in Community Medicine, Westminster Medical School, London.

E.S. Paykel, Professor of Psychiatry, St George's Hospital Medical School, London.

P. Sainsbury, Consultant Psychiatrist, MRC Clinical Psychiatry Unit, Graylingwell Hospital, Chichester.

M. Schreiber, Department of Psychiatry, Washington University, St Louis, Missouri.

P. Sint, Österreichische Akademie der Wissenschaften.

R.J. Turner, Consultant Psychiatrist, Mapperley Hospital, Nottingham.

INDEX